D0908316

In Defense of Openness

In Defense
of Openness

*Why Global Freedom Is the Humane
Solution to Global Poverty*

BAS VAN DER VOSSEN

JASON BRENNAN

OXFORD
UNIVERSITY PRESS

OXFORD
UNIVERSITY PRESS

Oxford University Press is a department of the University of Oxford. It furthers
the University's objective of excellence in research, scholarship, and education
by publishing worldwide. Oxford is a registered trade mark of Oxford University
Press in the UK and certain other countries.

Published in the United States of America by Oxford University Press
198 Madison Avenue, New York, NY 10016, United States of America.

CIP data is on file at the Library of Congress
ISBN 978–0–19–046295–6

1 3 5 7 9 8 6 4 2

Printed by Sheridan Books, Inc., United States of America

Contents

Preface

IN 2016, XENOPHOBIA had a triumphant year.

Donald Trump complained about foreigners stealing American jobs. He depicted low-skilled immigrants as a threat to the American economy and culture. During his campaign, Trump said he would build a wall to keep out dangerous Mexicans and would do everything in his power to keep out Muslims. Luckily, the Supreme Court is helping to stop President Trump, who means to keep his word.

When Bernie Sanders was asked about immigration, he agreed. He dismissed open borders as a "Koch brothers proposal," a "right-wing proposal which says essentially there is no United States."[1] Despite the mass of empirical evidence to the contrary, Sanders nonchalantly claimed that immigration would make almost everyone in the United States poorer.[2]

Trump and Sanders reject a society that is open to the world around it. Not only do they want immigrants to be rejected at the border, they also want domestic companies to be kept within. Before beginning his presidency, Trump began to threaten American corporations that would dare move their production abroad. Sanders, too, complained about outsourcing and its supposed harms to American workers. Both claimed that such moves were harmful and the United States has a right to prevent them.

Of course, Trump and Sanders are mere symptoms of a much broader popular movement.[3] Many people reject the idea that societies should be open, respecting the freedom of people to move themselves, their goods, and business in and out of society. They think that immigration and trade are bad, especially immigration from and trade with less developed countries.

These people ignore the overwhelming consensus of economists right and left to the contrary. They ignore hundreds of years of research showing otherwise.[4] In their eyes, drawing an imaginary line on map magically transforms mutually advantageous trades of goods and services into dangerous games of poker, where one side's gain comes at the other side's loss.

As we'll show in this book, these ideas are wrong. Mass immigration would not harm, but rather benefit developed economies. And it would enormously benefit people in the developing world, too.

We have a lot of work to do.

WHEN WE TURN to mainstream work on global justice, things don't get much better. There is a huge and growing philosophical literature discussing these issues. But much of this literature is—to be frank—perplexing, frustrating, and at times even embarrassing. If philosophers had conspired to advocate the very opposite of what mainstream institutional and developmental economists recommend, things wouldn't have turned out much different.

Consider an example. There is overwhelming evidence that economic rights and freedoms are necessary for development. And the evidence that mass global redistribution can cure world poverty is flimsy at best. Indeed, many left-leaning economists claim that the large-scale redistribution of wealth to poor countries with dysfunctional governments would actually make things worse. Despite this, most philosophers who write about global justice are either silent about economic rights and liberty, or, worse, try to debunk these rights so they can defend global redistribution.

The global justice literature often assumes (without argument) heterodox and discredited theories of why some nations are rich and some are poor. The dominant view among economists is that rich nations became rich because they had good institutions, while poor nations stayed poor because they had bad institutions. Of course, there is plenty of disagreement and debate about this issue. But economists largely agree that a number of basic institutions are necessary: strong protection of private property, neutral governments characterized by the rule of law, and free and open markets.

As we will argue in this book, the basic underlying insight here is that ending poverty and oppression requires turning societies into places where people interact on increasingly positive-sum terms. What makes societies thrive is for their people's productive powers to be harnessed for the common good. And this requires that socially beneficial activities, economic production, and peaceful interaction are what pays. In our view, the way to make the world more just is for this dynamic to extend as far and wide across the globe as possible.

Yet most of the global justice literature proceeds as if the differences in wealth we see around the world either resulted from zero-sum processes or can be solved by zero-sum processes. It assumes that the only way the poor can get rich is for the rich to give up what they have. Saving the poor must come at expense of the rich. If the problem is zero-sum, surely the solution must be zero-sum also.

To make these assumptions is to get the facts wrong. But it's not *just* the facts that are wrong here. Philosophers who take these views usually end up endorsing mistaken *moral* principles as well. They misdiagnose the problem and thus misdiagnose the cure. And as we'll see, there is a relationship between these mistakes. Ignoring the real problem makes one miss the real solutions.

We have a lot of work to do.

PACE TRUMP AND Sanders, and pace many of our philosopher colleagues, global justice is not about picking a side on us versus them. The Trump/Sanders nationalist idea—that we should pick us over them—is wrong. The standard leftist view—that we should pick them over us, making the poor rich by making the rich worse off—is *also* wrong. Both sides make a mistake.

Us or them? Answer: *Why not both?*

The policies we propose in this book have far more potential to cure global poverty than any of the policies typical philosophers of global justice advocate. At the same time, the policies we recommend to combat global poverty policies also *help* citizens of developed countries, rather than hurt them. The choice really is not between us and them. Policies can be positive-sum. Justice definitely is.

What justice requires, first and foremost, is for governments to allow and enable people to form mutually beneficial relationships with one another, to allow and enable people to make mutually beneficial transactions. It requires that governments allow their citizens to buy foreign products, hire foreign workers, and rent houses and apartments to foreign tenants. What justice requires is that everyone everywhere have a right to exit, a right to enter, a right to trade, and right to possess, use, and profit from productive property.

In short, what global justice requires, first and foremost, is global openness.

MANY THINK OF their nations and countries as akin to houses or clubs. But they really aren't. Asking Canada—which despite its rhetoric to the contrary, is highly hostile to immigration—to open its borders is not like asking homeowners to let poor people invade their basements. Rather, it's asking Canada, the United States, and every other country to allow people who want to rent their apartments to foreigners, hire foreigners, or buy products from foreigners, to do so.

If Westerners were well-informed altruists who cared only about the interests of the global poor and knew what really works, they would support the policies we defend in this book. If Westerners were well-informed egoists who cared only about themselves but knew how best to do so, they would still support the policies we defend in this book.

Neither, of course, gets the idea of justice right. Justice doesn't require endless sacrifice at the altar of the other, or equality, or compassion. Nor does justice allow us to ignore the plight of others in order to attend to our own. No one should be sacrificed, and the sacrifices won't work anyway.

Instead, justice is about making people better off *together*. It is about allowing and encouraging people to better themselves through bettering others, and to let them better others through bettering themselves. Global justice is about extending the range of positive-sum interactions around the world.

Us or them? *Why not both?*

In Defense of Openness

Positive-Sum Global Justice

Pockets of Prosperity

Aiden sits on the floor in his private bedroom. He connects one block to another. A $90 Lego Minecraft Nether Fortress emerges from the scattered pieces. His younger brother, Keaton, pesters him to share the Zombie Pigman action figure. Finally, Aiden relents, and Keaton smiles.

Both children have Band-Aids on their arms. Yesterday, they received flu shots. Neither has ever caught the flu, and perhaps neither ever will.

The next day, their parents cart them off, in leather-lined vehicles, to violin, piano, and acting practice. They spend the second part of the day playing with friends. Each day they eat three full and healthy meals, unless they ruin their appetites by sneaking Trader Joe's pumpkin bars from their pantry.

Several hundred miles away, Miles is playing with his new Thomas the Train toy. Losing Thomas is about the worst thing imaginable to him. Earlier today, his father took him to the local Museum of Life and Sciences. Miles played in the tree houses, saw some farm animals, and took a train ride himself. Hundreds of other kids were there also enjoying themselves. Miles is barely two years old, but has already received some of the best health care available in the world.

The three boys will get twelve years of high-quality elementary and secondary education, and then, we hope, complete four-year degrees at world-class universities. Afterward, they will likely have their choice of professions. They are more likely to suffer from a crisis of choosing which occupation best fits their interests than from chronic unemployment.

Many families are like ours. Their stories illustrate what can happen to people when they live in places with the right institutions. They are likely to lead long, prosperous, meaningful, and fulfilling lives of their own choosing—or at least as likely as one might ever expect to get. They are likely to be the authors of their own lives, rather than leading lives forced upon them by tradition, command, or necessity.

Almost every book on global justice begins by talking about how desperately poor some people are. We took a different path. We began by talking about how rich some people are. We don't do this to rub our good fortune in the faces of those with less. We do this to draw attention to how remarkable the existence and relative accessibility of this kind of wealth really is. Wealth, in other words, is the exception—it's the thing that needs to be explained, understood, and replicated.

In contrast, poverty is boring. Poverty is normal, in a statistical sense. It is not normal in a *normative* sense: it is not how things should be. It is normal in the sense that poverty is human beings' default, natural state. Almost everyone who has ever lived has been desperately poor, malnourished, and at risk of premature death. Aiden, Keaton, and Miles are highly unusual. When their parents suffer a misfortune—a car breaks down, the kitchen sink springs a leak, or even a parent loses a job—this has no noticeable effect on their lives. That's interesting and strange. Around the world most people, for most of human history, would have found cost-equivalent setbacks financially devastating.

Two thousand years ago, everyone everywhere was poor. This state of affairs seemed permanent. Religious leaders who advocated charity did so to nourish the soul or ease the burden of poverty, but did not expect that charity, or anything else, could eliminate poverty altogether. Poverty, it seemed, was here to stay.

But some places stopped being poor. In some places, there are only pockets of poverty among vast fields of wealth, where poverty is unusual, something to be gawked at, where depictions of extreme poverty captivate readers as much as descriptions of fantastic or alien worlds. In other places there are pockets of wealth, where the opposite is true. The key to solving world poverty is, probably, to figure out why some places became rich and then *repeat* or *spread* the causes of success.

The good news is that this is already happening. In the past 40 years, more people (in absolute terms and as a percentage of the total population) have been lifted out of extreme poverty than in all of history before. In 1820, about 95% of people lived in extreme poverty. In 1960, about two-thirds lived in extreme poverty. Now, less than 10% of the world does. Perhaps most remarkably, these numbers are proportions. Over the same period, world population has been increasing—especially in the poorest parts of the world. Even though there are many more people around, we've found ways of making sure fewer are starving.[1] This is a miracle, but hardly anyone notices it.

Adam Smith argued that we should measure the wealth of nations not by the size of the king's army or treasury, but by the fullness of the common people's stomachs and the opportunities available to their children. In 1776, when Adam Smith published *The Wealth of Nations*, most people around the world were still living in what we would now consider extreme poverty. Nevertheless, he realized, the typical inhabitants of some countries, such as the Netherlands or England, enjoyed about three times the standard of living of the typical inhabitants of others, such as Spain or France.[2]

The phenomenon—that some countries became rich quickly while others did not—is often called the Great Divergence. Smith's explanation for the Great Divergence is that the (now) richer countries had better institutions and policies, which in turn encouraged higher forms of economic productivity and growth, and these in turn made even the relatively poorest citizens of those countries richer. The (still) poor countries had bad institutions, bad policies, and a lot of violence. They're run by what we might call extractive elites, groups of people who make their money by extracting wealth and resources from their people. These things encouraged economic stagnation, which in turn ensured that the poor remained poor, just as they always had been.

Ending poverty requires institutions that protect and enhance people's economic productivity and innovation. Economic growth matters. Indeed, as we'll see, when it comes to fighting world poverty, it matters more than anything else.

To illustrate: on most reliable estimates, per capita world product— the total amount of yearly economic production worldwide per person— probably just barely doubled between 5000 B.C. and 1800 A.D.[3] Since then, it has increased by a factor of at least thirty.[4] Importantly—and this point will be critical—wealth has been created, not just moved around. In 2014 the United States produced more real output, by itself, than the entire world did in 1950.[5]

Imagine you could redistribute all the income produced in 1000 A.D. equally among everyone in the world. Even if you did that, the median, average, and modal standards of living would still be what the United Nations now considers extreme poverty. (According to Angus Maddison, world GDP/capita in 1000 A.D. was only about $450 in 1990 US dollars.[6])

Even John Rawls, the pre-eminent left-liberal political philosopher of the past 65 years, argues that we should not much worry about redistribution or egalitarian ideals of justice until we've reached a suitable level of economic development.[7] When the pie is tiny, it doesn't much matter how you cut it. Most people will get crumbs. If you want everyone to have a decent slice of pie, the important thing is to make sure, first and foremost, that there is a lot of pie.

Some people who read the stories of Aiden, Keaton, and Miles might react by thinking, "That's not fair! We need to take some of what those kids have and give it to those who have less." Others might think, "Good for those kids. We need to figure out a way to make everyone have that good of a life." It may not be obvious now, but these are two radically different ways of thinking about poverty. And once we see that, there will be little to recommend the first kind of reaction.

Global Justice as a Positive-Sum Game

Many philosophers who write about global justice defend things like new or stronger human rights protecting people's political and civil liberties. They claim to have discovered various socio-economic rights, like a right to a decent standard of living, access to high quality health care, even rights to be protected from social deprivation. They want to introduce more robust and more internationally oriented forms of democracy. And they propose, in one form or another, large-scale redistributive solutions to the problems of world poverty.

What sets us apart is the question of whether these kinds of proposals should be the *exclusive* or *primary* focus of a theory of global justice. Or, perhaps better, what sets us apart is what the global justice literature tends to leave out. What's left out is protection and recognition of the basic building blocks that make development even possible. There is overwhelming evidence that basic economic rights and freedoms—things like stable property rights, robust protections of freedom of contract, and a guarantee of the freedom of labor—are necessary for development.[8] The main point of this book is that these rights are absolutely *central* to global justice.

The lesson we take from the history of poverty and wealth creation is that people, societies, and indeed the world flourish more when people are rewarded for productive activities, the kind of activities that bring valued goods and services into the lives of others. They wither when what's rewarded are the kind of extractive activities that thieves, dictators, warlords, and oppressors like to engage in—the kind of activities in which one party's gain comes at the expense of another.

As we'll argue throughout this book, we think global justice requires that we expand and protect the ways in which people's relations can be seen as *positive-sum* forms of interaction, and avoid *zero-sum* (or, worse, *negative-sum*) forms. A zero-sum game is an interaction in which one person can win only if, and only to the extent that, another loses. For example, in poker, no money is made; it is only moved around. You can win $100 only if someone else loses money. (In a casino, playing poker is a negative-sum game, as the house takes a rake.)

A positive-sum game, by contrast, involves interactions through which people can gain without those gains having to be offset by corresponding losses for others. At their best, positive-sum interactions make all parties better off (or at least make no one worse off).[9] The paradigmatic case of a positive-sum interaction is trade. Typically, parties engage in voluntary trade because they expect to, and generally do, benefit from the exchange. They might want to make a profit, desire to obtain goods they personally value higher, or care about benefiting others. In one way or another, trading partners typically walk away from an exchange better than they approached it.

Thinking about justice in these terms allows one to see what's wrong with theories that focus on redistributive proposals as the main solution to the problems of global poverty. Redistributive policies, while sometimes justifiable, are zero-sum in nature. They move money from one place to another, attempting to make the latter better off by making the former worse off.

These zero-sum principles lie at the heart of major theories in the global justice literature. Cosmopolitan egalitarians argue that helping people in developing countries requires people in rich countries to strongly sacrifice their self-interest. Nationalist egalitarian theories resist, concluding that people in the First World do not have to redistribute to the Third World, yet also resist allowing people to move from the developing to the developed world. Both views accept the (as we'll soon see, *mistaken*) empirical claim that helping the world's poor must hurt the world's rich.

In our view, the goal should be to turn zero-sum forms of interaction into positive-sum ones, to replace the sources of poverty and oppression with sources of prosperity and productivity. To put it in slogan form: what solves zero-sum problems is changing the nature of the game, not changing who extracts how much from whom.[10]

To us, the main ingredient of global justice is freeing up people's ability to put their persons and goods to work where they see this as most valuable. It means opening borders—allowing people to move where their talents will be most valued. It means freeing up trade—allowing people to move their possessions where they will be most valued. And it means robustly protecting the economic freedoms and property rights that surround and protect their abilities to make best use of those opportunities.

In short, what global justice requires is *openness*. It requires that rich countries, and the institutions they control, *allow* foreigners to make mutually beneficial, voluntary trades with their own citizens. We will argue, on a variety of grounds, that everyone everywhere has a right of migration, a right to trade, and right to possess, use, and profit from productive property.

Thinking about global justice in these terms fits with a broader view of justice to which we are attracted. In our view, when justice obtains, that's supposed to be a welcome thing, something to celebrate rather than bemoan. (And the reasons for celebration are more than merely the fact that justice would obtain.) The point of justice, among other things, is to make our world a good place for everyone to live in.

If justice is achieved, we can see others as people we are glad to welcome into our communities—local, national, or the human community at large. We can see others as people who bring something to the table, people who will end up making our lives go better and not threats to our own lives, goals, and freedoms. We can celebrate the birth of others' babies and the arrival of new immigrants, because they bring us fellow cooperators rather than mouths we will end up having to feed. And, perhaps most importantly, when justice obtains, we can see ourselves as people others have reason to welcome, people who offer promise, advantage, and progress.

We defend these conclusions out of humanitarianism, out of concern for the plight of the world's poor. We fail to do right by others, and especially the poor, when we don't recognize their contributions, productive potential, and resourcefulness. We fail to do right by people when we picture them as mouths to be fed, rather than the cooperators and contributors that they would like to be. We fail to do right by them when we treat them primarily as consumers rather than producers.

As anyone who has ever visited a developing country will know, the world's poor are extremely enterprising.[11] They find ways, against great odds, of providing for themselves and the people they care about. Their cities are bustling with commercial activity, from small vendors to people collecting cardboard boxes on the street, and those searching garbage dumps for metals to sell. These people are not helpless victims. They are people who work hard, make plans, and find ways to survive and better themselves as well as others. They are victims, to be sure, but the main perpetrator is not a global order that fails to provide for them. It's a global order that fails to welcome them and allow them to make their contributions, and the local orders that feed upon them like parasites.

False Starts

Theories of justice can go wrong in a variety of ways. They can invoke mistaken moral principles. Or they can invoke mistaken empirical claims, leading them to misapply correct moral principles. Or they can go wrong by making their principles not sufficiently sensitive to the empirical conditions in which they are supposed to apply.

This will be a recurring theme throughout this book. That ending poverty requires positive-sum forms of cooperation may seem like a mere empirical claim. But it makes a difference morally, too. Knowing what actually has a history of making a difference helps one appreciate what's morally appropriate to demand of others. And flawed moral principles often look attractive because they match flawed empirical views.

Many people believe that global justice requires mass redistribution from rich to poor countries. We'll take a close look at their arguments in later chapters. We've noticed that many of the people who are attracted to these redistributive views find them appealing at least in part because they also hold empirically inaccurate beliefs. They often endorse one or more of the following claims:

- The reason some countries are rich and others are poor is that natural resources are unevenly (and therefore unfairly) distributed around the globe. The rich are rich because they have or had access to more or better resources than poor countries.
- The reason some countries are rich and others are poor is that the rich countries *extracted* resources from the poor countries. The history of colonialism is a key causal explanation of economic development.
- We can easily end world poverty if rich countries simply redistribute a large enough portion of their wealth to the developing world.

These, of course, are *economic* claims. But they play an important role in many people's normative thinking. In one form or another, they represent what we're calling zero-sum analyses of poverty and development. They regard world poverty as a simple problem of resources being misallocated: too much here, too little there.

Once claims like these are accepted, and the zero-sum framework is established, the natural next step will be to search for moral justifications for redistributing wealth in order to fix the misallocation.

But these empirical claims are false starts. They misdiagnose what caused the Great Divergence, and they misidentify what steps actually have a chance of solving world poverty. The Great Divergence did not result from there having been a common pool of resources and, at some point, the rich taking more than their fair share, taking what belonged to others, and so on. The causes of prosperity have to do with turning the zero-sum forces of extraction into positive-sum forces of real production and innovation. Whatever might be the correct principles of justice must fit that point. They must include and empower the productive powers of the world's poorest, enabling them to better themselves and others.

Changing the intuitive appeal of redistributive solutions to global justice, then, requires setting straight the empirical misconceptions that give these proposals their intuitive force. The next section does this.

The Fact of Growth

It bears repeating: everyone used to be poor. Almost all people everywhere throughout human history lived under what we now would refer to as "extreme poverty." Economist Brad Delong estimates that in 5000 B.C., per capita world product—the total amount of yearly economic production worldwide per person—was only about $130 (in 2002 USD), and barely doubled to $250 by the year 1800.[12] Economist Angus Maddison, whose historical data is widely used, offers higher numbers: $457 USD (1990 dollars) in 1 A.D., rising to $712 USD in 1820.[13] The exact numbers are somewhat disputed. But it's not disputable is that extreme poverty was once widespread and normal, and now it is not. Until recently, almost everyone everywhere was poor.

When the history of economic growth is drawn on a chart, as in Figure 1.1, it looks like a hockey stick.[14] We condensed the period from 1 to 1500 A.D. (and all of human history before that) because, despite rising and falling empires, golden and dark ages, the lines hardly move. Had we not done this, the picture would be even more dramatic. From the beginning of time until about 250 years ago, pretty much nothing (in terms of income per capita) happened. There were occasional blips and dips, as a good harvest might feed a few extra bellies, or a bad war might leave them starving, but the norm was that everyone was poor. As John Maynard Keynes put it:

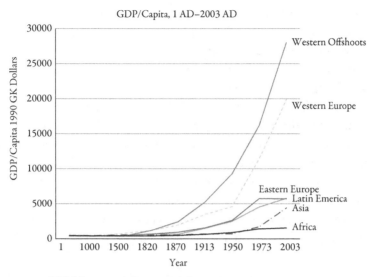

FIGURE 1.1 GDP/Capita, 1 A.D.–2003 A.D.
Source: Maddison 2007, 70.

From the earliest times of which we have record . . . down to the beginning of the eighteenth century, there was no very great change in
the standard of life of the average man . . . Ups and downs certainly.
Visitations of plague, famine, and war. Golden intervals. But no pro-
gressive, violent change. Some periods perhaps 50 per cent better than
others—at the utmost 100 per cent better than before—in the four
thousand years which ended (say) in A.D. 1700.[15]

Then something changed. The stagnation ended. In the past 200 years, per
capita world product has increased by a factor of at least 30.[16] Absolute
levels of wealth grew faster than the population at large. People—as in entire countries—got richer. Today, some of the richest countries in the world
(e.g., Singapore) enjoy average standards of living that are 80 times that of
the poorest countries (e.g., Burundi).[17] Average people in the United States
consume per week roughly what most people in sub-Saharan African countries consume per year.[18] There is a huge gap between the wealth, income, and
standard of living of the people in the richest countries and that of the people
in the poorest countries.

   This was not always so. In 1821, the gap between Western Europe and the
world average was only about two to one, while the gap between the richest
and poorest countries was only about five to one.[19] If we go back further into

history, the gap closes. Indeed, early medieval Europe was poorer than China at the time. In 1000 A.D., every person in every geographic region had roughly the same (poor) standard of living.[20]

Note the shape of the curves in Figure 1.1. Yes, Western Europe and the Western European offshoots grew faster than the rest of the world, and, yes, as a result, the gap between Europe's standard of living and the rest of the world grew. But notice that even the poorest regions enjoyed *some* growth. It's not that Western Europe and the European offshoots grew rich while the other countries became even poorer. It's not as though Western Europe grew rich at the rate others grew poor, which would suggest a zero-sum reallocation of a fixed stock of existing wealth. Rather, the other countries for the most part started off as poor, and got *slightly* richer over time, while the European countries and their offshoots started off as poor, and got *much* richer over time.

The Quality of Institutions Trumps Everything Else

When Thomas Pogge, perhaps the leading theorist of global justice, writes about global justice, he defends one of his preferred redistributive proposals by pointing out that the world's rich have unilaterally excluded the poor from their fair share of the world's natural resources. Pogge thinks this unjust because people worldwide have a claim to "a proportional resource share."[21] Redistribution is justified, according to him, in order to set straight this unequal access to resources.

Sometimes remarks like these are offered as an explanation of why rich countries became rich. However, as such, they simply don't hold up.[22] As economist David Weil summarizes the empirical literature in his textbook *Economic Growth*, "the effect of natural resources on income is weak at best."[23] Natural resources can help, but they can harm development as well. For instance, China after the 1950s was and remains poorer than Singapore or Hong Kong, though the latter have *no* natural resources to speak of. The USSR was poorer than the United States, though the USSR had better natural resources. In Adam Smith's time, the Netherlands and England were richer than France, though France had more and better natural resources. And so on.

Indeed, while natural resources can sometimes spur growth, they frequently *inhibit* growth. Economists refer to this problem as the "resource curse." Countries with a high concentration of easily extractable natural resources frequently suffer from economic stagnation. There are competing theories of why this is so (though these theories are largely compatible, as they identify what might be jointly contributing causes). One theory holds that countries with abundant natural resources "do not develop the cultural attributes necessary for economic success," in part because necessity is the mother of invention.[24] Another theory is that countries that enjoy resource booms tend to just consume the sudden influx income in an unsustainable way. They don't develop capital, but eat away the extra income until it's gone. Yet another theory, called the Dutch Disease theory, holds that a sudden abundance of resources leads to contractions in manufacturing.

But the most popular theory (or, more precisely, the theory thought to identify the most significant set of causes) is that when a country enjoys abundant resources, this encourages governments to act in destructive ways. Government officials can just extract resources for their own selfish ends, and can afford to ignore or oppress their own people. Fighting over control of the resources can lead to civil war. But the dynamics needs not be so violent or nasty. "Nicer" governments might create unsustainable welfare programs, programs they can only afford so long as commodity prices for that resource stay high.[25]

Contrary to resource-based explanations, the dominant view in development economics is that sustained economic growth results from having good economic and political institutions.[26] Institutions, Nobel Laureate Douglas North writes, "are the rules of the game in a society or, more formally, are the humanly devised constraints that shape human interaction."[27] These rules can set the terms for social interaction in different ways, ranging from the harmful to the productive. The view that setting these terms in the most productive manner is the key to explaining growth has quickly become dominant in economics.[28] While no one thinks that institutions are *all* that matters, their important is widely seen as paramount. As economist Dani Rodrik summarizes, "the quality of institutions trumps everything else."[29]

Of course, the field of economics is as full of disputes as any other. And it's by no means uncontroversial what kinds of policies might lead to development. Still, economists largely agree on a number of basic conclusions, such as that countries with robust systems of private property, protected by the rule of law, and governed by strong, inclusive states, offer much better prospects for significant and sustained development than those that lack such protections.[30]

Figures 1.2 through 1.5 illustrate some of these correlations. Note that we are not trying here to demonstrate or prove that these findings are correct. Our goal here is articulate some of the main results of social scientific inquiry that theories of global justice ought to incorporate. We are reporting their findings and summarizing their reasons, but readers should refer to the

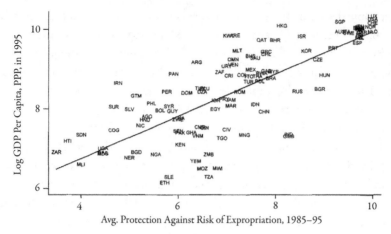

FIGURE 1.2 Average Protection Against Risk of Expropriation, 1985–1995
Source: Acemoglu and Robinson 2005, 403.

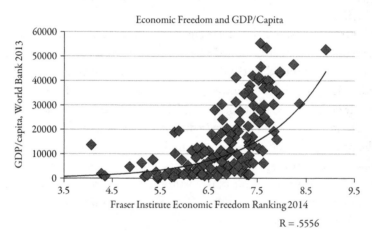

FIGURE 1.3 Economic Freedom and GDP/Capita
Source: World Bank 2013, authors' calculations.

economics literature directly if they want to see a rigorous demonstration of these conclusions.

Figure 1.2 appears in a review paper by Acemoglu and Robinson. It illustrates that countries with better protection of private property tend to be richer.[31]

Figures 1.3 and 1.4 use data from James Gwartney, Robert Lawson, and Joshua Hall's *Economic Freedom of the World* 2014 and 2016 annual reports.[32] Each year the Fraser Institute, a Canadian think tank, rates countries according

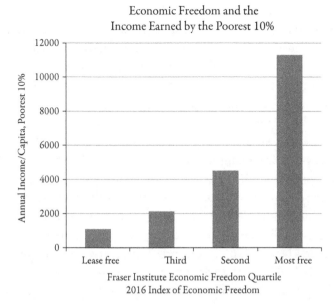

FIGURE 1.4   Economic Freedom and Income Earned by the Poorest 10%
Source: Gwartney et al. 2016.

to their commitment to economic freedom, taking account of such factors as access to sound money, free trade, ease of starting and doing business, ease of investing capital, the protection of property rights, and the degree of government control or manipulation of the economy. The most economically free countries, according to the report, include Australia, New Zealand, Canada, and Switzerland. Many of the Scandinavian countries—which some Americans mistakenly refer to as "socialist"—beat the United States overall on economic freedom, and others beat it on many central aspects of economic freedom. (The *Wall Street Journal*, together with the Heritage Foundation, produces a similar index, and gets similar results.[33])

Figure 1.3 shows the correlation between *overall economic freedom*, as rated by the Fraser Institute report, and GDP/capita, as measured by the World Bank.[34] Figure 1.4, which is taken directly from the Fraser Institute report, shows the relationship between economic freedom, and the absolute level of income of the poorest 10%.[35] Note that Figure 1.4 measures income *before* internal transfers or welfare payments take place. The freest countries are also the richest countries, and generally have the most generous welfare systems. Thus, Figure 1.4 understates how well the "poor" do in the freest countries.

Figure 1.5 is similar to Figure 1.3. Each year, the World Justice Project produces a Rule of Law Index, which rates countries by the degree to which countries adhere to the rule of law, aggregating such factors as checks and balances on government power, the absence of corruption, openness of government, protection of human rights, provision of order and security, effective regulatory enforcement, and proper and effective provision of civil and criminal courts.[36] In Figure 1.5, we plot the Rule of Law Index score for various countries, as assigned by the World Justice Project, against GDP/capita (as measured by the World Bank), and find a robust correlation.

Again, these charts merely show correlations. They are not enough on their own to demonstrate causation. We place them here only to show readers just how robust the correlations are. At the same time, there is evidence that the relationships illustrated here are causal—it's not just that richer countries happen to do a better job protecting private property, but that protecting private property leads to increased prosperity.[37]

One way to illustrate the power of institutions is to examine countries that have recently become more capitalist, or less capitalist, and then see how these changes affect their development in the short term. In a recent paper, economist Peter Leeson examines what happened to countries that become more capitalist between 1980 and 2005, and compares their performance to countries that became less capitalist in that same period. The countries that become *more* capitalist also enjoyed about a 33% increase in real per capita income, about five extra years of life expectancy, about a year and a half of extra schooling per capita, and saw dramatic increases in how democratic they are. The countries that became *less* capitalist saw their income stagnate,

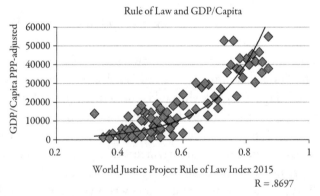

FIGURE 1.5 Rule of Law and GDP/Capita
Source: World Bank 2013, Authors' calculations.

life expectancy drop, and became less democratic. (They did, however, enjoy about half a year's worth of extra schooling per person.[38])

The basic mechanisms that produce these results are fairly well understood. As Daron Acemoglu and Robinson argue in their important book *Why Nations Fail*, the main difference between good and bad institutions concerns the degree to which they foster extractive activity or encourage cooperation and productivity. The main difference, they argue, has to do with whom the institutions empower, and thus whom the institutions benefit. What they call *inclusive* institutions empower people across society, and thus tend to benefit all. By contrast, *extractive* institutions empower only some, and thus tend to benefit only those small groups of people at others' expense.

On the political side, inclusive institutions require a state that strikes a tricky balance between a reasonable level of centralized power and pluralism. Pluralist governments represent many different groups and interests in society, through free and competitive elections, and governed by the rule of law. Such inclusive political institutions avoid the destructive outcomes that fall on the opposite extremes on a spectrum of political violence. On the one extreme, there is anarchy and civil war. These are the result of insufficient political centralization. On the other extreme, there is tyranny, oppression, and rent-seeking. These are the result of too much concentration of political power. Societies that find themselves too close to either extreme tend to contain extractive political institutions.

On the economic side, inclusive institutions secure people's rights to private property, including private property rights over productive resources, and allow these to be held broadly across society. These allow societies to experience the kinds of specialization, exchange, investment, and innovation that increase productivity. Acemoglu and Robinson write:

> Inclusive [economic] institutions ... are those that allow and encourage participation by the great mass of people in economic activities that make best use of their talents and skills and that enable individuals to make the choices they wish. To be inclusive, economic institutions must feature secure private property, an unbiased system of law, and a provision of public services that provides a level playing field in which people can exchange and contract; it must also permit the entry of new businesses and allow people to choose their careers.[39]

Extractive economic institutions, by contrast, are those that limit or altogether prevent the ability of people across society to individually own private and productive property, engage in commercial and profit-seeking activities, and enjoy the fruits of their investments and innovations. Such institutions stifle productivity. The effects are ugly:

> Nations fail today because their extractive economic institutions do not create the incentives needed for people to save, invest, and innovate. Extractive political institutions support these economic institutions by cementing the power of those who benefit from the extraction . . . In many cases, as . . . in Argentina, Colombia, and Egypt, this failure takes the form of lack of sufficient economic activity, because the politicians are just too happy to extract resources or quash any type of independent economic activity that threatens themselves and the economic elites. In some extreme cases, as in Zimbabwe and Sierra Leone . . . extractive institutions pave the way for complete state failure, destroying not only law and order but also even the most basic economic incentives. The result is economic stagnation and—as the recent history of Angola, Cameroon, Chad, the Democratic Republic of Congo, Haiti, Liberia, Nepal, Sierra Leone, Sudan, and Zimbabwe illustrates—civil wars, mass displacements, famines, and epidemics, making many of these countries poorer today than they were in the 1960s.[40]

All this illustrates the importance of the political and economic institutions that facilitate production, exchange, and innovation. The rights, rules, and liberties that make up such institutions form the basic engine of development. They are the things that make it possible for people to leave behind the conditions of poverty and oppression. They help societies move away from the zero-sum logic of extraction and toward the positive-sum logic of growth and prosperity. A good theory of global justice would take these points *very* seriously. It would give pride of place to individual property rights, the freedom to exchange, and the liberty to move and migrate. The theory of justice we develop in this book does just that.[41]

Our Argumentative Strategy

This book is divided into three parts. The first part identifies and defends three elements of a more open world. What unites these elements is that they each are instrumental in widening the scope of potential positive-sum interactions in which people can engage. They protect and empower people who want to bring their persons and goods to others who might desire them around the world, on terms each party can see as beneficial. As we'll argue, this means recognizing people's rights to migrate and trade freely around the world.

We begin this first part of our argument by defending, on intuitive, moral, and economic grounds, the right of people to move where they please, just as Jason and Bas are free to move anywhere in the United States at will. This is the purpose of chapter 2. Chapters 3 and 4 then rebut a range of objections to the idea that borders should be opened. Chapter 5 then makes a similar—intuitive, moral, and economic—case for free trade. In chapter 6, we defend this again from a variety of objections. Finally, in chapter 7 we argue that the basic rights undergirding the right to trade freely, rights that we call people's *productive rights*, ought to be recognized as core human rights.

In chapters 8 through 10, we respond to a number of arguments claiming that global justice must be much more redistributive in nature. In particular, we address three strategies one might take to defend such an approach—strategies that focus on what we might call the past, present, and future.

The first of these, discussed in chapter 8, takes a backward-looking approach, arguing that large-scale redistribution is justified because people in the developed world owe people in the developing world compensation for past imperialism and colonialism. Chapter 9 looks at arguments which try to defend such redistribution in order to correct the injustice of today's unjust world order. And in chapter 10 we examine the forward-looking argument that bases global redistribution on the interpersonal duty to prevent future suffering.

Finally, chapter 11 responds to what we regard as the most pressing objection to our view. The objection claims that since increased growth would exacerbate climate change, it should be avoided altogether, or at least be limited as much as possible to only the developing world. While we share the objector's concern about the dangers of climate change, we argue that this does not undercut our conclusions.

Throughout this book, we will rely upon common-sense moral intuitions and ideas rather than any grand moral or political theory. Thus we will not be attempting to show what Kantianism, Rawlsianism, utilitarianism, or some other grand theory implies about global justice. Instead, we will begin with widely shared principles and ideas. When we challenge common-sense *conclusions* about global justice, we will do so on the basis of more basic and strongly held common-sense moral ideas, beliefs or empirical arguments.

As part of this method, we will use thought experiments that set up analogies between moral theories and more familiar interpersonal cases.

The use of such thought experiments is familiar: it allows us to test whether different proposed theories are consistent with deeply held and shared moral beliefs.

But that's not the only reason we have chosen to rely on this method. The other reason is that such examples help engage our moral imagination. They allow us to stay alive to the fact that the questions we're asking concern real people, living real lives, making real decisions in ways they see as most appropriate given the circumstances. This is important because when questions of global justice are put in the abstract, these facts are easy to lose sight of. Powerful psychological heuristics encourage us to think of foreigners in simplified, and often unfair ways—as monolithic groups of people, a "they" who, in one way or another, threaten whatever makes us an "us." We want to guard against these dynamics by drawing attention to the fact that these are people, persons who have much to offer, if only given a chance.

As a result of this method, we avoid relying on idiosyncratic or easily dismissed moral principles or empirical premises. We think it's deeply problematic when philosophical treatments of justice rely on highly controversial views, say, about the connection between justice and material equality. And we think it's deeply problematic when theories of justice prescribe solutions that evade, ignore, or cherry-pick the empirical evidence about the conditions most conducive to the creation of prosperity and economic and political development.[42]

One might think that a book defending global justice as global freedom would have to do something of this kind, too. It might have to deny moral duties of assistance, or would rely upon implausible ideas about libertarian self-ownership. Others have offered arguments of this kind,[43] but this is not our approach. Instead, we will argue that the conclusions of global openness we defend are consistent with—indeed demanded by—widely shared interpersonal moral intuitions.

2

The Moral and Economic Case for Free Immigration

WE REMEMBER AS elementary school children the celebrations when the Berlin Wall came down. It was a symbol, and proof by existence, of what was wrong with communism. The Soviets and their stooges had to *force* their people to stay. The West did not. People yearn to be free, and life in the West was better, much better, than life behind the Iron Curtain. It took a system of guarded walls and fences to keep them imprisoned within that totalitarian system. Now, that symbol was smashed. East Germans were free to seek a better life.

But even as the Iron Curtain broke apart, other walls did not. Brutal regimes rarely build walls to keep their subjects in these days. But the West has built its own walls to keep out those who might try to leave them. The message is clear: "We believe that everyone should have the freedom to leave their home countries in search for a better life. But do it somewhere else."

A High-Stakes Lottery

The city of Nogales is cut in half by the US–Mexican border. People born on the Mexican side face radically different life prospects from those born on the American side. A few miles make the difference between having the option to choose between life in Arizona, California, New York, or Texas and life in Sonora, Chihuahua, and Sinaloa. By Organisation for Economic Co-operation and Development (OECD) estimates, this is a difference between a median household income of $41,355 and $13,085.[1]

Of course, life in many countries in the world is much worse than in Mexico. People born in Sierra Leone, for example, must set their sights lower.

Per capita income is $340, with 72% of the population living on less than $1 per day.[2] The difference is not just the lack of money. To stay alive in Sierra Leone for more than 46 years is already to beat the odds.[3] Where we are born affects our health, the chances of our children surviving past the age of five, our life satisfaction, and so on.[4] As Joseph Carens pointed out more than 30 years ago: where we are born is like a high-stakes lottery.[5]

Indeed, it's hard to imagine the stakes being higher. As we have seen, the life prospects we face are highly sensitive to the institutions under which we live. But institutions are inert. When good institutions take root, they often survive for long periods of time. Once bad ones appear, they also tend to survive. Bad institutions incentivize political and social elites to keep them bad—their extractive ways of life often depend on it.[6]

Consider two possible ways to mitigate the effects of this lottery. First, we might follow the advice of people like Paul Collier and try to export the right institutions to the people that need them most through military interventions.[7] We'll set that option aside here as it requires a kind of nation-building that is extremely unlikely to succeed. While we have something of an idea about what good institutions look like—stable property, competitive markets, democracy, the rule of law—we have very little idea of how to bring them about. And there are structural reasons why it may not really be possible for "us" to simply export good institutions to other parts of the world.[8]

The other option would be to allow the people who are born under bad institutions to move to those places governed by better ones. After all, the lot we draw in our high-stakes lottery need not determine where we spend our lives. Unfortunately, in our world, most people are denied that option. States put up fences and walls, manned by armed guards. They patrol their coastal waters and monitor airports. As a result of these policies, over 3,000 immigrants died in the Mediterranean Sea in 2014 alone.[9]

States around the world strive for the birthplace lottery to determine people's life prospects as much as possible. This chapter argues that this practice is highly unjust. As we will see, borders ought to be as open as they might reasonably be. The argument we present combines the force of two sources of pressure for open borders. The first of these focuses on the economic benefits of freer migration, for both immigrants and receiving populations. The second shows that the requirement to open borders matches our intuitive moral judgments. Together, these build a prima facie case that freeing up migration is a key step toward a more positive-sum world.

The Economic Argument for Open Borders

Imagine a world in which the following were true:

Strawberry Restrictions

1. Desperately poor people have only one thing to sell, strawberries.
2. Only rich people buy strawberries.
3. The very rich are free and able to travel anywhere in the world to buy strawberries in search of the best deal.
4. The poor are required to stay put—they may only sell strawberries from their homes. They are forbidden, literally at gunpoint, from looking for a better deal elsewhere.

If an evil demon wanted to hurt strawberry sellers and rich buyers, he might want to impose conditions 1 through 4. Under such conditions, the price of strawberries will be artificially low. Conditions 3 and 4 reduce competition among buyers, making sure that strawberry sellers can't go looking for a better deal. They can only accept whatever deal comes to them. Thus, they will get stuck having to accept bad deals.

The same reasoning applies to the sale of labor. We have an economic system in which everything—financial instruments, money, factories, information—can be globalized and move freely across borders; everything, that is, *except poor, unskilled labor.* As a result, poor, unskilled laborers are unable to travel in search of opportunities. They are *forced* to sit and wait for opportunity to find them.

It is no surprise, then, that the only opportunities that find them involve low wages and sweaty conditions. Our immigration laws make the most vulnerable members of the world sitting ducks for exploitation. Just as the strawberry restriction laws ensure that strawberry sellers get a bad deal, immigration restrictions ensure that poor, unskilled laborers in developing countries get a bad deal.

The reason to focus on the plight of poor laborers should be obvious. While not being as free to move as they should be, rich and skilled people do have considerably greater opportunities to do so. And the harms of immigration restrictions for the poor are much more severe. Like the rich, they are prevented from moving to other places to find work. Unlike the rich, they have few alternatives to obtain a good standard of living when they're prevented to move. At the limit, it may threaten their lives.

Still, would-be immigrants are not the only ones who lose. The people on the other side of the border (rich and poor) who would like to hire, cooperate, and interact with them lose too. As do the owners of the stores where the immigrants might spend their money, the buildings immigrants might rent, and so on. Even the rest of us who don't directly interact with migrants lose as a result of migration restrictions. Of course, when those of us in the developed world are denied the right to trade with would-be immigrants, we suffer much less than they do. But we still lose.

A number of economists have tried to estimate the overall economic losses that result from immigration restrictions, and the results are staggering. In a meta-analysis paper titled "Economics and Immigration: Trillion Dollar Bills on the Sidewalk," Michael Clemens reviews various peer-reviewed published estimates and finds that the estimated *gains* from open borders would amount to 50–150% of current world product, with the mean estimate being about 100% of world product.[10] World product in 2014—the total value of everything everyone produced—was about $108 trillion.[11] A world of open borders would have a total world product of about $216 trillion. On this analysis, we are foregoing no less than an entire planet's worth of economic output.

Admittedly, some of these estimates use some unrealistic assumptions, such as that that nearly every worker will move in search of better jobs. In real life, people care about things other than making more money. They want to be near friends, family, and want to avoid feeling foreign. When Eastern European countries like Poland and the Czech Republic joined the European Union's zone of free movement, many opponents of open borders feared a tidal wave of immigrants looking for higher wages in the West. The tidal wave never came, though part of the reason for that was that restrictive labor laws made it hard for immigrants to get jobs elsewhere.[12]

Still, Clemens points out that even if we use the much more conservative assumption that only a small fraction of people would move, the gains would still amount to $20 to $60 *trillion* to the world economy. That is year after year, and with compounding growth on top of that. Much of this would go to the poorest workers, and much would go to everyone else. No one, not even the most bullish foreign aid-enthusiasts, believes that international aid could come anywhere near these results.[13]

This is not to say that opening borders will be great for *everyone*, or impose no costs of its own. A total increase in global standards of living can be accompanied by losses for particular people, especially in the short term. Some people might lose their jobs because more efficient workers have arrived.

And even if those people benefit in the long run too, as they likely will, it is in their short-term interest to limit the freedom of others to move.

But from an economic point of view, such losses do not threaten the case for opening the borders. Suppose we make a cost-benefit analysis between the options of open and closed border regimes, using Clemens's estimate that an open borders regime would add at least $20 trillion to world product. And suppose that we identify certain *negative* economic consequences of open borders, including the losses to those workers who would be displaced as economic costs of free migration and other costs as well (perhaps free migration would put so much pressure on our infrastructure that we would have to make improvements). Using a hypothetically high estimate (not one taken from any empirical paper), let's imagine that these costs would rise up to $5 trillion per year.[14] The costs of immigration would then still not be an *overall* compelling reason for closing borders, as we have potentially $20 to $60 trillion or more in gains to make up for these costs (which would compound year after year).

Popular opinion has it that freeing up migration would have bad economic consequences. In the next chapter, we'll examine some of the purported economic downsides of open borders. But at first glance, this seems the exact opposite of the truth. What is disastrous, economically speaking, is our current system of restrictions. By limiting people's freedom to move around the world, and preventing people from making mutually beneficial trades, we are forfeiting staggering benefits to migrants (who would see their earnings multiply in ways otherwise near impossible) and the rest of the world. For that reason alone, there is a strong presumption in favor of open borders.

The Intuitive Moral Case for Open Borders

The economic argument for open borders is powerful by itself. However, there is also a powerful deontological argument for freeing up immigration. The first step in this argument is to establish who has the burden of proof. As we will show, those who prefer to restrict immigration must offer us some compelling justification. That is, states must have good reasons for keeping people out. Absent such reasons, people have a right to move freely.

Consider this thought experiment, from Michael Huemer:

Starvin' Marvin
Starvin' Marvin heads to the market looking for food. Marvin has little to trade. However, suppose there are people at the market willing to trade food for whatever Marvin has. Unless someone stops him,

Marvin will get to the market, make the trade, and eat. Imagine, how-ever, that Donald forcibly prevents Marvin from getting to the market. Donald posts guards to keep him out. The guards continually capture Marvin and turn him away. As a result, Marvin can't barter for food, starves and dies.[15]

In this situation, Huemer contends, Donald clearly did something morally wrong. He did not simply *fail to help* Marvin—as when people walk by a beggar without giving some money. Donald *actively hurt* Marvin, using vio-lence, by preventing him from making a trade with a willing partner.

Note that our intuitions aren't particularly conflicted about this. We all agree that unless Donald has some very good reason for doing this, he se-riously and deeply wrongs Marvin. Sometimes there can be such reasons. Should Marvin have a dangerous, communicable disease, Donald may be jus-tified in restricting his freedom as a way of protecting the people on the mar-ketplace.[16] But that is just the point. Unless there *is* such a reason, preventing Marvin from getting to the market is wrong. We need a justification.

Immigration restrictions seem analogous to the case of Marvin. When countries keep immigrants out, they are not just failing to help them. Some people in rich countries want to hire poor foreigners, and the foreigners want the jobs. But governments post armed sentries around their borders, using force to stop those foreigners from making life-saving or life-changing trades with willing partners. As such, they actively hurt some of the most vulnerable people in the world by forcing them to remain in poverty, oppression, and even life-threatening circumstances. Unless they have some very good justi-fication for doing so, then, immigration restrictions are deeply wrong as well.

You might balk at this analogy. Perhaps you think it unfairly loads the dice against immigration restrictions; after all, it's not as though forbidding someone from immigrating usually kills her.

Maybe. Let's consider some slightly different thought experiments, then, that set aside the threat to Marvin's life and focus more generally on restricting people's movement. To keep things simple (for now), each of these takes place within a single country. Later we will ask whether changing our focus to inter-national movement makes a difference.

Individual Restrictions I
Jane lives in rural Montana. She wants to leave as she is poor and there are not many jobs around. After careful consideration, Jane decides to move to Texas. A willing landlord in Texas is happy to rent her

an apartment, and some employers in Texas want to interview her. However, when Jane shows up at the Texan border, she finds Jim blocking the road. Jim, who has long lived in Texas, tells Jane to leave. Jane politely explains that all she wants is work hard and live in Texas, but Jim is unfazed. When Jane tries to enter Texas anyway, Jim pulls out his gun and forces Jane to turn around.

In individual restrictions I, it seems clear that Jim seriously wrongs Jane. Indeed, it's plain that that Jim grossly violates Jane's rights, in this case the right to move around freely. He has no business interfering with Jane in this way. As long as she does not threaten or wrong anyone else, Jim should leave her be. When he forces her to turn around, it's Jim who is in the wrong, not Jane.

Asking Jim to step aside, again, is not asking him to *help* Jane. A failure to help is not what's wrong in this example. Jim does not simply fail to help Jane; he actively and coercively *interferes* with Jane (and with the people who want to make trades with her). Jim uses violence and threats of violence to stop Jane from interacting with others who wish to associate with her. At first sight, then, the conclusion from the starvin' Marvin example applies here as well. Unless Jim has some very good justification for his interference, he seriously wrongs Jane (and Jane's potential trading partners as well).

You might still think that our intuitions in this case are due to Jane's circumstances, in particular her poverty and lack of opportunity in rural Montana. That is, perhaps you agree that Jim wrongs Jane but think that this is not because Jane has a presumptive right to freedom of movement, but rather has such a right only because of her dire circumstances.

It seems obvious that Jane's poverty lends force to her claim to enter Texas. But it would be a mistake to think that this means that Jane's poverty does all the work. Even when people are not poor, it is still wrong to interfere with their freedom of movement. Consider the following variation.

Individual Restrictions II
Jason lives in Northern Virginia, has a great job, but is getting tired of the traffic. Bas lives in North Carolina and has been telling Jason about how wonderful a place it is to live. Jason decides to move to North Carolina. This was not Bas's intention, and so he decides to prevent Jason from coming. When Jason tries to come anyway, Bas meets him on the road with his gun and threatens to shoot Jason unless he turns around.

Again, the restriction is wrongful. Even though Jason had a wonderful life in Washington, DC, Bas still violates his rights when he prevents Jason from moving. Bas uses force to stop Jason from interacting with others who wish to interact with him.

The point seems clear, then. The kinds of force and interference involved in limiting people's freedom of movement stands in need of justification. Unless Bas, Jim, or Donald have some very good reason for stopping Jason, Jane, or Marvin, they need to step aside and let him be on his way. By analogy, the same seems true for modern governments and immigrants.

Unless there is another difference between these cases and immigration restrictions, of course. One such difference might be that restrictions enforced by the state and restrictions enforced by individuals are not the same thing. Perhaps, in other words, the state is special in some way not yet considered.

One reason might be that states are (or are at least supposed to be) the agents of their people. And maybe that status gives them the permission to restrict the freedom of people like Marvin and Jason. Of course, an agent can't have more powers than the principal might bestow on it. So we should ask whether the people, as a group, have the right to restrict people's freedom of movement in this way. If they do, at least in principle, then whenever states act as agents of their people, they might indeed have the right to keep out immigrants.

This will not do. Compare:

Group Restrictions I
Jane once more wants to move to Texas. This time, Jim suspected that Jane wanted to come and notified his neighbors. The group decides they don't like Jane coming, and tells Jane to go home. When Jane tries to enter Texas anyway, they pull their guns and force her to leave.

It is clear that Jim and his neighbors again wrong Jane. The fact that they act as a group does nothing to change this. No new rights or permissions have appeared. Unless the group has some good *other* justification for restricting Jane they should leave her be, just as was the case when Jim acted alone.

Of course, it is possible that there is some further fact about groups that gives them the right to restrict others' freedom—other than the mere fact that they are a group, that is. What might this be? A popular suggestion is that states are special because (*when*) they are democratic. But this, too, seems problematic. Consider:

Group Restrictions II

Jane once more wants to move to Texas. Again, Jim suspected that Jane might come and notified his neighbors. They took a vote and the majority agreed that Jane needs to go home. Together they meet her at the border, tell her they don't want her there, and pull their guns when Jane tries to enter anyway.

Again, the restriction remains wrong, even though it is carried out by a group that is deciding things democratically. Jim and his neighbors simply lack the *right* to tell Jane where she can go. If a group lacks the right to make that decision for her, then a group making that decision in a particular (democratic) way also lacks that right. Jane can move about freely *unless* there is some good, independent justification for preventing her.

Of course these thought experiments do not *prove* that immigration restrictions are unjust. For one, they may still not be completely analogous to that case. Some may think, for example, that the examples leave out what's most important here. Perhaps states can keep people out not merely because they are groupish or democratic, but because of some other, closely related feature. Perhaps the difference is that they have a right to self-determination. Or perhaps it's because of the value of the welfare state. Or perhaps it's something else.

We will discuss (and reject) many of these proposals in the following chapters. However, for now, our argument is a different one—it's about who bears the burden of proof. These examples show that it lies squarely with the defenders of immigration restrictions. They have to show that there *is* some such further difference between the thought experiments and immigration restrictions, that states really are special in a way that overrides the normal presumption in favor of freedom of movement. The examples are meant to show only that *ordinarily* we cannot permissibly use this kind of force against innocent people. And so, absent a successful argument showing that states are indeed special, the point stands that people are (like Jane) free to move.

One might object that invoking these intuitions is unfair. The thought experiments leave out one important feature that you may think makes all the difference: Marvin, Jane, and Jim (and Jim's neighbors) are already living in the same country. Perhaps they are even all citizens of the same country. And *that*, one might think, is exactly what makes all the difference in the world. There are meaningful moral differences between how we treat fellow citizens and foreigners. And among these differences might be the fact that citizens have a *right* to be here, but foreigners do not.

But this reply will not do. For it assumes an answer to precisely the question that we are asking. Our question is *whether* states are justified in making these distinctions between inhabitants (citizens and residents) and outsiders. And we cannot answer that question by pointing to the distinction itself. Or, at least, we cannot use that distinction without *also* offering an argument for why that distinction is morally meaningful—the kinds of arguments we'll consider later.

The Presumption of Liberty

The examples illustrate that at least intuitively, people seem to recognize a moral presumption in favor of liberty. According to that presumption, unless some good justification can be offered, we ought to refrain from coercively interfering with other people's lives.

One might worry here that this presumption is really just a *libertarian* idea. And, if true, that would be a problem. We have some sympathy for libertarianism, but it *is* a controversial political philosophy.[17] We wouldn't want to rest our case for global openness on the truth of libertarianism.

However, the presumption of liberty is not unique to libertarians. If it's to be identified with a background ideology at all, that ideology is liberalism in general. All liberals share the view that acts of coercion, including government coercion, call for justification. Indeed, this may be the defining feature of liberalism, both in its left-wing and libertarian variations. As Gerald Gaus explains,

> The liberal tradition in political philosophy maintains that each person is free to do as he wishes until some justification is offered for limiting his liberty . . . As liberals see it, we necessarily claim liberty to act as we see fit unless reason can be provided for interfering . . . A person is under no standing obligation to justify his actions . . . Interference with another's action requires justification; unjustified interference is unjust.[18]

The underlying idea here can be traced back to an idea of moral equality. As equals, we are free to live as we see best, without first having to ask permission from others. Other people have no authority over us to demand that we explain ourselves before we get to live our lives. Of course, again, sometimes there may be good reasons for restricting our liberty. But, by default, *all* restrictions on liberty are presumed wrong and unjust until shown otherwise.

Nevertheless, some people have sought to challenge this presumption. According to David Miller, for example, if there is a presumption of liberty, it cannot be very weighty. It may be overridden for relatively minor goals. Writes Miller:

> Of course there is always *some* value in people having more options to choose between, in this case options as to where to live, but we usually draw a line between *basic* freedoms that people should have as a matter of right and what we might call *bare* freedoms that do not warrant that kind of protection. It would be good from my point of view if I were free to purchase an Aston Martin tomorrow, but that is not going to count as a morally significant freedom—my desire is not one that imposes any kind of obligation on others to meet it.[19]

To Miller, the freedom to migrate is similar to his freedom to purchase an Aston Martin: nice if you can have it, but not something that merits much protection. People only have a right to "an *adequate* range of options," where adequacy is understood in terms of generic human interests. As a result, people have a right to move around freely insofar as this is generally necessary for having a decent life. But this does not include the freedom to move around the entire world. That freedom is nice if you can have it, but does not merit much protection.[20]

Miller thinks that countries can exclude immigrants for a variety of reasons, including relatively trivial ones like the desire to maintain a specific culture or the current size of their population.[21] Such reasons can suffice to keep immigrants out *because* there isn't much of a presumption to be overcome. As long as foreigners have "adequate" freedom of movement, this is enough to keep them out.

The key claim in Miller's argument is his proposed distinction between "bare" and "basic" freedoms, where liberties being bare means they do not merit much protection. But this claim is seriously problematic. For one, it leads to a host of unacceptable implications. Miller does not see much problem with countries prohibiting otherwise perfectly innocent consumer goods, such as his freedom to buy a fancy sports car. As long as these do not serve morally basic interests, even fairly trivial reasons can suffice to deny people this liberty.

Compare this suggestion in other contexts. Suppose, for example, that the French decide that analytic political philosophy sullies their culture. Could the French state permissibly ban this book, and much of the global justice literature with it? Although we would like to believe that reading this book serves generic human interests, it almost certainly does not. It seems, then, that Miller's view would allow the French to forbid bookstores from selling his and our books. Similarly, the American government could ban Indian films, the Indian government could prohibit American films, and so on.

Note that nothing here turns on it being the government that is doing the interfering. Miller's point, remember, is not that the government somehow has special standing, but rather that these "bare" liberties do not carry much moral weight. Thus, suppose Jason decides that Bas has spent too much time watching sports, perhaps because it takes away valuable time he could be spending on writing philosophy. To be sure, the liberty to watch sports is not of serious weight—many people live fine lives without it. And to be sure, writing philosophy is a valuable thing. Yet clearly, Jason would be wronging Bas, and seriously so.

When we apply Miller's ideas to the context of migration, further problematic results follow. For instance, it implies that governments may not only restrict immigration into their own societies for certain reasons, but into other societies as well. Suppose the United States began sending back immigrants traveling to Mexico via American airports, or vigorously patrolled the Gulf of Mexico, to prevent these immigrants from tainting Mexican culture. If the US government is justified in preventing immigration to the United States for this reason, it must also be justified in stopping immigration elsewhere for the same reason.

It is plain, of course, that countries doing this would be seriously morally wrong. Yet Miller's argument lacks the resources to explain why this is so. It won't do, for example, to say that the US government wrongs Mexico here because it is violating Mexican sovereignty. This misdiagnoses the case. The United States is not only wronging Mexico; it is wronging the people trying to immigrate into Mexico. And this cannot be explained by invoking Mexican sovereignty.

Once we give up on the idea that restricting people's freedom of movement calls for serious justification, we have opened up the door for many more restrictions than are acceptable. Better, then, to maintain what seems intuitively right in any case: that the presumption of liberty is real.

How to Argue for Closed Borders

The purpose of this chapter has been to establish that at first glance, immigration restrictions seem like rights violations. When immigration restrictions are imposed by rich countries, they do not simply fail to help would-be immigrants. They forcibly prevent them from making life-saving and life-changing trades with willing others. Unless they are backed up by some compelling justification, such restrictions are wrong.

In the next two chapters, we'll examine a range of arguments that attempt to defeat this presumption in favor of free movement. As we'll see, in the end these arguments fail. Before we turn to this, however, let us quickly review what it would take to defeat this presumption.

Most arguments against open borders claim that this would cause some bad thing (or the loss of some good thing). And they conclude that borders should therefore not be open. To make such an argument successful requires at least two steps. First, it requires real evidence that open borders would indeed produce the bad thing, or harm the good thing. However, as we'll see, often such arguments are either highly speculative or simply mistaken about the facts.

Second, even if there is evidence that the bad thing would happen, we still need a good philosophical argument showing that avoiding the bad thing or obtaining the good thing is important enough to restrict people's freedom of movement. As we saw earlier, even if it's a bad thing for Jason to move to North Carolina (at least, in Bas's eyes), it's not bad in a way that licenses Bas to force Jason to stay out.

One way to test this is to ask whether avoiding the bad thing or getting the good thing would also justify imposing *other* illiberal or anti-democratic restrictions on people's freedoms. If an argument works equally well justifying other policies that are plainly unacceptable (like forced birth control, religious control, or internal migration restrictions), this counts as a strike against the argument. Unless one can carefully explain why these arguments *only* call for restrictions on immigration, and nothing else, the argument ought to be rejected.

3

Economic Objections to Open Borders

THE PRESUMPTIVE ECONOMIC case for open borders appears powerful. The deadweight loss from labor mobility restrictions are on the order of $20 to $60 trillion a year, and perhaps much more. If these estimates are even close to correct, restricting international migration represents an economic disaster. It would be the single most inefficient thing governments do.

A smart reader might say that things cannot be that simple. If we want to know the *net* cost of immigration restrictions, then this deadweight loss is only one entry on the ledger. Before we can conclude that it's economically a bad idea overall, we need to look at other things as well. Free migration may have costs, and we need to measure these against the putative benefits.

In this chapter, we examine a number of standard economic objections to open borders, such as the claim that open borders would depress domestic wages, cause crime, put too great a strain on the welfare state, or undermine support for basic liberal values. These objections rely on *causal* claims: claims that increased immigration would in fact have these bad effects, the kinds one defends with social scientific evidence.

Our discussion, in general, consists of two steps. First, we look at whether the social scientific evidence is actually in favor of, or against, these objections. Second, we ask whether these bad effects, if indeed they would occur, are sufficient to justify restricting immigration.

Protecting Domestic Wages

One of the most popular arguments for restricting immigration is that allowing foreigners to come would depress domestic wages. This is consistent with our claim that opening borders will lead to massive economic gains overall. Almost everyone can win, and win big, while some people lose. If domestic markets suddenly have access to many more laborers, the price of labor will decline. That's great for those who get to enjoy the benefits, but not for the laborers themselves. Or so the argument goes.

The key issue in this argument is whether immigrating workers are *substitutes* or *complements* for existing domestic workers. If immigrants are substitutes—if they will compete for the same jobs as current domestic workers, but at lower cost—they could indeed depress wages, at least to some degree. But if they are complements—if they have different skills and do different jobs—then they are in fact likely to *increase* domestic workers' wages.

When economists study this issue, however, their findings generally do not offer much support for the objection. Even when it is assumed, for the sake of argument, that immigrant workers are substitutes for domestic workers, economists find that the negative effects on wages are relatively small, temporary, and limited to a small subset of domestic workers. That is, while most workers see wages increase, some, typically the least educated, will see their wages decrease. But even these negative effects are temporary.[1]

When these pessimistic modeling assumptions are lifted, trying harder to estimate whether immigrants actually are substitutes or complements, the results are more positive still. On these more realistic scenarios, immigrants increase rather than decrease most domestic workers' wages even more strongly.[2] Economists Rachel Friedberg and Jennifer Hunt conclude that "despite the popular belief that immigrants have a large adverse impact on the wages and employment opportunities of the native-born population, the literature on this question does not provide much support for the conclusion."[3]

The empirical evidence thus seems to indicate that large-scale immigration would be a large boon for the domestic economy, and that most workers would see their wages rise rather than fall. That said, some domestic workers—particularly low-skilled workers—might see their wages fall somewhat in the short term. The moral question, then, is whether these harms could justify restricting immigration. But again, it's difficult to see how protecting the wages of low-skilled workers in rich countries could justify such restrictions.

Consider the following thought experiment:

George and Jorge

Jason pays George to mow his lawn. One day, Jorge calls Jason and tells him he'd mow his lawn for less money. Jason is happy about this and tells Jorge it's a deal. He thanks George for his services, and informs him he'll use Jorge from here on. George is angry, thinking that Jorge "steals" his job, and tells Donald about the incident. Donald posts armed guards around Jason's neighborhood, and forces Jorge to go home.

It seems clear in this case that Donald seriously wrongs Jorge. We might feel bad for George, of course. He did lose his job, and losing one's job really hurts. But George has no *claim* to being hired by Jason, nor does he have a claim to being hired over Jorge.

The example, of course, is simply a special case of the starvin' Marvin thought experiment we saw before. What's added here is only *why* George wants to keep Jorge out. George wants to keep "his" job. However, as the thought experiment shows, that is generally not a good enough reason to justify coercively interfering with other people. It thus seems like this argument simply lacks the power to justify immigration restrictions.

It seems, then, that if Donald is not justified in preventing Jorge from competing with George, governments are also not justified in preventing immigrants from competing with their domestic workers. Or at least, they are not justified in preventing them *for the reason that* they will be competing. If immigration restrictions are justified, some other argument is needed.

It's worth noting here that the language of "stealing jobs" is seriously misleading. If it looks like George loses "his" job when Jorge arrives, that is only because the government was forcibly preventing people like Jorge from doing business with people like Jason before. The state quite literally forbade, through the use of force, Jason and Jorge from making a mutually beneficial deal. Once we open borders, that is no longer true. This might mean that some people will lose business, and they will be worse off as a result (at least in the short term). But all this shows is that they were, in effect, enjoying an economic rent from closed borders—their income was artificially inflated compared to what the market otherwise would have supported. They enjoyed artificially high incomes at the expense of the poor.

Of course, on the flip side, others will gain from opening borders. Jorge's income was artificially depressed compared to what the market would otherwise support. And he's much better off when borders are opened. The *moral* question is whether we can protect domestic workers' inflated incomes by forcibly keeping would-be immigrants' incomes down. It's the question of whether we can (strongly) prioritize the well-being of fellow citizens over the well-being of foreigners. Perhaps we can. But merely pointing out that domestic workers' income will go down is simply to restate that their incomes are inflated because foreigners are not allowed to compete. It does not help to answer the moral question.

The Welfare State

Another major argument against open borders is that it would bankrupt modern welfare states. Modern rich democracies, such as Norway, the United States, or the Netherlands, have expansive welfare states. Even though the "poor" in these countries enjoy pre–tax-and-transfer incomes that are much higher than the world average, the governments of these countries still regard these incomes as too low, and issue generous packages of welfare benefits including subsidized medical care, education benefits, training, unemployment insurance, pensions, food stamps, housing subsidies, and more. A vast influx of immigrants, the argument goes, would bankrupt countries with such policies.

These worries are at least somewhat overblown. Studies of the fiscal impact of existing immigrants—calculated as the difference between the taxes and other contributions they make and the costs of the public benefits and services they draw—consistently find that the net impact of immigrants ranges from positive to almost zero.[4] Moreover, the economic studies we discussed earlier claim that increased immigration is expected to be a spectacular economic benefit, bringing significant economic growth. If so, then the receiving countries should expect a larger tax base and an increased ability to pay for welfare services.

That said, immigrants arrive poor, while the growth arrives later. And perhaps, even after all of this growth, it may be impossible to give every new immigrant the huge subsidies and welfare payments the citizens of welfare states now enjoy. So, for the sake of argument, let's pessimistically assume that the countries receiving immigrants cannot afford to pay a single penny more toward social insurance, education, or other social services. Let's also assume that the countries will not split the current budget for these welfare services with any incoming immigrants. What then?

It seems like there is an obvious solution here. If modern welfare states really cannot afford to give immigrants welfare benefits, that does not mean they should keep them out. After all, immigration would still benefit them, and us, tremendously. A better option would be to let them immigrate, but deny them welfare benefits. The solution is to build walls *around the welfare state*, not walls around the country.[5] This may sound callous. But note that it's far less callous than forbidding immigration altogether. Instead of denying immigrants safety, better employment opportunities, and welfare state benefits, this option only denies them the latter.

We would not defend this proposal, all things considered. In our view, it's unjust for a government to create different formal classes, with only the higher class being eligible, by birthright, for benefits. However, if forced to choose between this and the ongoing injustice of closed borders, we'd prefer a more open world, with two-tiered societies.

Suppose, by contrast, that one feels really strongly about avoiding the two-tiered society. Would that justify closing the borders? This is a puzzling position. Presumably, the worry about treating people as second-class citizens is a worry about treating people poorly, making them vulnerable to abuse, discrimination, and other wrongs. But those worries are not at all alleviated by closing the borders. In obvious ways, they are exacerbated. In practice, the effect of keeping people out of prosperous welfare states is to condemn them to much worse conditions; higher risks of abuse, violence, and discrimination; and lower standards of living overall. This proposal aims to avoid two-tiered societies by creating a two-tiered world.

Immigrants themselves seem prefer life in two-tiered societies over life in a two-tiered world. Indeed, they prefer this in rather large numbers. The millions of so-called illegal immigrants presently living and working in countries like the United States effectively *are* second-class subjects. They enjoy far less protection of the law, and already do not enjoy the social services on which this argument focuses. Nevertheless, these people seem to strongly prefer this option to being stuck at home.

Maybe proponents of this argument would say that this line of thinking is mistaken. (Would they say that these immigrants *themselves* are mistaken?) Perhaps they'd say that equal treatment within welfare states is more important than allowing poor people around the world to seek a better life. Even if so, this argument contains a fallacy. If we really cannot simultaneously have (a) welfare states (b) in which everyone has equal access to their provisions, and (c) open borders, the refusal to reject (b) does not entail the rejection of (c). The correct implication of the impossibility of combining a welfare state with an open society may be that the welfare state is best scaled back to more sustainable levels.

Proponents of the welfare state no doubt recoil at the thought. Perhaps they think that the commitment to equality is especially important within societies, and that this requires keeping the welfare state. However, this proposal really attempts to purchase equality at a tremendous price. After all, open borders would cause a massive economic boon, benefiting current citizens of receiving countries and greatly benefiting immigrants. The present argument holds that since it's impossible to give everyone under open borders equal welfare benefits, we should prefer a policy—closed borders—that makes everyone (much) worse off.

We find it hard to see why anyone might find this option attractive. Suppose we make it less abstract. Imagine offering a poor Haitian the following explanation of your opposition to opening the borders: "Sure, if you came to the United States, your income would go up by a factor of 10, and our income would go up as well. However, we can't afford (or don't want) to pay for your kids' schooling, so you'll just have to stay poor, and your kids will have to stay uneducated, in Haiti. Justice prevents us from treating you as a second-class citizen, and so we'll just have to treat you as a *non*citizen. You're welcome."

Recall that we are conceding here, for the sake of argument and probably contrary to the facts, that immigrants pose a net drain on the welfare state. Once we recognize that immigrants are not mere consumers of benefits but contributors as well, whatever little appeal these arguments might have disappears altogether. Consider another analogy. Perhaps it's true that treating people equally is more important than improving their lives. If parents have only one toy available for two children, and it's really impossible for the kids to share the toy, it might be better not to give it altogether rather than for one to have it but not the other.[6]

But this, too, is a case in which decisions about how to distribute goods have no effect on the availability of goods going forward, the overall well-being of the people involved, and so on. Immigration is decidedly not like that. Adding immigrants to a society is not a matter of merely adding more mouths to feed, increasing the number n in the 1/n slice of the pie each of us gets. Immigrants add to society at least as much as (and likely more than) they take from it. In this case, it is in the interests of the receiving groups to accept the immigrants.[7]

It is probably true that opening the borders while keeping current welfare state provisions intact would be unpopular. No doubt we'd see many media stories about newly arrived immigrants living off welfare. It might create moral hazard problems, incentivizing people to come for the welfare benefits rather than work. Perhaps this means that the wise choice would be to delay or deny immigrants access to such benefits. Or perhaps it means we should scale down the welfare state to sustainable (but equal) levels. Either way, it's clear that keeping borders closed would be the worst choice, both in terms of justice and in terms of its overall consequences. The welfare state argument for limiting immigration fails.

Illiberal Immigration

In terms of the practical problems surrounding immigration, perhaps the most important barrier to making immigration work is the successful integration of new people into existing societies. Different countries have different track records, and, perhaps more importantly, have remarkably different levels of success integrating different groups.

Notoriously, many in Europe are concerned about the integration (or lack thereof) of Muslim immigrants from Northern African countries like Algeria and Morocco. It is said that these immigrants are disproportionally involved in crime, experience high levels of unemployment, and fare worse educationally. In his attack on immigration *Reflections on the Revolution in Europe*, Christopher Caldwell summarizes some of the most worrying statistics, such as that "Muslims make up 50% of the population in many French jails, and up to 80% in certain prisons near the banlieues."[8]

Things are not much better in terms of employment and education. According to *The Economist*, youth unemployment for French-born citizens whose parents arrived from Africa is twice as high as for those with nonimmigrant backgrounds. No less than 30% leave high school without any diploma or qualification, almost twice the number of those without immigrant parents.[9]

Explanations for these depressing statistics are speculative. But many (especially in Europe) attribute these problems to something inherent in Islam, or at least the way it's expressed in Northern African societies. They see a certain antagonism in Islam and its associated cultures as the explanation for these problems.[10] Hence the purported problem of immigration: immigrants bring along their cultures,[11] ones that lack support for the rule of law, democracy, and freedom. As such, they threaten to undo core liberal values elsewhere, too.

The most thorough version of this argument has been offered by economist Paul Collier. Where we see the benefits of immigrants getting access to better institutions, Collier worries about the effects of immigration on those institutions themselves. He develops a model in which the increased migration he thinks we see today makes immigrants live in enclave-like communities, places resistant to integration into liberal society. As a result, allowing people to move freely from poor to rich societies undercuts the very institutions that make prosperity possible, and with it social stability and liberal freedom.[12]

For ease of discussion, let us call countries with "dysfunctional social models" (Collier's term) *bad countries*, and the stable, liberal, and prosperous societies that Collier wants to defend *good countries*. Finally, let us call the cultures that support the institutions of good and bad countries *good* and *bad cultures*, respectively.

Collier's main argument against immigration can be summarizes as follows:

1. When people from bad countries move to good countries, they infuse good countries with bad cultures.
2. Because good countries need good cultures, once enough people move from bad countries to good countries, the good country will become a bad country.
3. It is permissible to forcibly prevent people from turning good countries into bad countries.
4. Therefore, it is permissible to forcibly prevent people from bad countries from moving into good countries.

The argument relies on a couple of empirical claims. Most importantly, it presumes a different view from what we have called the institutionalist approach. That approach, recall, holds that the primary determinant of whether a country is prosperous or poor is the quality of its institutions. Insofar as culture matters, it is mostly a *product* of the presence of certain institutions.[13]

To be sure, there is evidence for this challenge to the institutionalist view. A number of studies find that the most important determinant of a country's economic growth is, in fact, the ancestry of its population. Once we correct for migration, this argument goes, where people come from has much more influence on how well a country performs than the quality of its institutions. Or, more accurately, the quality of institutions is itself a product of the quality of the people and their cultures.[14] These findings may support Collier's view that "migrants bring their culture with them."[15] Depending on whether they come from good or bad countries, this may be a good or a bad thing for the receiving country.

Consider an example, using money to make things more easily quantifiable.[16] Country A is poor, with everyone making only $1,000 a year. Country B is rich, with everyone making $50,000 a year. Let's take a pessimistic scenario in which allowing people to move freely from country A to country B drastically lowered the living standards of B's people, say to $30,000 a year (or, again, whatever the equivalent might be in terms of liberal values).

Collier argues that this drastic effect justifies B excluding immigrants from A. But note that saying this requires the *additional* assumption expressed in premise 3. It requires that we can prioritize B's standard of living over A's. Even though the people from B face a net loss of $20,000 a year (a great loss), A's immigrants experience a $29,000 *increase* (an even greater gain). The idea that B can keep out A's immigrants thus holds that one side's loss of $20,000 outweighs the other side's increase of $29,000.

The real question, then, is the same as with the argument from domestic wages. It's whether the people in B have the *right* to exclude the people from A—whether they have the right to prioritize avoiding their losses at the expense of others' potential gains. But that, again, is precisely the question we're asking. The question is *whether* B has a right to restrict immigration. Stating that people from B would face a loss if it lacked that right does not settle the matter. After all, people from A would face a gain. And we have already seen that absent some compelling justification, people have a right to freedom of movement. Collier's argument, which purports to show that B might lose, thus remains incomplete.

Perhaps you think that the example is still too rosy. Perhaps allowing the people from A to move to B would not just lower B's living standards by $20,000 (or the equivalent in liberal values), but entirely destroy its basis of prosperity or freedom, thus moving B all the way back to A's $1,000.

We can suppose that forcibly preventing immigration could be justified if it really were necessary to avoid this nightmare scenario. But there really is no reason to think this scenario is likely. For one, at best the arguments about ancestry are part of a broader overall picture. And in that picture, institutions still play an important role as well. If cultures help shape institutions, institutions help shape cultures, too. Immigrants often absorb the norms of receiving countries, and take these with them when they return home.[17] Second, and contrary to Collier's ideas about immigrant enclaves, empirical evidence suggests that immigrants today integrate better, not worse.[18] And the evidence that cultural diversity undermines social trust is at the very least questionable. These results run counter to the nightmare scenarios.

Historically liberal institutions and their predecessors have been remarkably robust. They have withstood profound changes in populations, cultures, and norms. That includes times in which there was much greater freedom of movement than today.[19] Of course, in the past people also feared a lack of support among immigrants for domestic cultures and norms. In the United

States, the same points were once made about Irish, Italian, Chinese, and Eastern Europeans immigrants, and many others. None of these groups actually threatened American liberalism. We see little reason to think that today's immigrants, people who would choose to uproot their lives in order to enter liberal societies, are different.

But suppose Collier is right, and suppose, even more strongly, that allowing immigrants from country X into country Y would be an absolute disaster for the institutions of country Y. At worst, this is reason to restrict immigration from X to Y. But it says nothing about immigration from *other* countries.

Extending the Economic Objections

The economic arguments for restricting immigration suffer from two general faults. First, they often invoke mistaken or exaggerated empirical claims, such as that migration is economically harmful. Second, even if the empirical claims were true, these arguments *presuppose*, rather than establish, that countries have the right to restrict immigration. They fail to show what they're designed to show.

There is, however, a third important problem with these arguments. The economic objections to immigration lack the requisite kind of *specificity*. That is, the defender of immigration restrictions needs to show why these arguments apply *only* to foreigners wanting to immigrate, and don't also justify a range of other policies and measures, ones that are plainly unacceptable.

Consider again the argument that immigration restrictions are justified in order to protect domestic wages. Suppose that, contrary to the existing evidence, mass immigration really did depress most workers' wages. Would this suffice to forbid immigration? Consider the parallel question: suppose that Virginia feared that allowing cheaper workers from North Carolina to compete would depress Virginian wages. Would this justify limiting immigration from North Carolina? Or suppose that the United States wanted to open more jobs to women, but someone objects that since women would compete with men these jobs, wages—the price of labor—will decline.

Clearly, people would balk at these suggestions. They would point out that the people living in Virginia do not have some special claim on the jobs in the state, that North Carolinians are wronging no one by moving, and that Virginian employers have the right to hire whom they want, including people from North Carolina. They would point out that women, no less than men, have a right to work, and that employers have the right to hire women as much as they have a right to hire men. No one would seriously regard these arguments as compelling justifications to the contrary.

It's easy to multiply examples. Suppose that someone made a parallel argument to Collier's about residents of predominantly black areas like Anacostia and Ward 8 in Washington, DC. Suppose they argued that, pointing to crime statistics, people from these areas lack support for liberal values like the rule of law and should be prohibited from exiting the city in search of a better life.

Most people would be horrified at such a proposal. And its advocates would be called racists. But the horror is not only directed at the racial problems. If, in the effort to keep down crime, Virginia announced that it would forbid low-income whites from high-crime, rural areas like West Virginia to immigrate, most people would again—and again correctly—conclude that this is highly unjust.[20]

The examples multiply because the economic arguments discussed here are perfectly general in nature. They apply to foreigners and citizens alike. But, given that they are utterly unacceptable domestically, their defenders owe us an explanation why they are not *also* unacceptable when applied to foreigners. We need to know why countries are supposedly justified in doing things to foreigners that they would view as horribly unjust if done to their subjects.

This, again, is the question we are asking. If there *is* such a difference, if we really can do these things to foreigners without wronging them, we need an argument as to why. The economic arguments fail to pick out this difference. As a result, they fail to offer the right kind of justification.

4

Philosophical Objections to Open Borders

SO FAR, THE case for open borders looks strong. There exists a common-sense and liberal presumption in favor of allowing people to move freely and take jobs others are willing to offer them. Immigration restrictions are problematic because they forcibly prevent people from such making life-saving or life-changing trades with willing partners. Moreover, while open borders would have some costs and downsides, the overall consequences appear to be extremely positive.

In the previous chapter, we responded to a number of economic objections to open borders. This chapter discusses another set of objections: the most important arguments philosophers and political theorists have adduced in favor of immigration restrictions.

The Effects on Those Left Behind

The first set of arguments focuses not on the effects of immigration but of its counterpart, emigration. A policy of free movement might help the immigrants themselves and people in the receiving countries, some philosophers worry, but actually harm those left behind. And they argue that this can justify Western governments from prohibiting immigration from such countries. Here's how David Miller puts it. A policy of open borders, he writes,

> will do little to help the very poor, who are unlikely to have the resources to move to a richer country. Indeed, a policy of open migration may make such people worse off still if it allows doctors, engineers,

and other professionals to move from economically undeveloped to economically developed societies in search of higher incomes, thereby depriving their countries of origin of vital skills.[1]

Similarly, Thomas Pogge writes that "not many of those that rich countries admit are really amongst the worst-off." According to Pogge, immigrants are likely to be among the "more privileged" people from their societies—again because they are the ones that can afford the resources needed to cross borders. Immigration thus has the effect of leaving the very poorest behind to fend for themselves.[2]

Miller and Pogge see migration in a very different light than we do. Whereas we see the gains that stem from freedom of movement as an unqualifiedly good thing—good for migrants, good for the people around them, and good for the world in general—Miller and Pogge see the "more privileged" leaving a country as harming the people around them.

There is much wrong with these arguments. First, they get the facts wrong. It is simply not true that allowing people to leave poor countries harms others. In fact, empirically it turns out that the opposite policy, forcing the "more privileged" people to stay in poor countries, has negative effects. Such policies discourage people to invest in education and other forms of human capital accumulation.[3] Forcing doctors to remain in the Sudan does not automatically create more jobs for doctors. It just forces them into accepting jobs that are below their skill level. The possibility of leaving incentivizes people to invest in themselves, but only a small group of those who invest actually uses the option of leaving. We are all better off surrounded by people who *could* leave, even if they don't.

Allowing people to leave also tends to have positive effects on political processes. A number of studies have shown that allowing emigration has positive effects on the quality of democratic institutions. One reason is that emigration allows previously excluded people to participate more in politics, as may have been the case in India.[4] Another reason is that preventing people from leaving can threaten political stability. When elites have the option of leaving, they are less likely to resist the loss of political power at home.[5]

Economically, allowing exit has positive effects, too. The most straightforward and direct way in which those left behind benefit from the departure of others is through remittances. Those who leave send money home, which helps those left behind, including the very poor.[6] Over time, the largest share of remittances is sent to poorer families.[7] In light of this, claims like Pogge's that helping "needy foreigners" requires a commitment "*not* to the struggle to get more of them admitted into the rich countries, but *rather* to the struggle to institute an effective programme of global poverty eradication" is, well, bizarre.[8]

But what if the facts were different? If immigrants fleeing the extractive conditions of their homes means that they in some way hurt those who stayed behind, would that justify forcibly limiting their freedom? Can there be limits, for example, to the smartest and best educated people leaving, as those who worry about the "brain drain" would have it?[9]

Consider an example. Suppose Widad grows up in Sudan, an unjust, oppressive, and extractive regime. She receives medical training at the University of Khartoum and gets an offer to work as physician in Canada. In Canada, she and her family would enjoy a vastly better life. She would be able to send her children to better schools and offer them enormously better opportunities. And she will be able to send money to help her extended family back home. Nevertheless, it also means that the Sudanese won't have access to her medical skills.

For what reason might Widad be justifiably forced to stay put? One possible reason would be that the people in Sudan *need* Widad's services more than Canadians do. On this argument, the Sudanese greater need justifies denying Widad her freedom to choose where to live and work. But this is an extremely implausible idea. For one, it is highly implausible to think that others have some kind of *claim* on our services, such that their need limits our freedom of occupation. Few people live this way, and they plainly have the right to do so. We all get to live our own lives.

This does not mean we should not help others, of course. Nor does it mean that people who need help must be left to fend for themselves. But it does mean that there are clear and important limits to what kinds of help we can be *made* to provide. To see this, consider the only slightly different proposal that Canada should force *its* doctors to work in Sudan. (Or the proposal that Widad should be forced to work somewhere else, say in Bangladesh, if the need there was even greater.) This would obviously be unjust. But if we can forcibly limit people's freedom of movement because of the need of the Sudanese, it seems we can also forcibly limit their freedom of movement because of need elsewhere.

Perhaps, then, need is the wrong place to look. A more popular argument is that Widad has *special obligations* to the people of Sudan. The idea here is that the Sudanese people invested their tax payments in Widad's education. Gillian Brock writes:

There is a deep unfairness in allowing those who have been trained by an impoverished state to simply leave that state and sell their talents to the highest bidder; those who have sacrificed to train that individual deserve some reasonable return on their investment.[10]

Kieran Oberman agrees:

An obligation of repayment is owed by skilled workers who have acquired skills, during their adult life, at the poor state's expense. It obliges them to repay the costs of their training either with money or with their labor.[11]

As a result, the story goes, poor countries like Sudan can be justified in forcing people like Widad to stay.

Obligations of repayment can arise for several reasons. One obvious reason is as a result of agreements, such as contracts. Consider the following example:

Philanthropic Scholarship
A rich philanthropist offers Widad a scholarship to get through medical school. Among the conditions of the scholarship is that after graduating, Widad works for three years in a Sudanese hospital. Widad accepts.

In this case, it's plausible that Widad is obligated to stay in Sudan for three years after she graduates. The arrangement is similar to when the US Reserve Officer Training Corps (ROTC) agrees to pay for students' undergraduate or even medical degrees if ROTC students then agree to become military officers for a number of years. We see no problem with this type of agreement. It may even be, in appropriate ways, enforceable.

Could governments treat people's freedom to move in a similar way? Presumably, it would depend on their actual decisions. Sudan, for instance, has private universities, so if Widad knew that choosing a publicly funded education meant having to stay in Sudan for a few years, her situation would indeed be similar to the philanthropic scholarship example. Should she choose a private education instead, however, this argument would lose its force.

People like Brock do not propose making migration restrictions contingent upon the *choices* of would-be migrants to consume certain public services. It's not because of one education or another that they seek to prevent people like Widad from leaving. Rather, the idea is that people consume a host of public services, and thus *all* have the same burden of repayment Widad has in the philanthropic scholarship example.

But this is unacceptable. Widad's agreement matters because the requirement to repay cannot be simply foisted upon her. Such a possibility would makes us all terribly vulnerable. Consider the following example:

Coercive Philanthropist

Widad receives an email from someone calling himself a philanthropist. The email tells her that he will pay 50% of all her bills moving forward. In return, she will be forced to work for his company for three years. She can't refuse the offer. It's just fair.

Of course, Widad *does* enjoy a serious benefit in this example. Half of her expenses are covered by the philanthropist. Still, this benefit cannot justify the philanthropist *coercing* her in this way. His offer is not accepted by Widad, or at least it's not accepted in a way that counts as voluntary. If the philanthropist had given her a real choice, things would be different. But that's not what's going on here. The requirement to stay, defended by people like Brock, *is* merely foisted on people.

No doubt people like Brock and Oberman will be unimpressed. Their concern is that Widad is avoiding the taxes she would otherwise have to pay—her "repayment." And those taxes don't require these kind of voluntariness conditions either. If Widad can be forced to pay her taxes, why can't she be forced to stay as well? But this is no more promising. It's one thing to claim that people should remain tax-liable when they leave their countries. It's quite another to deny them the freedom to move from one place to another. While the former idea is contestable, it has its supporters. The latter, however, is radically different. It proposes to trap innocent people inside their countries. As we've seen, this is acceptable (if ever) only if further conditions of voluntariness are met.

We are *very* uncomfortable with the way these arguments depict people. There's something deeply perverse about seeing people like Widad as, quite literally, "public investments": people who represent a dollar figure lost, something to be recouped at all cost. Widad is a person, a human being with her own goals, desires, dreams, and commitments. She has a life to lead, and that life might lead her elsewhere. Sometimes this means that people who benefited her will not be repaid. It's okay. Sometimes it means people she benefited won't have the chance to repay her. That's okay, too. One day, perhaps, people might move to Sudan, bringing benefits without asking for repayment. Unless philosophers get in the way first.

People like Brock seem to think it desirable that anyone who receives a benefit must repay this. We do not. One of the reasons we endorse markets is precisely that they create so many positive externalities—benefits one enjoys without having to pay for them. We are not attracted to the view that all good things must come at a price. Such a view does not encourage people to produce good things. It's the opposite of what makes societies worth living in.

Brock writes that her conclusions hold mainly for "emigrants departing from developing countries, because this is where vulnerabilities and losses are most pressing."[12] If there is something perverse about treating Widad as a mere source of tax money, there is something even more perverse about responding to vulnerabilities and losses by imposing *additional* burdens on those already unfortunate enough to be living there.

Wellman on Sovereignty and Self-Determination

Perhaps the philosophically most powerful argument against open borders holds that states have the right to exclude immigrants as a part of their right to self-determination.[13] Just as clubs have the right to restrict members (even when allowing in a member would greatly benefit that member), so nation-states have the right to restrict who belongs in their club.

This kind of argument has several advantages. For one, it avoids the empirical problems we noted before. Rights-holders generally have considerable freedom to decide how to exercise their rights. There is no general demand that they exercise them smartly or in ways that produce the best possible outcomes. If states have the right to exclude people as a matter of their self-determination, then self-determining states can permissibly close their borders despite the serious gains that allowing immigration would bring. (This view does not entail that states *should* close their borders, it only entails that doing so is within their rights. It might be dumb for them to do so, just as it would be dumb for you to burn your life savings.)

Another advantage is that the idea that states have a right to self-determination is widely shared. The idea is deeply enshrined in international law; it's a cornerstone of much philosophy of international affairs, and it has broad popular support.

Neither of us has much faith that existing states actually have rights of self-determination.[14] But even if you agree, the argument here should still be of interest. Our skepticism of states is controversial, and it would be disconcerting if the case for open borders would rest on it. It's important to know what would follow for the case for open borders, should it turn out we were wrong about state self-determination.

In what is by far the best discussion of this question, Christopher Wellman has argued that self-determining states have a right to exclude immigrants because the right to self-determination includes a right to free association.[15] The intuition is powerful. Consider an interpersonal example. Suppose Bas decides he wants to marry Jason, but Jason turns him down. It would be plainly wrong for Bas to force Jason to marry him. Jason is a self-determining, or autonomous, person and as such has a right to choose with whom he wishes to associate. And that includes not associating with Bas (at least not in this way). For Bas to respect Jason as a self-determining agent, he has to respect his right of free association. Of course, Bas's life might go much worse as a result, but Jason still has the right to say no.

What's true for Bas and Jason is also true for individuals and organizations. If Bas wants to join the local country club, but they turn him down, he cannot force them to accept him. They have a right to self-determination, which includes the right to decide with whom to associate, and with whom not to. Of course, again, Bas might be worse off as a result, but the club still has a right to exclude him.

Finally, the same holds between countries. The United States cannot unilaterally force Canada to enter into some treaty; Canada's right to self-determination gives it the right to choose whether or not it wishes to associate with the United States in that manner.[16]

The final step in Wellman's argument is to claim that the same is true for immigration as well. Just as Canada has the right to reject associating with other countries in the form of treaties, so too does it have the right to reject associating with individual people. If this is true, and immigration is indeed a kind of association, then states with a right to self-determination have a right to reject immigrants.

We can summarize this argument as follows:

1. The right to self-determination of states gives them the right to choose with whom they wish to associate.
2. Immigrants associate with the state.
3. Therefore, states with a right to self-determination have a right to choose whether or not to allow immigration.

The argument looks plausible, but has to be rejected in the end. To see the problem we need to unpack the idea of self-determination a little, for there are two importantly different ways that idea can be understood. And this distinction is crucial to Wellman's argument, as it viciously equivocates between the two meanings.

The key difference is between the nature of the *agent* whose self-determination is in play. Wellman's argument relies on an extension of this idea from the context of individuals (like Jason) to collectives or group-agents (like a country club or Canada). It's this idea of group self-determination that can be understood in two different ways.

On the one hand, we can think of a group having self-determination as the combination of the rights of self-determination of its individual members. Here, it's rights and status that are the result of the transferred rights and choices of its members. Call this the *individualist* understanding.[17] On the other hand, we might think of self-determination in a more thoroughly *collectivist* way. Here, groups possess rights not merely in virtue of the (directly transferred) rights of their members or citizens, but in virtue of their status as groups per se. Groups are thus seen as independent or self-standing agents, entities capable of acting freely, and thus having a right to self-determination all of their own.[18]

The difference matters. The individualist understanding of self-determination makes sense in certain contexts. This is most clearly the case for voluntary groups, such as when people join together to form a country club. The members of such clubs freely accept the terms of their membership by deciding to join and remain in them. Thus, even those who oppose a certain decision freely accept being subjected to it by virtue of their continuing membership. As such, the members of voluntary groups can be said to collectively exercise their individual autonomy.

However, this understanding will have no application to the question of *state* self-determination. For the members of states (people like us) decidedly do *not* freely accept the terms of association. States, as many have pointed out, are not like clubs.[19] They impose their rule on people (with force), and do not let them leave without having to uproot their entire existence. Such terms would never be accepted for clubs or voluntary associations, the kinds of entities for which the individualist understanding of self-determination is relevant. In the state, there often is no clear connection between the individual members' wills and the collective.[20]

On the individualist reading, then, premise 1 of the argument becomes false. Individualist self-determination does not apply to states. For Wellman's argument to succeed, he has to rely on the collective understanding of self-determination. And indeed Wellman is explicit on this point, stressing that "group autonomy [is] something that can be exercised by a collective as a whole rather than individually by persons in a group," that self-determination "exists when the group as a whole rather than the individuals within the group stands in the privileged position of dominion over the affairs of the group," and (writing with Andrew Altman) that the right to self-determination is "irreducibly collective."[21]

Understanding the argument in collectivist terms might render premise 1 true. But now we have to read premise 2 in a collectivist sense, too. The crux, then, is whether immigrants seek to *associate* with the state *as a collective*— and not, for example, with its members as individual persons. (It's plain that premise 2 is true on the individualist reading. Clearly, immigrants want to associate with individual people in the state. That's why they're coming.)

At the very least, saying that immigrants seek to associate with the state is an odd way of speaking. It's not as if they're proposing a kind of treaty, as we saw in the example of Canada. That is a clear case of association, but immigrants propose to do something quite different. They're not looking to associate with the state (as a collective entity, separate from its members). If anything, they're looking to *join* the state, to become one among the many parts that make up its collective body. Such joining or merging with an entity is a different matter from associating with it (at least insofar as we view the matter, from the point of view of the collective). The latter consists of two separate entities joining in a relation, while the former consists of one entity being incorporated by the other.

When immigration succeeds, it is unnatural to say that we are still dealing with two separate entities, the group-agent Canada and the individual immigrant, now standing in a newly formed association. The natural thing to say is that we are now dealing with a single collective body that has gained a new member. The upshot of this is that when immigrants join a state, they are not entering into an association with the state as a whole.[22]

This difference is reflected in the way that processes of treaty-formation and immigration are organized. Because entering into a treaty involves associating with groups as collective agents, treaties call for negotiations with state representatives, such as the foreign minister or secretary of state; they are then signed in name of the country as a whole. The same is not true in the case of immigration. Such negotiations would be beside the point, since immigrants do not seek to associate with the collective body of the state but to become constitutive elements of it.

There are important differences between immigrants and associating parties, too. Compare someone (call him Ahmed) successfully immigrating into a country like Canada, with Canada successfully joining the United States in some treaty. Wellman thinks that Ahmed and the United States are similarly placed with respect to Canada. But this is false. For while Ahmed becomes part of any association in which Canada (as a whole) enters, because he has become a part of that Canadian state, the reverse is not true. The United States does not also become party to all other Canadian associations. If Canada and the Netherlands enter into a mutual defense treaty, the United States does not thereby become obligated to come to the Netherlands' defense. Ahmed, by contrast, does become obligated, in just the same way all citizens do.

The problem with the argument is this. If we understand self-determination in the collectivist manner, as Wellman says we should, premise 2 is false. But if we understand the argument in the individualist way, rendering premise 2 true, then premise 1 is false. And if we understand premise 1 in the collectivist way and premise 2 in the individualist way, the argument is invalid. The argument fails.

This is a good thing, too, as Wellman's argument would support some rather troubling additional conclusions. If states have the right to decide who to accept and reject as members, this right would also apply to their own citizens. Thus, should the state decide that it no longer wants to associate with people of a certain race or ethnicity, this argument would justify removing them from the territory or forbidding them from having children. Plainly, this is unacceptable.[23]

The value of self-determination lies elsewhere else, then. Instead of offering control *over the population* that governs itself, it offers that population—whatever it may be—control over *how it governs* itself. There's a difference. Self-determination may be an ideal supporting democracy, sovereignty, and the like. It's not an ideal supporting closed borders.[24]

Prioritizing Co-Citizens

A third attempt at justifying immigration restrictions focuses on the purported special relations that exist between co-citizens. On one version, defended by Stephen Macedo, borders can be closed because of special obligations of distributive justice that hold primarily among fellow citizens.[25] Working within a Rawsian framework, Macedo argues that these obligations hold mostly within societies, and not across them, because co-citizens stand in a special moral relationship of collective self-governance.[26] This can justify closing borders in order to protect the least well-off in rich societies:

> If high levels of immigration have a detrimental impact on our least well-off citizens, that is reason to limit immigration, even if those who seek admission seem to be poorer than our own poor whose condition is worsened by their entry. Citizens have special obligations to one another: we have special reason to be concerned with the distribution of wealth and opportunities among citizens. The comparative standing of citizens matters in some ways that the comparative standing of citizens and non-citizens does not.[27]

There is something very odd about those who claim to care about distributive justice worrying more about inequality among people in rich societies, all of whom may be in the top decile of world income, as opposed to the far greater inequality between those people and the rest of the world, who live in much greater poverty.[28] But let us suppose, for the sake of argument, that Macedo is right and distributive justice holds primarily among citizens of the same nation-state. Would this justify restricting immigration?

It's hard to see how it could. Even if democratic states ought to prioritize the welfare of their own worst-off, this doesn't license doing just anything. When we carry out our duties of mutual aid, reciprocity, or beneficence, we must respect the rights and claims of others. We must comply with the claims that others have against us. While we are morally permitted to prioritize the welfare of our children over others', and buy birthday presents for our kids but not yours, we cannot actively interfere with the lives of your kids in order to get presents for our own.

Similarly, when wealthy countries restrict immigration, they do more than simply prioritize their citizens over foreigners. They are not merely distributing resources. Rather, as we have seen, they're imposing restrictions on others that actively and forcibly interfere with their liberty, lives, and well-being. They are actively imposing harm. The question, then, is whether the relations of priority to which Macedo points can justify these harms—or whether such harms pose a limit to the ways in which states can prioritize their own citizens.

Domestically, of course, such priority relations cannot justify restrictions on freedom of movement. Consider an example. Suppose (contrary to fact) that it turned out that internal restrictions on labor mobility somehow tended to maximize the welfare of the least advantaged workers. Perhaps forbidding citizens who live in rural areas from taking jobs in cities or more populous states within the same country would somehow stop some (imaginary) race to the bottom. We doubt that anyone would think that this would justify laws preventing people from moving from a town to the city. If we really had to choose between liberty and distributive justice in this way, people still have a right to move where they want, even if that comes at the expense of promoting certain goals of distributive justice.

If claims of distributive justice do not justify restricting the freedom of movement of co-citizens, why are things different for foreigners? One answer, suggested by Michael Blake, is to say that governments owe a guarantee of freedom to their own citizens, but not to foreigners. According to Blake, the difference between the freedom of movement of citizens and foreigners is that the former, but not the latter, is part of a bundle of rights and protections the state must offer its subjects in order to be legitimate. Any legitimate state must offer its citizens the freedom to move. But this does not mean it must offer noncitizens the same freedom. Since they are not subject to its rule, they need not be accorded the same kind of concern.[29]

This is a very strange view. What's plausible about the Rawlsian position is that in order for the state to justifiably subject people to its coercive power, the state must guarantee those people certain liberties. But Blake suggests a quite different position: that people must be guaranteed certain liberties *only* if they are subjected to the state.[30] This latter idea, that our rights and freedoms need to be given to us, things to be granted only after first being coerced by some state institution, is extremely implausible.

Indeed, this line of thinking threatens the very starting point of the kind of Rawlsian theory it desires to express. The idea here is that basic freedoms are afforded to people as a condition of state legitimacy, not fundamental moral requirements that people might claim against the state. But if that is true, it becomes obscure why state coercion needs to be justified in the first place (by offering these protections). If there is no fundamental presumption against coercion, a presumption that precedes the creation and coercion by the state, then why would the creation and coercion of the state require justification?

Arguments like this only gain traction if we first assume that people— being autonomous, free, and equal—cannot without justification be subjected to this kind of coercion. But that stipulation, of course, is just to assert that there's exactly the kind of presumption against coercion that makes immigration restrictions morally problematic. If the state as such needs justification, then, it follows that closing its borders for outsiders needs justification, too.

Coercion as such does not distinguish between citizens and outsiders. And this should be obvious. When a state restricts outsiders from entering, it plainly *does* exercise coercion against them. To this extent, it rules over them. Certainly, they are required to comply (and are *made* to comply) with its laws. If a necessary condition for a state imposing coercion is that it must respect and guarantee certain basic liberties, then on its face this should apply to everyone the state coerces, including the would-be immigrants who are forced to stay away (as well as its own citizens, who are coercively prevented from making voluntary and mutually beneficial trades with would-be immigrants).

Again, what we need is an account that shows that the (supposedly unprotected) freedom to immigrate into a particular country is categorically different from other (clearly protected) freedoms. The argument for priority for co-nationals works only if we already presume that immigration restrictions do not count as coercive infringement of people's liberty or as coercively imposed harms. There is no reason to grant this assumption, and so Macedo's argument fails.

Final Thought: Making Immigrants Welcome

Making the world more just requires opening up societies, increasing the opportunities people have for entering into positive-sum interactions. Freeing up international migration is a key—perhaps *the* key—part of that. When people become free to choose where they want to live and work, they become free to escape oppressive and extractive relations. They become free to avoid others who would force them into zero-sum interactions. And they become free to move into more stable and inclusive relations, ones where their productive powers are valued and can be put to good use.

The economic potential of the world opening up these mutually beneficial relations is staggering. There is simply no other policy available that comes even close to having the same potential to address world poverty. Even allowing poor foreigners short-term work in rich societies vastly outperforms aid in terms of development potential. A recent study compared the economic effects of short-term work by farmers from Haiti in the United States, where no US workers are available. Compared to the effects of more traditional assistance, the study found that the policy raised workers' earnings on average by a staggering 15 times.[31]

Over the past three chapters, we've seen a host of attempts by people to justify currently existing policies that stop this improvement from happening. While we seek to free up immigration around the world, these authors seek to stop poor people (and others) from leaving their situations behind. These arguments fail. There exists an important moral presumption against coercively interfering with their freedom, and none of the arguments we have discussed succeed in overriding that.

A hostile reader might respond by looking for yet another theory about why borders should be kept closed. No doubt people will come up with new theories. There is no one master argument that defeats all possible arguments for closing the borders. However, after this many failures, an honest thinker should begin to wonder *why* all these arguments fail. Perhaps there is an underlying reason why none of them succeed. In our view, the underlying reason is clear. When innocent people seek to interact with willing others in ways that are productive and mutually beneficial, justice does not ordinarily allow *other people* to set up barriers between them.

When immigrants seek to bring their productive powers to others who welcome them, it is no surprise that in general they boost—and not lower—local wages and living standards. But this is not a *given*. Whether and to what extent immigrants are positive-sum contributors to society depends in large part on how society chooses to welcome them. We can allow and encourage immigrants to make themselves be welcomed as contributors. Or we can set up things that do the opposite.

When countries confine immigrants to refugee camps or migrant centers, they deny them the possibility of being productive. When countries actively prevent immigrants from working during lengthy and burdensome immigration procedures (procedures that can last up to a decade), they put them in a position where their skills atrophy. Such policies are as irrational as they are unjust. When Turkey issued identity cards to Syrian refugees, local wages went up. In Lebanon, where refugees were prevented from working, the same was not true.[32]

Societies make it difficult for immigrants to be contributors in less draconian ways, too. Some technically permit immigration, but make it very unlikely that immigrants can succeed. Many countries "protect" native workers from the competition of immigrants by excluding immigrants from the job market. Intentionally or not, restrictive labor and business regulations in Europe have contributed to the formation of an underclass of second- and third-generation immigrants living in poverty and without opportunity. When roughly a quarter of people under the age of 24 are unemployed, as they are in places like Sweden and France, immigrants and their children are the first to lose out. It's no surprise if integration slows down.

The point here is not only about treating immigrants fairly, although it is that, too. Governments owe good conditions for integration to their *own* (or prior) subjects as well. When laws, rules, or regulations prevent immigrants from working and integrating, natives are denied the possibility to work with new people, meet new people, buy from new people, and otherwise enjoy the significant benefits they could offer, if only given a chance. There is no fairness in living among people who are prevented from being productive members of society.

Current situations in countries dealing with immigration problems, then, are likely not very reliable guides to what a more just practice of open borders would look like. Things such as crime rates, unemployment, or support for liberal values among immigrants are not fixed matters. They are *endogenous* variables—they respond to the policies we choose. In a just world, a world of open borders, societies would welcome immigrants as productive citizens, and actively lower the economic barriers they might encounter. They would make it easier for immigrants to assimilate by making it easier to find work, start businesses, and become educated. In such a world, immigrants would very likely make themselves be even more welcomed too.

It is a deeply tragic fact about our current world that migration, which can and should be an enormous benefit to us all, is now often characterized as a "burden"—indeed, a burden that is to be distributed between receiving countries supposedly unlucky enough to receive them. It's a great moral failure that leads to such a perversion, to seeing honest people as burdens to be spread around, instead of opportunities to celebrate. This failure lies as much with those who receive immigrants as it lies with those who arrive.

5

The Moral and Economic Case
for Free Trade

ADAM SMITH WROTE *The Wealth of Nations* to debunk the economic philosophy of mercantilism. Mercantilism's guiding thesis was that countries get rich by maintaining a positive cash flow—to send out products in return for gold (or cash). Mercantilists saw trade in starkly zero-sum terms. In their eyes, to export goods for money is for a country to win, because cash is flowing into the country, making it richer; to import goods is to lose, because cash is flowing out, making it poorer.

Smith's insight, which has been reinforced by generations of economists from David Ricardo to Paul Krugman, was that this line of reasoning involves a major mistake. Both imports and exports can play an important role in making countries prosperous, depending on the way their economies function at a given time. In the long run, people and countries get richer by being productive, making better goods, and making them cheaper. The trick with trade is to find forms of exchange that foster this. When foreigners make goods relatively more efficiently, it makes sense to import them. Exports are best when it's relatively more efficient to produce things at home.

When people are free to trade, they tend to import and export when doing so best serve their needs. Producers and consumers can look for deals abroad that are cheaper, higher quality, or more innovative. And they can sell their products abroad when what others offer is worse. Trade restrictions like tariffs or subsidies protect less productive and less competitive enterprises—the kind that would not survive if people were free to seek out the more efficient ones. This does not contribute to the goal of making societies and people better off. It makes goods more expensive, even when it bolsters exports, and thus works toward impoverishing a society overall.

Stated in these terms, Smith's point may seem obvious. And yet most people in his time and ours advocate policies that achieve the opposite. The average American today remains a proto-mercantilist.[1] Many, on both the left and the right, prefer to buy things made in America, look askance at companies that outsource their manufacturing, and want to see companies that move abroad penalized.

Most philosophers who write about global justice are either silent about free trade or, worse, disparage it and instead advocate zero-sum transfers. This silence or opposition is a serious mistake. As we will argue, global justice requires free trade. It requires that people be free to buy and sell abroad as well as domestically. Our argument will take three steps. In this chapter, we show that there is a strong moral and economic presumption in favor of the right to trade freely. In the next, we address a number of philosophical arguments that might be thought to outweigh this presumption. Then, in chapter 7, we connect this case with the basic rights of productivity and exchange that make trade possible, and argue that these rights qualify as central *human* rights.

The structure of the argument thus mirrors the chapters on migration. We'll start here by providing the basic moral and economic case for free trade. This case shows that there exists a presumption in favor of people having the right to trade with others without coercive interference. However, again, these rights are not absolute. If free trade were a disaster, that would override the presumption. Fortunately, the contrary is true: free trade generally produces very good consequences for most people. As a result, those who would advocate for trade restrictions bear a heavy burden of proof.

What Counts as Free Trade

By "free trade," we mean a policy in which governments or private agents do not coercively interfere with economic exchanges between geographical areas. Nearly all countries have *internal* free trade. Virginia does not impose quotas on crabs imported from Maryland; North Carolina does not impose tariffs on peanuts imported from Virginia. Hardly anyone advocates internal trade restrictions—even though most of the arguments people offer for restricting international trade apply equally well to internal trade.

There are a number of ways in which countries restrict international trade. The most obvious include:

- *Import quotas:* limits on the amount of a good that may be imported from another country.

- *Bans/embargoes:* an import quota of zero units of a good.
- *Tariffs:* allowing imports, but requiring either the seller or buyer to pay a fee, raising the price of that good and making it less competitive with domestic goods.

Governments can restrict trade in less obvious ways as well, including but not limited to:

- *Subsidies:* taxing citizens and transferring their income to domestic producers, allowing those producers to lower their market price. For instance, most wealthy countries subsidize domestic agriculture; as a result, their consumers do not buy as many agricultural products from the developing world as they otherwise would.
- *Regulations:* many regulations imposed on imported goods have the (often intended) effect of restricting or reducing imports, or artificially making those imports artificially expensive and uncompetitive.[2]

To be in favor of free trade needn't mean one is a libertarian. After all, almost all economists support free trade in the sense we have in mind here, and yet the typical economist in the United States is a moderate Democrat.[3] Nor is our argument directed against all forms of regulation of economic activity. Whether (or what kind of) regulation is a good idea is an open question, one we do not address here. Instead, our argument is more focused. We are concerned with those practices that reduce *international* economic exchange in particular. Regulations can but need not take that form.

Critics of free trade often contrast this with *fair* trade. The problem with free trade, they argue, is that it allows for workers in poor countries to be exploited, coerced, at times even enslaved, in order to make products as cheap as possible for rich consumers. However, as stated, this contrast rests on a mistake. The free trade position is not simply about maximizing consumer surplus in rich countries, at whatever cost. Free trade is about allowing people on both sides of the trading relation to interact with each other on free and voluntary terms. Even if governments put no tariffs on a banana that has been produced by a forced laborer, there is nothing "free" about buying that banana.

Protecting voluntary exchange, in other words, first and foremost means recognizing that people have rights against coerced or nonvoluntary exchange. These include rights over their property and persons—rights that strongly protect people against being forced to work, having their crops expropriated, and so on. In an important way, then, the free trade argument simply extends the idea that there's something deeply wrong with forced labor or exploitation. Just as those production methods wrong people by coercing them and violating their rights, so too do other forms of coercive interference with economic exchange. If we believe in the rights of workers to choose their employment free from force, we should also believe in people's rights to buy and sell their products free from force.

Of course, fair trade supporters may think that freeing up international trade is not enough. They might argue that rich consumers should pay more for their bananas (even more than it would cost to have their bananas produced without rights violations), and support better working conditions for people in poor countries. Perhaps they are right, but this is not our concern in these chapters. Our concern is with opposing coercive interferences of economic exchange, and this is perfectly consistent with consumers choosing to pay more to get the kinds of goods they value.

Why Protectionists Bear the Burden of Proof

Most people recognize that the case for rights to domestic economic activities, including exchange, is strong. We take this to be obvious in the domestic context. Few if any people advocate for trade restrictions within their own countries.

Intuitively, that's plainly the right way to go. To see this, consider a variation of the thought experiment we offered in the context of migration. This time, Marvin is trying to trade within a single country.

Starvin' Marvin, FedEx Edition

Starvin' Marvin, who lives in rural Mississippi, is hungry and poor. He makes something people want to buy. Marvin finds a buyer in Chicago and, unless someone stops him, will send them his goods, making enough money in the process to feed his family. Marvin puts the item in a FedEx box and sends it to Chicago. When it arrives, you show up, and either throw the item away or send it back. You announce that from now on, you won't let Marvin send anything to Chicago. (Or, alternatively, you say that you'll let people in Chicago buy things from people like Marvin, but only if one of them first pays you a significant amount of money, enough to convince Marvin's customer to look elsewhere.) As a result, Marvin doesn't complete the trade, and stays poor.

As before, it seems you have done something seriously wrong. You did not simply *fail to help* Marvin, you *actively hurt* him. Someone in Chicago wants to buy things that Marvin made. Marvin wants to sell. The money could be the difference between him having something to eat today or not. You forcefully prevented him from making a beneficial trade with a willing partner. While it's not your fault that Marvin was poor to begin with, it *is* your fault that he and his family stay poor. You should, at the very least, not prevent Marvin from helping himself. You ought to let Marvin and his customer complete their trade.

Supporters of trade restrictions think that domestic cases like this are importantly different from international trade. We cannot, they might say, compare the case of Marvin from Mississippi to cases of trade with people in other countries. Should Starvin' Marvin live, say, in Mauritania, then interfering with him might be justifiable. However, intuitively, Marvin's location seems to make little difference to his rights against interference. And the same is true of his customers. (Marvin might be looking to send things from Mississippi to Mexico.) After all, if you were visiting Mauritania and stopped Marvin from completing a trade *there*, you'd still be acting wrongly.

The case against free trade, then, has to be more precise. It has to be that there is something special about international trade—trade that *crosses* national borders—that allows governments to interfere with people like our Mauritanian Marvin and his Chicagoan customer. In the next chapter and in the following section, we will inspect a number of arguments that aim to establish why this case might be special. For now, our point is more minimal: unless such an argument can be made successfully, there seems to be a presumption in favor of leaving Marvin and his customers alone. At least initially, people like Marvin are free to trade as they please.

It might be thought here that the example does not really show that interference with trade is wrong. Perhaps you are wrong to stop Marvin's trade because he is poor and your interference would *harm* him a lot? But that is a mistake. To see this, suppose that Jane, after several years of struggling, built a successful business online. And suppose that you prevent the (now) rich Jane's products from being delivered to her customers. It still seems like you are doing something morally wrong. Of course, your actions harm Jane much less than they did Marvin. Maybe that means the case of Marvin is more urgent. But your interference with Jane remains wrong nonetheless.

In fact, interfering with exchange is prima facie wrong even when nothing significant whatsoever is at stake. Consider the following example.

Two Memoirs

Suppose billionaires Carlos Slim Helu and Bill Gates self-published memoirs on their personal websites. They each make their memoirs available for $10, and each makes it clear they plan to use any money they receive for the billionaires' poker games they host. Bas wants to read one, but is indifferent between the two. He flips a coin and, as a result, picks Helu's memoir. However, before he can buy Helu's memoir, Jason shows up with a gun and says, "I forbid you from buying Helu's memoir. I insist you buy *American*."

Here Bas is actually indifferent between the two memoirs. And both sellers would hardly notice a $10 loss of income and are planning to spend it in a trivial way. Nevertheless, Jason still acts wrongly. Jason should not coerce Bas, even though Bas reading Gates's memoir involves no real setback for anyone involved.

It seems, then, that there is a strong prima facie case for free trade. And that case seems to extend to international trade as well as domestic trade. People in one country want to buy things people in other countries make. And the foreigners want to sell.[4] Often the money will make a real difference to their lives, sometimes even the difference between being able to eat or not. But governments coercively interfere with this by posting legal barriers around their markets, stopping foreigners from making life-changing trades with willing partners. At first glance, it seems that they should—like you—stay out of the way.

Sometimes people think it's obvious that governments can interfere with people like foreign Marvin selling goods. After all, when Marvin sells his products, he replaces someone else whose livelihood might depend on being able to sell. Marvin, people might say, is "stealing" that person's business or job. Those other sellers are harmed, potentially seriously harmed, by Marvin's showing up. In the short run, competitors are competitors.

However, citing such harms will not do much for the defender of trade restrictions. If we are going to ask about the harms and benefits of new competitors entering the marketplace, we need to think about both sides of the exchange relation. And—even setting aside the harm done to Marvin when he's prevented from making his sale—this means thinking about his consumers as well. When you prevent Marvin from doing business in Chicago, you do not just impose a cost upon him. You also impose costs upon his would-be consumers, people who preferred Marvin's products to his competitors'.

Is it permissible to use force to shut down a competitor, if the competitor outcompetes you for something you want or need? In general, the answer is obviously no. An Olympic athlete who hires people to beat up a competitor plainly does something wrong. A business owner who thrashes a competitor's store plainly does something wrong. A job candidate who prevents another candidate from making it to the interview plainly does something wrong.

Consider the following case, which modifies an example Robert Nozick offered in *Anarchy, State, and Utopia*:[5]

Suitors

Robert and Steve both want to marry Gjertrud. She goes on a date with both men, and decides to pursue a relationship with Robert. She prefers Robert's better looks and keen intelligence. Suppose this leaves Steve devastated. He feels life is not worth living without Gjertrud's love. He ends up spending his days miserable and alone.

Few people would take seriously the idea that Steve can interfere with Robert and Gjertrud. Nor would they say that Robert and Gjertrud owe Steve compensation. And we wouldn't think kindly of Steve if he lobbied his congressperson to prevent Gjertrud from marrying Robert. Such suggestions are absurd and borderline evil, notwithstanding the fact that Gjertrud and Robert in some sense greatly "hurt" Steve. (Would anyone even say that Robert "stole" Steve's potential spouse?)

Thought experiments like Nozick's point out something odd about arguments for interference with economic freedom. Such arguments often suggest that we can restrict economic liberty for certain kinds of reasons—or that those reasons are enough to force those who do better under economic freedom to compensate those who do worse. But the very same reasons plainly do not justify similar forms of interference in other contexts. Making Robert compensate Steve for "outcompeting" him is absurd.

What this shows is that many putative arguments for restricting economic freedom don't actually do much independent work. Arguments that invoke reasons like the harms of competition, or the "stealing" of jobs, *presuppose* rather than *prove* that the economic freedom of foreigners has lower moral status. Only when we already assume that people like foreign Marvin are not entitled to economic freedom in the same way as domestic Marvin can we see complaints about competition by the former as having a kind of force that complaints about the latter plainly lack.

The point is the same, then. Obviously, we should not just assume that foreigners have lower moral status. After all, our question is *whether* people like foreign Marvin have the same kinds of rights to economic freedom as people like domestic Marvin. It's possible, of course, that the restrictionists are right. Perhaps foreigners really do lack the rights to trade that compatriots enjoy. But if they are right, we need an argument showing us why. Without such an argument, the presumption in favor of free trade stands, and people ought to be left as free to trade internationally as they are domestically. The burden of proof rests squarely with the defender of trade restrictions.

The Economics of Free Trade: Why the Protectionists Have a Hard Job

As a profession, economists have long favored free trade. Paul Krugman, in an article written during what he called a "golden age of innovation in international economics," puts the point as follows: "The essential things to teach students are still the insights of Hume and Ricardo. That is, we need to teach them that trade deficits are self-correcting and that the benefits of trade do not depend on a country having an absolute advantage over its rivals."[6]

Krugman worries that most intellectual discussion outside of economics departments portrays countries not as potential trading partners who mutually enrich each other, but as competitors. He fears a view of trade that sees different parties as vying for a fixed amount of goods, rather than together creating more. Yet it's a basic fallacy to think that countries compete in the same way that, say, athletes compete when they're trying to win a race.

Such mistaken views about trade are common. Recently, economists and laypeople were surveyed on their respective views of economics.[7] Vanessa Sumo summarizes: "When economists strongly agree on an issue, the general public usually disagrees with them."[8] The vast majority of Americans believe that "buy American" policies help create American manufacturing jobs on net, while only about tenth of economists agree. The overwhelming majority of economists believe that NAFTA has benefitted Americans, while the public disagrees, thinking it benefitted Mexico at the expense of the United States. Things were no different 20 years ago. The 1996 survey of Americans and economists found the same divergence between what lay Americans and economists thought about trade.[9]

Part of the explanation for this divergence is the fact that the way trade benefits both parties involved can be quite counterintuitive. An important part of explanation of this is the theory of comparative advantage. To explain it to readers unfamiliar with this idea we'll outline Ricardo's model, setting aside more advanced and sophisticated models developed over the past 40 years.

Imagine that a few hundred years from now, Earth is vastly more productive and technologically advanced.[10] Suppose we Earthlings discover how to build starships with warp drives. Right after we test our warp drive, the Vulcans make contact with us. Suppose, for the sake of argument, that all Vulcans are more talented than all Earthlings in everything. The dumbest Vulcan is smarter than the smartest Earthling, the weakest adult Vulcan is stronger than the strongest Earthling, and so on. Suppose the Vulcans are also better at doing everything—growing corn, making computers, designing fashion—than Earthlings are. Everything we can do, they can do better.

It might seem like Vulcans would have no reason to bother trade with us. The average American might suppose that trading with Vulcans would just put us all out of work, because everything we can do, they can do better. The average philosopher, as we'll see, might worry about the unfairness or disadvantage that trading would pose for us Earthlings. Economists, by contrast, would expect that except in unusual circumstances, both the Vulcans and Earthlings would gain immensely from interplanetary trade. To do so, each planet should specialize in its comparative advantage. That is, they should specialize in whatever form of production has the lowest opportunity cost.

To illustrate, suppose Earth needs to use 12 million workers to produce one starship per year, or it needs 2 million to produce 1 trillion tons of food per year. Suppose the smarter, stronger, and more logical Vulcans need only 1 million Vulcan workers to produce one starship per year, or 1 million to produce 1 trillion of food per year. How would trade affect the standard of living on both planets?

Let's begin by imagining that the planets don't trade, and then compare this to a situation in which they do. First, consider the case where both planets produce everything they need themselves. Each planet decides to have 12 million of its workers manufacturing starships and 12 million growing food this year. (To simplify, we ignore any other goods other workers might produce.) Table 5.1 shows the most they can produce and consume without trade.

Now suppose, that in anticipation of trading, both planets decide to specialize in their comparative advantage. Earth stops making starships, and all 12 million former starship workers start producing food instead. The Vulcans don't specialize quite as much: they just shift 2 million of their food workers

Table 5.1 Production on Earth and Vulcan without Trade

Planet Labor Allocation (Starships, Food) in millions	Starships	Food, trillions of tons
Earth (12, 12)	1	6
Vulcan (12, 12)	12	12
Total Production	13	18

Table 5.2 Production on Earth and Vulcan with Specialization in Anticipation of Trade

Planet Labor Allocation (Starships, Food) in millions	Starships	Food, trillions of tons
Earth (0, 24)	0	12
Vulcan (14, 10)	14	10
Total Production	14 (+1)	22 (+4)

Table 5.3 Consumption on Earth and Vulcan after Trade (Vulcan trades one starship for 3 trillion tons of food)

Planet	Starships	Food, trillions of tons
Earth (0, 24)	1	9 (+3)
Vulcan (14, 10)	13 (+1)	13 (+1)
Total Consumption	14	22

toward producing starships. As Table 5.2 illustrations, the total production of each good now increases as a result of specialization.

Of course, Earth is now without starships, and the Vulcans no longer have as much food to eat. Imagine, then, that the Vulcans decide to trade one starship for 3 trillion tons of food. Table 5.3 shows that this will make everyone better off than they had been under autarky, when there was no specialization or trade. We don't need to know how much Earthlings and Vulcans value food for this exercise, because, as Table 5.3 shows, both planets have at least as much of both goods after trade.

It turns out, then, that trading is beneficial for *both* the Vulcans and the Earthlings. Even though the Vulcans are more efficient in producing everything Earthlings could make, the Earthlings still gain from trading with them. And even though the Earthlings are worse at producing anything the Vulcans can make, trading with them is beneficial for the Vulcans, too.

Nothing changes, of course, if we replace "Vulcans" and "Earthlings" with "Rich" or "Developed County" and "Poor" or "Developing Country." And, equally obvious, our point is not that people in the developing world are less intelligent or more irrational than people in the developed world. Rather, the point is that, in general, trade allows each party to specialize in producing those things at which they are relatively speaking most efficient (even if they are not the most efficient at producing them in absolute terms). When trade is restricted, we lose those benefits. Each party will be worse off.

Of course, there are a number of caveats and objections in place here. For example, trade in the example moves the parties to what we might call a Pareto-superior outcome. Situations are said to be Pareto-superior when they improve at least one person's welfare without hurting anyone. In the case discussed earlier, we see such an improvement—no one loses while everybody wins. However, in real life, this is rare. When one company invents a better mousetrap, it makes its customers better off. And that is a step along the road of progress. But this is of little solace to the mousetrap manufacturer who loses his business as a result.

The same is true for free trade. Even though allowing people to exchange freely makes almost everyone better off in the long run, some people (especially those who enjoy economic rents from trade restrictions) will face losses, at least in the short run. Less competitive businesses at home and abroad will be out-competed. That's the point, of course, but it does hurt.

Similarly, it's not always true that both parties would benefit from allowing free trade. In principle, there can be cases where a country might benefit from restricting trade. We can describe examples where protecting infant industries would help spur development, or in which strategic policies of protectionism (e.g., government-backed cartelization) could benefit the home country (again, at the expense of others).[11]

However, it's one thing to say that in principle such protectionist measures *could* pay off. It's quite another to say that in the real world, we should pursue them. One problem here is that we face serious epistemic barriers. While on the blackboard we can describe infant-industry protection working to a country's advantage, in the real world we aren't well equipped to know which infant industries are worth protecting, how much protection they should have, when those protections should be relaxed, or which forms of protectionism will realistically benefit us more than they hurt us.

Closely related to this is the problem that protectionism will enable massive amounts of destructive rent-seeking—that is, attempts at gaining private economic benefits through political means.[12] Suppose a government announces that it is willing to restrict free trade in the special circumstances where such restrictions benefit rather than hurt its domestic economy. Every industry will clamor for protection, of course. Every industry will claim that they are one of these special, unusual cases. Perhaps if a government were staffed by omniscient, omnibenevolent administrators, we might want to trust them to go looking for these exceptions. But governments are staffed by real people, overseen by real politicians. And we would expect to see those politicians claiming that this or that restriction, which their constituents and lobbyists just so happen to favor for selfish reasons, just so happens also to be for everyone's good.

In the real world, then, when we're picking among policy proposals, free trade is far more likely to benefit a wide range of people, rich, middle class, and poor. When economists attempt to measure the deadweight losses from existing trade barriers, their estimates range from as little as a fraction of a percent to as high as 5% of world product. It's reasonable to assume, then, that we'll be losing out on about $2 trillion of additional production this year as a result of tariffs, subsidies, and import quotas.[13]

Of course, this is not nearly as high as the efficiency losses from existing restrictions on labor mobility we discussed in chapter 2. But that is in large part because previous reforms have made trade barriers much lower compared to current barriers to migration. Economist Douglas Irwin conservatively estimates that (not counting other trade restrictions) US tariff policy alone resulted in a static deadweight loss of about 1% of GDP per year starting in 1861, and then dropped to about a tenth of a percent as the United States liberalized trade by the 1960s.[14]

This way of stating things, however, tends to understate the overall welfare loss. Think of your bank account. If your bank account accumulates interest at 3% per year, it will, thanks to compound interest, double in about 23 years. At a 2% interest rate, it will take about 35 years. At a 1% interest rate, it will take about seventy years. The point is that when we suffer a deadweight loss to the economy, we don't just lose wealth *this* year; we also lose the wealth in future years that we would have enjoyed through compound growth. (The same, of course, applies to the losses from immigration restrictions.)

Such losses can be staggering in the long term. To illustrate, suppose from 1930 until 2005, the United States had had just one percentage point less economic growth per year (i.e., suppose it grew at 2.5% rather than 3.5%). In that case, by 2005, US GDP would be *half* the size of what it actually was. Assuming the population is the same, that would make the United States closer to Malaysia in terms of GDP/capita than the country it is today.

The economic case for free trade, then, is strong and reinforces the moral case. Not only do people have a prima facie right to exchange goods without coercive interference, allowing them to do so generally works to the benefit of everybody. When governments impose trade restrictions, they are facing a serious burden of justification. Unless we hear some very good reason why trade should be restricted—why they can use force to benefit domestic companies at the expense of others—such restrictions should be condemned as unjust.

Rawls and Freeman on Economic Liberty

Some philosophers, most famously John Rawls and his chief interpreter Samuel Freeman, resist that the right to trade is protected in the way we are describing here.[15] They deny, that is, that the liberty to enter in economic exchanges is basic in the sense of requiring some kind of protection. If that view is true, then it might seem to follow that trade restrictions do *not* stand in need of the kind of justification we claim.

When Rawls talks about "basic liberties," he has in mind those liberties that societies have a duty to recognize, uphold, and support in various ways. According to his first principle of justice—the Liberty Principle—each citizen should enjoy a "fully adequate" set of basic rights and liberties.[16] This set includes a wide range of civil liberties, such as freedom of conscience, sexual freedom, and freedom of religion, speech, assembly, and lifestyle. It also includes political liberties, such as the right to vote and to run for and hold office if elected. It includes legal procedural liberties, such as a right to a fair trial, habeas corpus, due process, and freedom from arbitrary search and seizure. And, finally, it includes some economic liberties, such as the right to own personal property and to choose one's own profession.

However, Rawls does *not* include many other economic freedoms as basic liberties. He does not include any of the productive rights we will discuss and defend as human rights in chapter 7. And he does not regard the right to own, use, and exchange one's private productive property as protected in the same way. The Liberty Principle does not protect people's freedom to make and enter into contracts; to buy and sell goods or services on terms to which all parties consent; to negotiate the terms under which they work; to manage their households as they see fit; to create things for sale; to start, run, and stop businesses; to own factories and businesses; to develop property for productive purposes; or to take risks with capital or to speculate on commodities futures.

Why not? Rawls's final philosophical test for whether a right qualifies as basic liberty or not has to do with whether it has the right connection to what Rawls calls our "two moral powers." These two moral powers are 1) a capacity to develop a sense of the good life, and 2) a capacity for a sense of justice. The first power is the capacity to "have a rational conception of the good—the power to form, revise, and to rationally pursue a coherent conception of values, as based in a view of what gives life and its pursuits their meaning."[17] The second power is the capacity to "understand, apply, and cooperate with others on terms of cooperation that are fair."[18]

According to Rawls, these powers are what make human beings *moral beings* worthy of special consideration. And rights are justified as the essential preconditions of realizing and exercising these two moral powers. As Samuel Freeman explains the connection:

> What makes a liberty *basic* for Rawls is that it is an *essential social condition for the adequate development and full exercise of the two powers of moral personality over a complete life.*[19]

Freeman stresses that a liberty is basic only if it is necessary for *all* individuals to have that liberty in order to develop the two moral powers.[20] Let's call this the *Rawls-Freeman test*.

The Rawls-Freeman Test
Some liberty X qualifies as a basic liberty just in case X turns out to be an essential social condition for all citizens to adequately develop and fully exercise their two moral powers over a complete life.

In his book *Free Market Fairness*, John Tomasi argues that Rawls ought to have included robust economic liberties such as the freedom to engage in free trade, the freedom to own productive property, and other such capitalist economic liberties among the set of basic liberties. Tomasi's main way of arguing for this conclusion is to amend Rawls's own arguments. Rawls argues that freedom of expression is among the basic liberties, and gives various reasons why this is so. Tomasi responds by giving almost identical arguments on behalf of, say, the right to own one's own store. Rawls argues that freedom of religion is necessary for people to develop their conception of the good life, to be true to themselves and who they really are. Tomasi shows that this is also true of economic liberty.

Tomasi's point, in short, is that if people are going to be the authors of their own lives, it's not enough that they get to choose whether and how to worship, for whom to vote, and with whom to associate. They also need to be able to conduct their own economic affairs. After all, the economic sphere is a massively important part of life, and many citizens will not be able to re-alize their conceptions of the good life without having extensive economic freedom.[21]

Freeman objects that Tomasi's argument rests on a misunderstanding of Rawls's theory. According to Freeman, these liberties do not qualify as basic liberties because they fail the Rawls-Freeman Test. Even if owning a factory, say, were essential to *some*, or even *many*, people's conception of the good life, that doesn't mean that *all* citizens need those liberties. And that's what's re-quired for economic rights to count as basic liberties.[22]

We agree with Freeman that economic liberties fail the Rawls-Freeman Test, as stated. To illustrate, people in Denmark and Switzerland enjoy much more economic liberty than people in Russia. But this doesn't mean it's im-possible, or even particularly difficult, for Russians to develop a sense of jus-tice or a conception of the good life. Most Russians clearly do. In fact, only a handful of countries allow citizens to have the range of economic liberty Tomasi thinks important. Nevertheless, lots of people around the world manage to develop their moral powers. Economic liberties, then, clearly fail the Rawls-Freeman test.

However, this appears to be a Pyrrhic victory. The argument Rawls and Freeman offer for rejecting capitalist freedoms as basic liberties applies equally well against the civil and political rights they believe *pass* their test. Consider: Rawls and Freeman think people have a basic right to extensive freedom of speech, freedom of participation, to vote and run for office, and so on. But just as it is implausible that *all* citizens must enjoy the full range of economic freedoms in order to develop their two moral powers, so it is also implausible that literally all must enjoy these civil liberties to do so. Again, there are plenty of countries that (severely) restrict these liberties, yet many people living there develop their moral powers.

As far as we can tell, Rawls and Freeman never actually attempt to show that their favored liberties pass their test. They try to illustrate why certain rights—such as the right to free speech or vote—might be basic liberties by arguing that these might be *useful* for developing the two moral powers, or that constraints on these rights might make it difficult to develop them.[23] They might say, for instance, that a person will have difficulty assessing different conceptions of the good life if the government forbids her from reading about alternative lifestyles.

The point is fair, of course, But, again, it cannot be enough to satisfy the Rawls-Freeman Test. It wouldn't be *impossible* for people to develop a conception of the good life, and for some it may not even be that hard. It would be a tall task indeed, one that would probably require extensive evidence from empirical psychology, to show that it would literally be impossible to develop the two moral powers without the full range of freedom Rawls wants us to have. We don't see any such evidence.

Pace Rawls and Freeman, very little liberty is strictly speaking necessary for the typical person (let alone *all* people, as Freeman would have it) to develop the two moral powers. People in deeply authoritarian or totalitarian regimes have a harder time than we do in accessing the proper evaluative horizons. And they may have a harder time developing their moral powers. But even in such countries, it's perfectly possible. Aleksandr Solzhenitsyn developed his two moral powers despite living in a totalitarian regime and being imprisoned in the gulag. Indeed, he may have developed his two moral powers as much as he did precisely because he was deprived of his basic liberties. The stoic philosopher Epictetus probably developed his two moral powers more than almost anyone who has ever lived, and he managed to do so while literally being a slave. The same might be said about Booker T. Washington, Frederick Douglass, and many others.

The Rawls-Freeman Test, then, implies that almost nothing counts as a basic liberty. For practically no freedom is actually necessary for all people to develop their moral powers. But this is absurd. For one, it would mean that the test *refutes* Rawls's own liberal theory of justice, a theory that set out to strongly affirm a number of basic liberties. The Rawls-Freeman test looks simply too strong.

In response to this, Rawls and Freeman might modify their test. Perhaps the point is instead that something counts as a basic liberty only if it is necessary for all individuals to develop their two moral powers *or* for them to fully exercise those powers over a complete life. This gets around the problem we just described. Sure, hardly any liberty is necessary for all individuals to develop their moral powers, but a great deal of liberty is needed to adequately *exercise* these two moral powers.

Most civil and political liberties will probably pass this revised Rawls-Freeman Test. However, it now seems as if there's an equally good case to be made for the economic liberties. As Tomasi shows, a wide range of economic freedoms (such as extensive freedom of contract and the right to own private property in the means of production) are needed for people to fully exercise their moral powers throughout their lives. After all, Tomasi's arguments almost exactly mirror Rawls's and Freeman's.

Tomasi is a Rawlsian. He accepts Rawls's basic theory of justice, but thinks he has discovered a mistake in how Rawls applies his own theory. Rawls should have held that citizens have a basic right not only to extensive set of civil and political liberties, but also to an extensive set of economic liberties of the sort we are defending here. Tomasi sees himself as correcting a mistake: Rawls missed what his arguments really implied.

We are not Rawlsians, so we're not much concerned with removing the warts and blemishes from the theory. As far as we can tell, Freeman is correct that, strictly speaking, Tomasi's list of economic liberties fails to pass the Rawls-Freeman Test. But again, pace Freeman, that's because the Rawls-Freeman's Test is implausibly strict. When we interpret the test as strictly as Freeman does (criticizing Tomasi), pretty much nothing passes the test.

We see that as reason to reject the test. We are much more confident in the claim that people have at least some basic liberties than we are in the Rawls-Freeman test, which we never found all that plausible to begin with. But, alternatively, if one were to weaken the Rawls-Freeman test, it's unclear how one can, in a nonideological or question-begging way, avoid Tomasi's conclusions. Either way, Rawls and Freeman have given us no plausible reason to reject the presumption in favor of free trade.

How to Argue Against Free Trade

The point stands, then. At first glance, protectionist restrictions seem to be rights violations. When people or governments impose such restrictions they do not simply fail to help would-be buyers and sellers; they forcibly prevent them from making mutually beneficial trades with willing partners. When they do so, they are forcing them to trade with people they would rather not, imposing themselves by cutting off relationships that otherwise would have formed.

If a country placed *internal* trade restrictions on its own citizens, by forbidding people in Virginia from shopping for coats in Maryland, almost everyone would recognize this as a violation of their rights, even their human rights. But many see trade restrictions between countries differently. Perhaps, in the final analysis, they are right, but they do bear the burden of proof. They must show that there is a real difference between these two kinds of trade, a difference sufficient to explain why it's impermissible to coercively interfere with one but not the other.

In the next chapter, we'll examine a number of arguments that purport to show why there really is such a difference. For now, let us note what such arguments must accomplish in order to be successful. First, the defender of trade restrictions will need to produce *real evidence* that free trade does indeed produce a certain bad thing they are worried about, or comes at the expense of some good thing they want to protect. And second, we need a good philosophical argument showing that avoiding the bad thing, or getting the good thing, is morally important enough to justify restricting trade.

In general, showing that coercion would produce good consequences is not sufficient to show that it's justified. If free trade threatens to undermine France's distinctive culture, say because it allows the French to consume too much American pop culture, that may make it a bad thing. But culture as such is not a good enough reason for people to use force against French and American citizens. The argument needs to offer something more—it needs to appeal to values or principles that are *in general* capable of justifying force.

6

Philosophers' Objections to Free Trade

WE HAVE SEEN that there is a strong presumption in favor of allowing people to trade as freely with foreigners as they can trade with their fellow citizens. If this presumption holds, then justice allows people not only to enter (subject to reasonable laws and regulations) into mutually beneficial exchanges domestically, but also internationally. If the presumption holds, that is, a just regime of international trade is as free as just regimes of domestic trade.

Of course, presumptions are just that, presumptions. They can be overridden by strong countervailing reasons. In this chapter, we consider a number of influential attempts to show that there are such reasons. As we'll see, they all fail and the presumption in favor of free trade stands.

The Exploitation Objection to International Trade

Jason has gone through a range of fancy guitar amplifiers over the past years. His Marshall JVM 410H and matching 1960A cabinet was built by well-paid workers in Bletchley, in the United Kingdom. His Mesa Boogie JP-2C was made by well-paid workers in Petaluma, California. In contrast, his EVH 5150 III was made by workers somewhere in Vietnam, who no doubt were paid much less than their counterparts in Petaluma or Bletchley. Perhaps by buying the EVH amplifier (which was significantly less expensive than the Marshall or Mesa), Jason inadvertently helped to exploit poor Third World laborers. Could the US government be justified in preventing people like Jason from doing things like that?

One of the major objections to free trade is that it enables (and even incentivizes) corporations to exploit workers in poor countries. Free trade leads to those workers being exploited in sweatshops. Governments, this objection goes, ought to impose trade restrictions not to protect domestic industries, but to protect poor workers around the world from unjust exploitation.

The idea of exploitation is notoriously difficult to make precise. But the general worry is clear enough. To exploit someone, roughly speaking, is to take unfair or pernicious advantage of that person's vulnerability. Consider the following paradigmatic case:

Drowning Man
Bob's boat capsizes in the ocean. As hungry sharks circle him, his strength gives way, and he realizes he will soon drown. Just then, Charlie appears in a fishing boat. He says to Bob, "I'm willing to save your life, but only if you give me 90% of your life savings and 90% of your future earnings." Bob would rather be poor than dead, and agrees.

In the drowning man transaction, Bob was going to die, and Charlie offers him an option that didn't previously exist. What's more, Charlie makes Bob's situation better, not worse. Before Charlie arrived, Bob was facing certain death. Now, he can stay alive, albeit poor.

Bob agrees to the deal because he expects to benefit from it. It may even be, depending on the circumstances, that Bob actually benefits much more from the deal in absolute terms than Charlie does. (For example, suppose Charlie is already fabulously wealthy, so getting 90% of Bob's future income does him little good.) Still, despite this, everyone except perhaps the most hardcore libertarians judge that the transaction in the drowning man example is exploitative. And most people would judge that such deals ought to be prohibited for that reason.

Some people regard offering poor workers a job in a sweatshop to be equivalent to the drowning man situation. Sure, the worker may be better off with the job than without it. But according to the objection, the employer takes unconscionable advantage of the worker's misfortune to offer that worker a raw deal. Some might go so far as to claim that developed countries should impose trade restrictions or penalties on imports made via sweatshop labor.

Before tackling this objection head-on, we begin by reminding readers that the sweatshops we see around the world do not result from unrestricted international free trade. Rather, remember that we have significant international trade in *goods*, but not free trade in *labor*. As we discussed at length in chapters 2 through 4, under the current system of globalization capital is free to move anywhere in search of a good deal, but labor is not. Laborers have to stay put and wait for deals to come to them, and so it's not surprising that they get a bad deal. Immigration restrictions artificially depress the wages of the world's poor, and exacerbate the sweatshop phenomenon. That's wrong.

We are not Pollyannas. Free migration—even though it would vastly increase world GDP—is not quite a panacea. Even in a world of free migration, some sweatshops would exist somewhere, at least for a while. However, right now, the debate is framed as if the defender of global freedom has to defend sweatshops, while those who propose restricting countries and their economies can use sweatshops as an arrow in their quivers. Our point is that this is mistaken. Current immigration laws are highly restrictive and illiberal, and defenders of freeing up labor markets have little burden to defend the status quo. The lousy conditions sweatshop workers currently have to accept are to a significant degree artifacts of unjust restrictions on labor mobility.

Suppose sweatshops are wrongly exploitative and unjust. It would not follow, as a matter of logic, that we ought to close them down, or restrict free trade in order to prevent them from arising. To see why, consider the following thought experiment:

Innocent Ivan

Innocent Ivan has been unjustly convicted of a bogus crime and sentenced to death. The executioner offers Ivan the choice of *how* he will die: 1) death by boiling, 2) death by starvation, or 3) death by guillotine. Ivan chooses the guillotine. However, right before Ivan is executed, Justin the Justice Wizard says, "It is unjust for Ivan, an innocent person, to be executed by guillotine!" Justin then cast a magic spell that destroys the guillotine. The executioner shrugs and tosses Ivan in a vat of boiling water, Ivan's #2 choice.

Justin the Justice Wizard did indeed prevent Ivan from suffering the injustice of being killed by guillotine. However, Justin didn't prevent an injustice from befalling Ivan, or make Ivan's life any better. Instead, he simply removed Ivan's best option—unjust as it may be—and replaced it with an even worse one. Of course, this does nothing to deny that killing Ivan by guillotine was unjust in the first place. But it does show that in certain cases, stopping an injustice can itself be a horrific injustice.

The bigger point is this: we shouldn't take away a victim's best option on the grounds that it is unjust unless we can replace it with an even *better* option. Ivan probably cursed Justin with his last breath, as well he should. Even though Justin prevented him from suffering one particular injustice, Ivan should regard Justin as his enemy.

How is this relevant to sweatshops? Matt Zwolinski argues that when people choose to work in a sweatshop, this is usually evidence that they consider it their best alternative.[1] Accordingly, simply taking steps to eliminate the sweatshop is usually a bad idea, especially if the person's other options are all very bad. Rather, we should only take steps to remove sweatshops only if doing so supplies workers with an even better option. (We are not unaware, of course, that sweatshop workers are sometimes forced to work. And, as we stressed in the previous chapter, forced labor in no way constitutes free trade.)

To illustrate, consider this variation of the thought experiment:

Sweatshop Worker

María, a 17-year-old uneducated woman in Honduras, has few options. She can turn to prostitution. She can try to find a rich lover to take care of her. She can scavenge metal at the local dump. Or she can work as a nanny, under the table, making very low wages. Then along comes a contractor that manufactures shoes for a number of multinational corporations. This contractor offers her a sweatshop job sewing sneakers. The job pays only $1.31/hr. and requires long hours. Still, María chooses this job over her other options. However, right before starting, Justin the Justice Wizard stops the contractor from selling goods overseas. The contractor closes up shop.

When María accepted the sweatshop job, she was desperate and lacked an adequate range of options. We might not want to say that her choice to work there was fully voluntary or autonomous. We might even say that María was exploited and that this is unjust. Still, as Zwolinski reminds us, María made a choice. María may be poor, but she's not a fool. If she chooses the sweatshop over her other options, that is strong evidence that she considers working in the sweatshop her *best* option. Thus, Zwolinski says, we must be very careful about using things like boycotts, nongovernmental organizations (NGOs), and government policy to influence working conditions. These actions could just push María's employer to move to a different location, perhaps hiring higher-skilled labors in a more capital-intensive production method. That would not help María.

Zwolinsk's point depends on the assumption that workers usually know enough to choose what's best for them. Of course, this may not always be true. Perhaps María is a fool, or ignorant of her options, or wont to act irrationally. In that case, maybe we would want to protect her from herself. However, it is much less likely that *all* or even *most* sweatshop workers are fools, ignorant, or irrational. It's much more likely that people in Honduras know more about their situation than you and we do, judging from the comfortable confines of our Western (rejection of) consumerism.

One way to investigate whether or not sweatshop workers are acting rationally is to look at what their alternatives actually are, and how sweatshops compare to these. Economists Benjamin Powell and David Skarbek examined apparel worker wages in countries accused of having sweatshops, looking specifically at companies that were accused of running sweatshops. They found that in almost all countries, sweatshop workers earn significantly more than the national average. Even workers at sweatshops that rich consumers in places like the United States are protesting tend to earn at least the national average.

What's more, Powell and Skarbek add, saying that apparel workers beat the average wage ignores the fact that even in these poor countries, people working at sweatshops are often immigrants from other, even poorer countries. When we thus compare worker wages to what they could have received in their home countries, the case for sweatshops looks even stronger. However bad sweatshops may be, they are generally far superior to workers' existing alternatives.[2] Zwolinski discusses similar findings, adding that in places like Nicaragua, the Dominican Republic, Haiti, and Honduras, sweatshop workers make something like three to seven times the average national income.[3]

This view of sweatshops is not unique to libertarian economists like Powell and Sharbek, but is shared even by left-wing economists like Jeffrey Sachs and Paul Krugman.[4] Most academic commentators now acknowledge that there is a strong economic, consequence-based case for using and allowing sweatshops. Economists say that sweatshops pay better—often significantly better—than the alternatives, and so dramatically improve the lives of workers, despite having what we in the First World would consider miserable working conditions.

Further, sweatshops are typically a temporary phenomenon. Businesses set up sweatshops where labor is abundant and opportunities are scarce. But the normal course of development is that sweatshops start the process of industrialization and development. Over time, worker productivity rises, and more and better kinds of jobs become available. That has been the case so far with the industrialized countries of the world, and it appears to be the case also with the currently developing countries.

Those who criticize free trade on the grounds that it causes or incentivizes exploitation should thus be wary of simply *restricting* overseas trade. Even though exploitation happens and is unjust, such restrictions often do more harm than good.

In response, one might propose more targeted regulations, such as regulations that require companies to pay their workers a better wage. However, whether these more targeted restrictions avoid the problem again depends on whether requiring importers to pay their workers a certain amount actually helps those workers. Perhaps it could. Normally, in a competitive market, workers expect to receive a wage close to their marginal product. However, in monopsonistic or semimonopsonistic markets—that is, markets where there is only one or only very few employers—employers have sufficient bargaining power that they can pay workers significantly less than their marginal product.

Do we have reason to think sweatshop employers are doing that, or that forcing them to raise wages will actually raise their workers' wages? Sweatshop managers might respond the way we want by raising the wages of all their current employees. Or, they might respond by moving to a more capital-intensive method of production, raising the wages of some (usually the more productive) employees, but firing the others (and thus delivering them an even worse option than being exploited in a sweatshop). Or they might fire all of their current employees and move the factory to a more developed country with a better infrastructure and political environment (which, again, would deliver their current employees a worse option).

Suppose, however, that companies actually raise their workers' wages. Would that help people like María from the sweatshop worker example? Again, it depends. Consider an analogy with a domestic example. Suppose that in response to criticism, Walmart decided to double its wages: instead of paying its floor-level associates between \$8–11/hr., it will pay each of them \$16–22/hr., plus benefits. Would this move be good for Walmart workers? One thing is clear: it would pay better to work at Walmart after the change than before. Anyone who currently works at Walmart and who keeps their job would see their salary double, and therefore would be better off.

But it doesn't follow that the kinds of people who currently tend to get Walmart jobs would benefit from Walmart's decision to double its wages. According to the Bureau of Labor Statistics, here are some other median hourly wages in the United States:[5]

1. Chemical technicians \$22.04
2. Real estate sales agents \$21.20
3. Carpenters: \$20.96

4. Desktop publishers $19.76
5. Agricultural and food science technician: $18.05
6. Dental assistant: $17.75
7. Tax preparers: $17.57
8. Motorcycle mechanics: $16.69
9. Library technician: $15.81
10. Emergency medical technicians and paramedics: $15.71

Now think about the kinds of people doing these jobs. They tend to have significantly more skill, experience, education, and other kinds of human capital than most of the people who now work at Walmart as cashiers. They might be more conscientious on average, too, as shown by the fact they were able to develop the skills necessary to work wood, prepare taxes, repair motorcycles, or assist in medicine.

So what might happen if Walmart started offering to pay cashiers and shelf stockers $22/hr.? As Walmart raises its pay, it starts to attract skilled, higher human capital workers from other fields. That's not to say that any particular library technician making $15.81/hr. will quit and go work at Walmart as soon as Walmart pays $15.82/hr. (And, of course, if Walmart raises wages, the companies that employ these other workers may have to raise wages too to compete.) Rather, the point is that as Walmart raises wages, the kinds of people who compete for Walmart jobs changes. As wages go up, workers with greater skill, human capital, and experience start to compete for these jobs. A dental assistant who gets laid off might now apply at Walmart. With more productive, more reliable, or lower-risk workers available, it's possible that some and perhaps many of them may beat out the workers currently getting Walmart jobs.

We can call this phenomenon *job gentrification*. Just as artists, hipsters, and yuppies can squeeze poor people out of their traditional neighborhoods, so can better-skilled workers squeeze low-skilled people out of their traditional jobs. If Walmart increases its wages significantly, this will be very good for the people who end up working at Walmart. But that doesn't mean it will be good for the kind of people who currently are getting the low-paying jobs at Walmart.

In the sweatshop worker example, María had few skills and few options. Suppose that in response to international regulations and pressures, the factory where María works decides to pay workers a "living wage" of $4.50/hr. If so, in order to avoid losing money, or at least to maintain profitability, the factory needs to ensure that workers have a marginal productivity greater than

$4.50/hr. These factories will thus likely switch to more capital-intensive, less labor-intensive production techniques. And this may mean that María will be out of a job. Perhaps the factory will hire people like Ana, who has a high school diploma, six years of job experience, and some computer skills. That would be great for Ana, but not for María. In the developed world, we might, if we're lucky, see how our regulations have improved working conditions (after all, average hourly wages went up), and think we've done justice to María. But, quite likely, what we don't see is that María lost her job.[6]

There is much to dislike about sweatshops. We'd strongly prefer a world in which everyone can afford to turn down these jobs. But if we genuinely care about helping the poor in our world, we must not remove what may very well be their best option unless we replace it something even better. Imposing trade restrictions does little to achieve that end.

Hassoun's Argument

In *Globalization and Global Justice*, Nicole Hassoun registers a different kind of skepticism about the case for free trade. One of her arguments is that the simplest model of free trade, the one students learn in introductory microeconomics textbooks, has some unrealistic assumptions.[7] Once we try to make the model more realistic, she says, free trade might not benefit everyone. Instead, it might actually benefit some at the expense of others (including the world's poorest).[8]

"Might" is doing a lot of work in Hassoun's objections. By no means has she refuted decades of work in trade theory, or shown that trade generally or even commonly suffers from these problems. Rather, the point is relatively banal: free trade does not *guarantee* optimal results.

This is true, of course. But it is also not the point. No institution can guarantee good results; even *legal guarantees* that a state will produce some end can fail or even be counterproductive to producing that end. The point isn't to look for guarantees. Rather, it's to ask which institutions tend to liberate and enrich people, and which tend not to. It's easy to imagine targeted protectionism, done in the name of fairness, liberating and enriching people without causing unjust harms to others. It's very hard to actually do so.

In her book, Hassoun offers a quick overview of the Econ 101 model of free trade, and then notes that the model is too simple. From this she concludes that the model does not have much power at all. But this is not a strong argument against free trade. Economists have developed many more advanced models and theorems to deal with the more complicated cases at which Hassoun hints, yet none of this is generally taken to defeat the case for free trade. Perhaps Econ 101 does not by itself make that case, but in order to reject free trade one has to do much more than merely reject the simplest version of this story.[9]

Hassoun then offers a very odd critique of the Ricardian model. She compares two examples, involving a rich and a poor country trading two goods (xylophones and marsupials). She notes that how much better off each becomes, after specializing and trading, depends on the exchange rate between the two goods. In both examples, the rich country specializes in producing xylophones while the poor country specializes in producing marsupials. In one example, the rich country gets a 25% gain in xylophones and a 20% gain in marsupials, while the poor country gets a 33% gain in xylophones and a 50% gain in marsupials. In the other, apparently problematic example, the exchange rate between marsupials and xylophones is less favorable to the poorer country. There, the model predicts that the richer country will get a 25% gain in xylophones and a 33% gain in marsupials, while the poorer country will get a 33% gain xylophones but no gain or loss in marsupials.[10]

We might prefer the first situation to the second. But it is weird to present this as an *objection* to free trade. Even when the exchange is less favorable to the poor country, what ends up happening is that it has the *same* number of marsupials it would have had under autarky, but ends up with 33% more xylophones than it would produce under autarky. The worst-case scenario is that specializing in marsupial production means getting a bunch of additional goods. Free trade thus still made the poorer country much better off. In her worst-case scenario, free trade is awesome.

Hassoun worries, although she does not show, that free trade might enrich many people but fail to help the very worst off. She notes that some economists share this concern, even if it is not the mainstream view. Still, even if she were right, that would hardly be a count against free trade. At most, it would mean that it lacks one count for it.

Imagine we had a magic wand that permanently cured everybody of the common cold, except for the bottom 1% of income earners in the world. The humanitarian thing to do would be to wave the magic wand. Similarly, imagine we had a magic wand that makes everyone significantly richer, except for the bottom 1% of income earners in the world. The humanitarian thing to do would still be to wave the magic wand. Sure, we might want to give priority to the worst off, but if the growth isn't coming at their expense, it's hard to see why it would be problematic. (Recall that life slightly above the very poorest conditions is still one of very severe hardship.)

Hassoun's most potentially persuasive case concerns the problem of intellectual property in drugs. She worries that if drug companies are given temporary monopoly rights on selling the drugs they invent, desperately poor people in the developing world might not be able to afford these life-saving drugs. She recommends that companies participate in a special fair-trade scheme designed to increase access in the developing world.[11]

We will not discuss Hassoun's proposal at length here. We bring it up only to note that it's a distraction from the real issue. There is a big philosophical and economic problem about whether intellectual property should exist in the first place, and if it should exist, exactly how it should work. For any ideology, there are people who take all sorts of positions.[12] The question of whether we should have free trade is a *different* question. Even if everything Hassoun says about drug patents is correct, this is not a matter of whether we should have free trade. Rather, it is an issue of how intellectual property rights ought to work—which things should be rights-protected within that system of free trade.

Suppose Bas and Jason disagree about how rights in real property ought to work. Maybe Bas thinks that untouched property should revert back to the commons after 10 years, and that property rights can be overridden for reasons of economic efficiency. Suppose Jason disagrees. He thinks that untouched property should revert back to the commons only after 25 years, and that property rights can be overridden only in emergencies. Their debate is plainly *not* about free trade, but about the nature of property. The same is true about Hassoun's arguments about intellectual property rights in drugs.

James's Critique

One of the most sustained recent critiques of free trade comes from Aaron James. While James acknowledges many of the points we have raised, he argues that these do not suffice to make a moral case for free trade. In his view:

> Strictly speaking, economic theory implies only that trade barriers have an opportunity cost: net national income is not as great as it would be under freer trade. That is *some* reason to be interested in freer trade, but not necessarily a conclusive reason, let alone a conclusive reason for completely free trade. For why not favor substantial trade up to some liberalization threshold, for the gains over self-sufficiency, but forgo further national income gains to protect would-be losers from harm, or to slow the breakneck pace of historical change?[13]

James is right about one thing: the economic argument (which is, at base, a humanitarian or welfarist argument) creates a presumption in favor of free trade. We'd add that the deontological argument we made in the previous chapter strengthens that presumption. But, again, there can be countervailing considerations that outweigh this.

One argument James offers is reminiscent of the point we saw Rawls and Freeman make in the previous chapter: James disputes that there is any sort of pre-political right to free trade. Instead, he claims, international trade is "an *international market reliance practice*," something that gives rise to demands of "structural equity"—in effect, a demand that the gains from trade are roughly equally divided between nations.[14]

James challenges this thought by questioning what he sees as the main reason for removing trade barriers: domestic economic efficiency or the "augmenting of national income," as he calls it. James says that growth or efficiency arguments carry hidden moral assumptions. When a country lowers its tariffs, some win and others will lose. Whether this is a good or a bad thing is a moral question. It does not itself settle that removing the tariff is a good thing.[15]

This much is true, of course. However, James infers from this that the case *for* and the case *against* tariffs face the same burden of proof—that there is no presumption against trade restrictions. After all, just as when a tariff is removed, some will win and others lose; when a tariff is instituted, some again win while others lose.

We need to be careful, however, about how we think about winners and losers in trade. Recall the thought experiment from the previous chapter, in which Marvin wants to sell something to a person in Chicago, but you stop him. In a free market, where anyone is free to sell things to willing buyers, Marvin's competitors might lose. In a closed market, in which Marvin's competitors lobby to prevent Marvin from being able to sell his products, Marvin and his customers lose, and his competitors win.

There's a level of abstraction at which these cases look the same, because both involve winners and losers. But this only shows that certain levels of abstraction *obscure* important moral differences. Intuitively, it seems rather obvious (on par with "don't kick people in the face for fun") that when Marvin makes his competitors lose by offering their customers something they prefer, that is very different from when Marvin's competitors make him lose by using coercion to stop people from buying things from him at all.

James seems to think otherwise, because he sees markets as "*constitutively embedded*" within a larger social environment governed by the state. And this means, he argues, that "the *very existence* of a market of that scope and kind depends upon the establishment and maintenance of those nonmarket institutions."[16] Without society, without a state that governs it, there can be no market:

> When property rights disintegrate and there is no "yours" and "mine" to exchange, we have not a *market*, in the relevant standard sense, but rather bartered exchange, chaos, war, or in any case a different kind of social thing. True laissez-faire is, in this sense, pure fiction. There could be no such thing as a purely self-organizing, self-sustaining, self-correcting market system of individual choices and exchanges (in this standard sense) without some constitutively embedding institutions or other.[17]

Both the absence and the presence of trade restrictions are part of a larger institutional and social environment. Might this mean that they face the same justificatory burden?

Claims like these are, by now, frankly trite. Despite much clamor to the contrary, no sensible defender of free trade denies—or needs to deny—the truism that the market is part of a larger social environment, governed by formal and informal norms, and so on. Few take pains to explicitly point this out, however, because not much turns on it.

To see this, consider an alternative "embeddedness" theory: modern society is constitutively embedded in a market environment. When the market disintegrates, and there is no economic interaction anymore, we have not a society like ours in the relevant sense, but rather a solitary, poor, and nasty existence. Such a society is, of course, a fiction. There have always been forms of economic exchange, and no real human society could exist without it.

This alternative theory shows, of course, precisely nothing. Yet it is simply the flip side of James's embeddedness assertion. But if it doesn't show anything, then James's story seems not to show anything either. It is simply the (also impotent) flip side of our (already impotent) story.

We cannot invoke our alternative story to argue that critics of free trade like James are mistaken. We cannot argue, in other words, that because current societies are inextricably embedded in an economic environment, one cannot appeal to social values in order to morally critique the market. To do so would be to assume that the market is to be held constant, and that society and the state ought to be organized around it. And to make that assumption is to assume exactly what is at stake—it assumes that the market is justified.

The same is true, then, of James's embeddedness story. The market is embedded within society and the law. Fair enough. But this no more shows that there are no moral limitations to what society or the state might do within the market than the opposite story shows that there can be no moral limitations to what the market does to society or the state. That would be to assume what is at stake—that regulating and limiting trade is justified.

What we are left with, then, is the simple—and highly intuitive—approach we have sketched out in the previous sections. State regulation, taxation, and enforcement by law are all potentially justifiable. But they *do* stand in need of justification. Sometimes there is good cause. But when there is not, free trade ought to remain the standard. People are, in principle, morally free to trade.

Perhaps James thinks that his arguments do not really depend on the embeddedness thesis, but on the point that international trade constitutes "a social practice." However, many of the same problems reappear with this point. James holds that a social practice exists, roughly, if the following conditions are satisfied: (1) two or more agents coordinate their behavior (2) in a generally understood way, (3) where expectations are governed, either formally or informally, and adjusted, despite potentially divergent interests, according to a shared organizing purpose or aim.[18]

It is questionable whether international trade satisfies all three conditions. James claims that the final condition is satisfied because, when trade barriers are removed, this is "for the generally assumed purpose of *mutual* national economic gain."[19] One might challenge that claim. But even ignoring this, note how weak these conditions are. According to James's account, driving a car in traffic counts as a social practice. The same is true of using language, playing video games online, and so on.

We are open to the possibility that the sufficient conditions for social practices really are this weak. For some purposes, that might make sense. But it does not make sense if these are *also* meant to be sufficient conditions for the application of claims of distributive justice. Perhaps there are problems of justice when some groups benefit from playing video games more than others. But it is absurd to claim that the injustice exists *because* playing video games is a social practice (at least in this weak sense). Perhaps there are problems of justice when some people benefit more than others from norms allowing free association or marriage for love. But it is plainly wrong to say that lonely people gain moral claims against happy couples for the reason that marriage is a social practice.

The conditions here are weak on purpose, of course. In order to show that free trade is morally problematic, James needs *omissions* (the absence of trade restrictions) to count as morally similar to actions like the imposition of a tariff. And so we end up where we began. The burden of proof cannot be avoided.

James's positive proposal, his desired alternative to free trade, is no less problematic. Perhaps most so is the fact that he treats *countries*, rather than individuals, as the relevant unit of analysis. In order to achieve justice in trade, James claims, countries should equitably split the gains of trade between them. It should be obvious by now that we reject this approach. In our view persons, not countries, are what matter morally. Making the world more just is about doing right by people, not the states that govern them.

It might be said, of course, that doing right by states *is* how we do right by individual people. That could be true. However, it cannot be plausibly said to be true of James's approach. To see this, consider the following example. Suppose we measure countries' gains of trade by looking at the per capita income differences that result from trade within them.[20] Here's one possible implication of James's view that these gains ought to be divided equally between countries. Imagine that country A's economy consists of 90% poor people who make $1,000, and 10% rich people making $10,000. Country B's economy has 10% poor people making $1,000, and 90% rich people making $10,000. And suppose that A's poor trade with B's poor, so that everybody ends up being $1,000 better off as a result.[21]

Here are the effects. Before trade, country A had a per capita income of $1,900. After trade, this became $2,800, a net per capita gain of $900. Country B went from a pre-trade per capita income of $9,100 to $9,200, only a $100 per capita increase.[22] The gains of trade, then, are unevenly distributed. Country A gained, *as a country*, significantly more than country B. It would follow, on James's view, that country A, which is the vastly poorer country, ought to transfer considerable resources to country B, the vastly richer. But this is bizarre. It makes no sense to penalize poor countries for taking steps toward development. That's a recipe for perpetuating the injustice of our world.

James attempts to avoid implications like this by claiming that his principle cannot require redistributions from poor to rich.[23] But apart from plainly being ad hoc, this fails to address the problem. By the same mechanics, a poorer country can catch up with a richer one because it gained more from trade, leading to the doubly odd outcome that redistribution is not only needed between equally rich countries, but that the direction goes from the formerly poorer to the formerly richer.

These problems are not the result of this or that particular example. If instead of per capita income differences we focus on percentages of country

GDP as a way to measure the gains of trade, the same results become possible. The trouble does not lie with one example or another. Measuring the justice of trade by comparing the effects on countries as a whole invariably allows for strange results like these. Generally speaking, it is possible for a country's per capita income to go up even when the income of every single person goes down, and vice versa.

The simple way of avoiding these problems is to reject James's idea that justice in trade is about equalizing gains between states, and accept what was always the more plausible view: trade matters morally as a free interaction between individuals. Once we adopt that view, there is no reason for the poor being bizarrely required to subsidize the rich anymore.

Might it be worth reviving James's ideas about fairness at some other level? Should we equalize the gains of trade between regions, companies, perhaps *individual* people? The answer remains no. The gains from trade each party enjoys are the net benefits that accrue to them as a result of exchange. To say that justice requires equalizing those net benefits, then, is to say that each party must on net benefit the same. However, net benefits are the difference between the value of the thing received and the cost of the thing exchanged for it. If we require people to equalize this difference, we create an immediate disincentive for each side to lower their cost of production. It won't be worth their while to invest in producing things more efficiently in order to increase their net gains from trade. Such increases are likely to be transferred away to their trading partners, and holding on to more expensive production methods will end up being subsidized by others.

The effect, then, is a tax on increased economic efficiency. Trading parties are penalized for improving their ability to produce the same things more cheaply. No matter whether this happens at the level of the individual or the state, that's a recipe for slowing economic development and growth. It most certainly does not help people around the world escape poverty or get better lives.

One reason James offers for wanting to equalize the gains of trade between countries is that people seem to *want* such policies. As he puts it:

If the "revealed preferences" of actual governments indicate what societies prefer, then such cases are common; many societies do not seem to prefer optimized national income at any social cost, since many sub-optimal trade barriers remain.[24]

The continued existence of trade barriers, he says, shows that societies might want to "slow the breakneck pace of historical change."[25]

Nothing of the kind follows. There's a large empirical literature on *why* people advocate what they do. And the reason is not that voters generally know the economic case for free trade, but reject it upon reflection. As we've seen, most people don't understand comparative advantage, see international trade as zero-sum, and advocate proto-mercantilist theories instead.[26] The reason Western countries have as much free trade as they do—why they have far *less* protectionism than their voters want—appears to be that their elected leaders are better informed and have significant leeway to ignore voter preferences.[27]

Compensating Losses from Liberalization

Right now, countries vary in how protectionist they are. Some have highly restrictive trade regimes; others have more open trade regimes. (We know of no country with a perfectly free trade regime.)

In general, everyone is better off in the long run in a free trade regime than under a protectionist regime. Or, perhaps more precisely, we might say that any individual is best off if he, and only he, is protected from competition, while there is free trade for everyone else. The temptation is thus for everyone to seek individual protection. But a regime in which there are lots of protections for many people ends up being worse in the long run for everyone than a regime without any protection. The situation is analogous to a prisoner's dilemma.

In the short run, liberalization will harm some people, relative to the status quo. Many people work in protected industries or businesses. They have their current jobs, or make their current salaries, in part as a result of protectionism. For example, Japan has high tariffs and engages in various forms of currency manipulation in order to make American cars and trucks overpriced in Japan. If Japan were to stop this unjust practice, some Japanese autoworkers would lose their jobs or be paid less, or some shareholders of Japanese corporations would lose capital.

This raises a question: Should the short-term losers of trade liberalization be compensated for their losses?

Some might think the answer is obviously no: after all, the workers or stockholders in question have been profiting from ill-gotten gains. They have taken advantage of unjust, inefficient, coercive restrictions on trade to enrich themselves at others' expense. Suppose Jason typically buys American pick-up trucks, because he wants to avoid the 25% tariff on imported trucks. Suppose that in the absence of the tariff, he would have purchased a Japanese truck. Now, suppose the tariff is lifted, and Jason buys a Toyota instead of a Ford. Ford might say that Toyota steals its business, and might think it's entitled to compensation. We might feel bad, if not for Ford the corporation, for some of workers in Dearborn, Michigan or some grandmothers who hold Ford stock and see it devalued. But keep in mind that Jason was only buying from Ford in the first place because the state quite literally used force and the threat of force to prevent Jason and Toyota from making their mutually agreeable deal.

When we liberalize trade some people will lose business, as they in effect enjoyed an economic rent. Their incomes were artificially inflated as a result of unjust coercion. Whether justice requires that they be compensated, or whether it's a good idea pragmatically, is a complicated question. It's not obvious that they do.[28]

At the same time, it's not obvious that they don't. Consider the following argument offered by Mathias Risse (though his version is more nuanced than what we state here). Individuals living in mixed and regulated economies make reasonable decisions about where and how to invest or develop their effort, human capital, physical capital, and financial capital, or about where to live, in light of prevailing conditions and institutions. They have little individual control over how much economic protection there is or will be, but they still have to invest and plan in light of what they reasonably expect the laws to be. We might hold it against a corporation or an entity for seeking a rent, but we can't really hold it against a person living in Dearborn for thinking it reasonable to learn how to build trucks, or deciding to stay in Dearborn rather than move elsewhere. If the state suddenly changes the rules, some such people will lose not because they did something wrong, but because they made reasonable decisions about how to live in the fact of unjust rules they cannot control. In such cases, Risse thinks, "individuals have a claim based on the risk they are encouraged to take in coordinated economies."[29]

Suppose the state is about to liberalize trade. One might imagine a Dearborn plant worker saying, "Look, I'm not claiming the tariffs were just. But the tariffs were there when I got here. I had to work somewhere, and it didn't look like the tariffs were going away. So, I learned to weld, took a job at Ford, and bought a house in Dearborn. If the state suddenly eliminates tariffs, I'm in big trouble. But I didn't do anything wrong. I only made these decisions because of how the state was behaving. I should be compensated."

A skeptic might respond, "Well, Dearborn plant worker, you should have kept your hands clean, rather than worked in a tainted industry." But the problem seems more complicated than that. In a market economy, pretty much everything affects pretty much everything else. Lifting tariffs might put a mom and pop Chinese restaurant out of business, or bankrupt a local dairy farmer. It affects some people in obvious and deep ways, and others in unobvious and slight ways. There may be no keeping one's hands fully clean.

Risse finds these kinds of arguments plausible. But, he thinks, at most it calls for the losers to be protected via social or unemployment insurance, government-sponsored retraining, and the like. The worker doesn't have a right to maintain the status quo or keep his job. Risse thinks there's a strong case for a left-liberal state that protects citizens from the worst downsides of the market. We won't rehearse the case here—it's a standard Rawlsian-style argument—but it doesn't suggest that the government should prop up inefficient businesses in perpetuity.

We suspect many readers, especially those on the left or with an economic populist mindset, are inclined to agree. However, note that we can construct a parallel case that they might reject. Imagine it's 1840. Suppose Jason manufactures cotton harvesting equipment, which he sells to slave-owning Southern plantations. Jason does not himself own slaves. If the government suddenly liberates all the slaves, as it obviously ought to do, Jason's income might drop dramatically. Does Jason have a claim to compensation or social insurance in the same way Risse thinks the Ford factory worker does? If there's a difference, what is it?[30]

Whether Risse is right or not is a complicated question. We don't take a stand here. Instead, we just note that we should keep two questions distinct:

1) Should we have free trade?
2) During liberalization, should the state compensate some of the losers from liberalization?

Answering yes to the first question does not commit you to any particular answer to the second.

7

In Defense of Productive Human Rights

MARX WORRIED THAT bourgeois economists and philosophers were overly concerned with "formal" liberty or "formal" equality. These formal liberties are mainly negative liberties protected by law. For instance, the government recognizes everyone's right to own a million-dollar home. But what good are such formal liberties to most people? Rights like that, Marx thought, really matter only to the rich. What matters is that people have actual *stuff*, not the protection of whatever stuff you might acquire.

From the armchair, this may sound like a damning critique of formal property rights. Surely, one might think, Marx has to be right. In principle, a political regime governed by the rule of law, with the robust protection of private property rights, which recognizes and protects people's rights to trade as they see fit, could also be a regime in which everyone is desperately poor. What good does it do a homeless person to know that the government would refuse to extract his private property, if only he had some?

If we get out of our armchair and look around, however, our view of merely formal liberties changes. As we discussed in chapter 1, a key reason why some nations are rich and others are poor is that the former have better institutions. In particular, rich countries have the rule of law, competitive political processes, and—crucially—robust protections of private property, trade, and a market economy. It's true that as a matter of logic, formal economic liberty does not guarantee that people will be well-off. But as a matter of empirical reality, formal economic liberty is one of the things poor people need most. It's a practical prerequisite for people being well-off to begin with.

No institutions *guarantee* prosperity. But certain institutions lead to it more reliably than others. And the absence of those institutions very reliably keeps people poor. This establishes at the very least that these institutions are of serious *instrumental* value—that is, valuable as a means to securing general prosperity. Might it establish more than that?

Could Economic Liberty Be a Human Right?

What is the *moral* status of legal protections of economic freedom? From the standpoint of justice, how should we think about states denying or respecting people's property rights, freedom of contract, exchange, and so on? Are these of only instrumental value, or could they matter intrinsically as well?

Human rights are among the main elements of global justice. A fully just world will be one in which everyone's human rights are fully respected. And a world in which everyone's human rights are fully respected is well on its way to becoming a just world. If economic freedom matters morally in a global context, perhaps these rights could qualify as human rights as well.

In both the philosophical literature and popular discourse, there has been a proliferation of proposed new human rights that aim at abolishing poverty. We hear defenses of human rights to subsistence, to freedom from poverty, against social deprivation, and so on.[1]

We can differentiate human rights in terms of their typical mode of justification. Let's call rights like these *consumptive* human rights. These are justified—if they are—primarily because of what right-holders get out of their enjoyment. The notion of consumption at play here is broader, of course, than merely the kind of market consumption that often plays a role in complaints about excessive consumerism. It refers to our enjoyment or benefiting from the provision of goods and services. We need shelter, sustenance, security, education, health care, and so on. Human rights are consumptive insofar as their justification relies on the delivery of these things.

In this chapter we defend a different class of human rights—what we call productive rights. Such rights are justified—if they are—primarily because of how they protect people in their capacity as producers. The notion of production, again, is broad. It refers to our capacity to work, create, build, invest, provide, collaborate, and bargain. These are the parts of life that matter primarily because of what we bring about through our activities. Human rights are productive insofar as they protect people in these capacities.

The distinction is not exclusive,[2] but one of emphasis. Consumptive and productive human rights aim, in different ways, to provide people with things they need to live on morally acceptable terms. One difference is between direct and indirect ways of bringing about the conditions of justice. Consumptive rights aim to do so directly, by mandating the provision of things like shelter or the means for subsistence. Productive rights operate indirectly, by enabling people to produce, create, or acquire.

The point of productive human rights is to respect people's agency in ways that consumptive rights omit. Most obviously, they represent legal protections that serve people's interests as active causes of not only their own survival, lives, and development, but also of the communities around them. The productive rights express the kinds of protections people are due in their roles as contributors.

We do not argue, then, that we should endorse productive human rights *at the expense* of the consumptive rights. Since the distinction between them is not exclusive, consumptive human rights can have productive value, and vice versa. Many of the productive rights we defend here have significant consumptive value as well. And many existing consumptive rights have productive value, too. The right to basic education, for example, might be justified because it enhances our quality of life, and because it enables social, political, and economic agency.[3]

Moreover, it's plausible that each class of rights cannot be satisfied fully without the other. While the two can be *made* to conflict, this is by no means necessary. A number of existing societies succeed in robustly protecting productive rights while also providing for a variety of consumptive rights, and the limits to human rights and state powers of regulation are already part of human rights law.[4]

The productive rights we defend include basic property rights and economic liberties. More precisely, they include:

(i)   rights to the exclusive possession of property;
(ii) rights to exclusive use of property, including the right to consume it by eating, drinking, inhabiting, and wearing it; the right to alter it through labor; and the right to use it for commercial purposes;
(iii) rights to reap income from one's property, for example through rents, investments, or use as collateral;
(iv) rights of contract, including labor contracts, and transfer of ownership by gift or sale.

These rights perform two key functions. First, some enable individual productivity, such as rights to control and use property, as well as rights to income and contract. These rights protect people against arbitrary expropriations of things like land, investments, or private pensions. And they help preclude labor bondage and the prohibition of economic exchange or self-employment. Others remove standard obstacles to productive behavior. These rights preclude prohibitive barriers to entry into the market, such as unnecessary and excessive licensing fees, the exclusion of groups on grounds of religion, ethnicity, and gender, as well as government corruption.

We will defend these rights as morally justified legal human rights. That is, we will understand saying that some right to X ought to be recognized as a human right to mean, roughly, that there is a legal right to X that morally ought to be established, protected, and respected by any state and the international community (including by states, NGOs, and supranational institutions). We do not defend these rights as moral rights in and of themselves. We are probably more confident than most that those rights qualify as such, but the argument does not turn on that issue.[5]

This list of rights has, of course, a very high level of generality. They are paradigm cases of productive rights, not a rigid or definitive statement, specified in all its determinate detail, of how people ought to be protected in their productive capacities. Productive rights allow for the further legal interpretation, application, and implementation at international, regional, and local levels. In this way, productive human rights are similar to other human rights. And that, of course, is precisely the point.

The Need for a Defense

In many (mostly Western) societies productive rights are relatively well protected. Why bother with a philosophical defense? Unfortunately, the right to property and rights to economic freedoms are highly controversial in human rights discourse and philosophical discussions. It's been this way since the inception of the human rights movement.[6]

That is not to say that these rights are altogether absent from key human rights documents. They are not—or more precisely, the right to property is not. (Economic freedoms are by and large absent.) For example, Article 17 of the 1948 Universal Declaration of Human Rights (UDHR) protects the right to hold property "alone as well as in association with others." The right is also listed in the American Convention on Human Rights (article 21) and the European Convention on Human Rights (protocol 1, article 1). And European Court of Human Rights jurisprudence upholds limited human rights to basic possessions, economic interests, certain contractual agreements, and claims of compensation against private and public parties.[7]

However, even the right to property has been highly controversial from the beginning. At the time of the UDHR's drafting there was strong ideological opposition. John Peters Humphrey, the Declaration's principal drafter and an avowed socialist,[8] along with the communist delegations sought to insert a socialist conception of personal property (excluding or strongly limiting private ownership of productive property), and even proposed a human right to an "equitable share of the national income."[9]

These efforts failed with the UDHR, but succeeded elsewhere. Article 23 of the American Declaration of the Rights and Duties of Man limits the right to property to what "meets the essential needs of decent living and helps to maintain the dignity of the individual and of the home." The 1960s International Covenant on Economic, Social and Cultural Rights and the International Covenant on Civil and Political Rights do not mention the right to property. Other productive rights are absent.

Of course, there are generally recognized rights against economic discrimination.[10] Article 15 of the International Convention on the Protection of the Rights of All Migrant Workers and Members of Their Families asserts the validity of Article 17 of the UDHR for migrants. Articles 15 and 16 of the Convention on the Elimination of All Forms of Discrimination Against Women require equal enjoyment of rights to property and economic freedom for men and women. However, these rights preclude the discriminatory implementation of whatever productive rights might exist. They do not affirm those rights in the first place.

The task of affirming these protections was largely left to regional documents and courts. And there the right to property was often significantly curtailed.[11] Human rights courts allow the widest national prerogatives to curtail, redefine, and expropriate private property. The African Commission has enforced the right in only a few isolated instances. The United Nations Human Rights Committee has not once found a complaint about property rights even admissible. This has not been for want of opportunity.[12]

Human rights law, then, is at best ambivalent about productive rights. However, the stance by philosophers is perfectly clear. The productive rights either receive little attention or are criticized as potential barriers to consumptive rights.[13] When philosophers speak of economic human rights, they now have in mind rights to adequate standards of living, food, clothing, shelter, basic health care, or paid holidays. A near consensus seems to exist that productive human rights are best left aside.[14]

As we'll see, this is a mistake. These rights ought to be defended as vigorously as any other human right. And they ought to be defended for many of the same reasons as we defend other human rights: they are essential to achieving a world without poverty, oppression, and abuse. They are essential ingredients of a fully just world.

Justifying Human Rights

The first step in the argument is to identify a way of defending productive rights. This section outlines a sufficient condition for justifying human rights. The condition consists of two parts, each of which reflects a strand of the most commonly accepted way of justifying rights: the interest theory of rights.

On this approach, human rights can be justified by demonstrating that they serve certain key and universal human interests, sufficient for holding others to be under a (corresponding) duty.[15] The two parts of the condition track different ways in which rights might serve people's interests. One is by serving basic and universal interests of right-holders themselves. Thus, a human right to shelter could be justified by showing that it will serve people's interests in maintaining their health, privacy, and safety, given the significance of these interests and the absence of defeating considerations.

The second is by serving key universal interests of people in society more generally. The right to freedom of speech might be justified by showing how it serves our shared interests in living in a society characterized by free and open debate. Even if the interests of individual speakers would be insufficient for this task (on the first condition), we can justify this right by showing how it serves these shared interests, again given their significance and the absence of defeating considerations.[16]

This second strand reflects the idea that human rights function as parts of a broader international legal system. And we can judge such systems in holistic ways. A justified system of human rights should form a coherent whole, something in which individual rights function in mutually reinforcing ways. If the inclusion of a certain right or set of rights strengthens the overall fabric of the human rights system, then this counts toward the inclusion of that right into the system. If (a) the system of human rights as a whole can be justified, and (b) a certain right or set of rights helps it work better, that is a strong reason for recognizing said right.[17]

These two conditions can be combined into the following jointly sufficient conditions. A right to X is part of a justified international legal system of human rights if:

1. its legal recognition and protection protects the basic and universal interests of the right-holder, sufficient to hold others under correlative duties; and
2. its legal recognition and protection in a society serves the basic and universal interests of people in society at large, sufficient to hold others under correlative duties.

Step 1: Serving the Basic Human Interests of Individuals

Productive human rights, recall, include rights (1) to the exclusive possession of property, (2) to the exclusive use and consumption of property, (3) the right to reap income from one's property, and (4) the right to transfer of one's property. Our first step is to show that these serve important and universal interests of right-holders.

The distinctive feature of these rights is that they serve people's interests by enabling them to bring things about through working, creating, acquiring, and so on. There are numerous ways they do this. This section highlights two specific interests: (a) the interest in providing for one's survival, and (b) the interest in control over one's life. These are not the only interests served by these rights, but they are among the most important ones.

Providing for Our Survival

Among our most fundamental interests is the interest in providing for our survival. The productive human rights serve this interest in ways that line up with the four classes of rights. We will consider these in turn.

(1 and 2) Rights to the exclusive use and possession of property protect the food we collect, the homes in which we find shelter, the clothes that protect us, and the tools we need to work in order to provide for these things. These rights offer assurance that our resources will not be taken away, damaged, or used up by others, thus protecting their availability to us. Such assurances are essential for the efficacy of people's efforts to provide for their own survival by acquiring resources through work or exchange. When we are not able to trust

that the resources we have acquired will be there when we need them, our interest in survival is to that extent set back.

Of course, the mere protection of what we have is not enough to serve our interests in survival. Homes are no good if you cannot live in them, food is no good if you cannot eat it, tools are no good if you cannot use them. Equally important, then, are rights to the exclusive use and consumption of our possessions. These enable people to reap their benefits by using them for sustenance, physical security, and other protections. Moreover, the right to use one's property for commercial purposes allows people to provide for themselves and their families by running small stores or selling goods on the local marketplace.

The exclusivity of both kinds of rights is key. First, different people have different and sometimes rival or conflicting needs. For our resources to meet our needs, we need control over how they are used. Only if these rights are exclusive can they assure that people's efforts to provide for their survival does not come at the expense of the like ability of others.

This is a key difference with nonexclusive ownership regimes, which make the availability of resources subject to the decisions of others. As a result, everyone's decision to use a resource necessarily diminishes the available stock for others. This results in well-known collective action problems that not only threaten the means of survival for each, but also disincentivize people from acquiring them in the first place. Because exclusive rights discretely apportion goods to owners, they can avoid these problems. Each owner's use of his or her resources does not affect the availability of other people's possessions.

(3 and 4) The third and fourth kinds of rights protect our ability to acquire resources through work, investment, exchange, and so on. On the one hand, rights to reap income of property are crucial to participating in both rudimentary and advanced economies. Many market activities require capital to get started. To be able to sell goods at the local market one needs to buy inventory, possess the means of transporting it to the market, own or rent a stand, et cetera. Inadequate protection of the right to reap income constrains these endeavors by restricting people's access to capital.

More generally, the ability to invest, save, and borrow enables people to spread the consumption of their earnings over their lifetimes in ways that are more efficient. We need to be able to safely put aside food, clothes, money, and other things during times of relative surplus in order to access them during times of relative scarcity. And we need to be able to access goods now that we will earn later. The right to reap income helps free up the requisite resources and thus serves to insulate people who lose their jobs, get sick, become temporarily disabled, or simply grow old from depravation.

Rights of transfer and contract, on the other hand, help people survive in two different ways. First, they enable people to sell their goods on local markets, run businesses, organize services, and engage in other kinds of commercial ventures. Moreover, they enable people to sell their labor. This is the only means of survival available to those who have nothing else to sell.

Second, the right to transfer and contract greatly increases the pool of resources people can enjoy. Most obviously, these rights give people the legal means to acquire resources they do not already possess, and reallocate some of their own possessions to chosen others. This bolsters the flow of resources through the economy and helps guide them to their most valued uses. Slightly less obviously, the right to transfer offers people their most reliable method of acquiring that which they do not produce themselves. This enables the division of labor and thereby significant increases in productive efficiency.

To the extent that these rights are curtailed, then, people's abilities to provide for their own survival (and that of their families and loved ones) are curtailed as well. In regimes that fail to protect or even limit rights to garner income and transfer, people become more dependent on the adequacy of other schemes or provisions—means that are typically not under their own control. As a result, the curtailment of these rights typically means that their ability to provide for their survival also becomes, to that extent, dependent on others. The productive rights thus crucially serve the interest in providing for our survival.

Control Over Our Lives

Second, productive rights serve people's interests in having control over our lives. Much of the value and meaning of life lies in the commitments we undertake, the plans we adopt, and the projects we develop in order to pursue and realize goods. We evaluate, alone and with others, the circumstances in which we live and how they interact with our preferences, needs, and dreams, and we update them when necessary. In a phrase, we have an important interest in being more than a slave of circumstance.

The productive human rights serve this interest in the economic sphere of life. We spend large parts of our lives working, consuming, and exchanging. These activities take up a lot of our time and form part of the conditions of what we can do with the rest of our lives. Unsurprisingly, then, many people see their work as central to who they are. They become invested in the businesses they start, spend their lives honing a craft, or are otherwise deeply involved in their work. For their endeavors to achieve their full depth and meaning, they need rights to garner income, trade, and enter into legally protected contracts.[18]

Rights to the exclusive possession and use of goods (1 and 2) offer people the ability to decide what happens within the part of the external world that is subject to their rights. Such control is essential to the ability to pursue meaningful projects, both economic and otherwise. Control not only makes these projects practically possible, but also protects them from outside interference. The means we use in our projects can become integral parts of them. The business owner's establishment, the retiree's savings, the worker's career choice are all constitutive elements of their projects.

Rights to reap income and trade (3 and 4) again enable people to acquire and use objects and resources in pursuit of their personal and joint projects. Without these, people are seriously inhibited in their ability to develop the kind of plans and commitments that make up a meaningful life. For many, productive activities such as trade or for-profit entrepreneurship are important parts of their career choices and life plans. For others, an important sense of well-being is connected to the ability to make our way in the world; to not depend on others, but be someone on whom others can depend. For yet others, these activities offer the means for pursuing their other, more cherished commitments.

The productive human rights thus offer people a greater deal of individual control over both the economic parts of their lives and their more general circumstances than do legal regimes that exclude or severely curtail these rights (like regimes of mere access or usufruct). Such nonexclusive alternatives invariably make our life choices and plans subject to co-determination by others, and thus fail to serve these interests to the same extent or even at all.[19]

Step 2: Serving Collective Interests

Our first justificatory step looked at the interests of individual rights-holders. The second step adds that we also have important interests in living in a society that legally protects productive human rights. We'll will discuss three key measures of this: (a) economic growth and income per capita of societies as a whole, (b) per capita income of the least well-off in society, and (c) average life expectancy.[20]

Our argument will combine strong theoretical reasons for believing this step is satisfied with supporting empirical evidence. That is, we'll first show why one should expect that these rights help make societies good places to live in, and then back this up with how actual societies tend to function when they do, and do not, protect those rights.

The theoretical argument is the flip side of how productive human rights enable people to provide in their own survival. Those rights channel self-help activities into mutually productive interactions. The conditions of mutual productivity are among the most important conditions for societies to leave extreme poverty behind. As we've seen, poverty typically results from societies becoming organized on zero-sum or negative-sum terms. When violence, extortion, corruption, and rent-seeking behavior take hold, we begin to move away from conditions of prosperity and toward poverty.

A central element of a society being a good place to live, then, is that the activities by which people make themselves better off don't come at the expense of others—and, vice versa, that the activities by which around them become better off don't come at their expense. Here's how Daron Acemoglu and James Robinson put it in their recent book, *Why Nations Fail*:

> Economic institutions foster economic activity, productivity growth, and economic prosperity. Secure property rights are central, since only those with such rights will be willing to invest and increase productivity. A businessman who expects his output to be stolen, expropriated, or entirely taxed away will have little incentive to work, let alone any incentive to undertake investments and innovations.[21]

Rights of exclusive use and possession (1 and 2) incentivize people to undertake such activities by promising them the material rewards of their efforts. Without secure property rights, people often can't afford to invest and increase their productivity. A worker, businessman, or trader who expects his output to be stolen or expropriated has little incentive to work, let alone invest or innovate. This prevents the replacement of less efficient firms with more efficient ones, and the rising standards of living that result.

Rights to reap income of property (3) are important because such innovations and efficiency gains typically require capital. The curtailment of these rights creates barriers to the most straightforward ways of accumulating capital, clipping the wings of the first two productive rights. Rights to exchange and contract (4) enable goods and services to be allocated in ways that fit the wishes and abilities of people across society. These rights are crucial to enabling the division of labor and specialization, both major determinants of economic development and growth.[22]

These observations are corroborated by empirical findings.[23] Consider Figures 7.1–7.4, drawn from James Gwartney, Robert Lawson, and Joshua Hall, *Economic Freedom of the World: 2016 Annual Report*,[24] which measure the impact of economic freedom on the three measures introduced earlier: (a) economic growth and income per capita, (b) per capita income of the least well-off in society, and (c) average life expectancy. Gwartney et al. measure economic freedom around the world as well as its relation to other freedoms and indicators of development. The report understands economic freedom as an index of data about protection of personal economic choice, government interference with markets and international trade, and the stability and legal protection of property rights. This index closely relates to the productive human rights discussed earlier. As such, its findings can, with due care and qualifications, be reasonably taken to provide information about the empirical effects of the protection of those rights.

Figure 7.1 compares the protection of economic freedom with growth in per capita GDP over a 24-year period. In line with these points, it shows a positive relation between growth and the protection of these rights.

Figure 7.2 shows the relation between economic freedoms and per capita income. This, too, illustrates the generally positive impact of productive rights.

The protection of these rights in practice positively relates to the development of societies as a whole and the material improvement of their people.

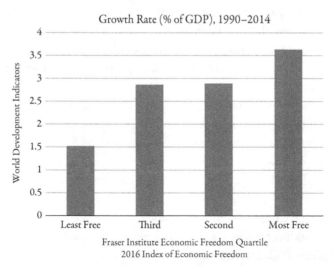

FIGURE 7.1 Growth Rate (% of GDP), 1990–2014
Source: Gwartney et al. 2016.

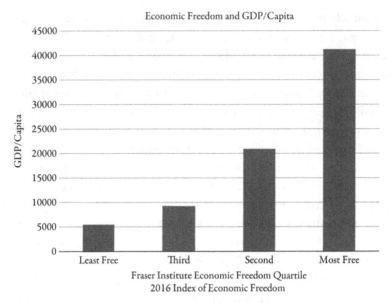

FIGURE 7.2 Economic Freedom and GDP/Capita
Source: Gwartney et al. 2016.

And such growth and rising per capita incomes are typically accompanied by rising levels of health, safety, education, leisure, and other parts of well-being,[25] thus serving people's interests across society.

Figure 7.3 illustrates the positive effect of these freedoms on the (pre-transfer/welfare payment) income of the poorest 10% of people living in such societies. It shows that the benefits that accompany the protection of productive rights are typically not restricted to only the rich or middle classes. They similarly (or more accurately: disproportionally)[26] benefit the least well-off, too.

Finally, Figure 7.4 looks at life expectancy, showing that people in countries with the most economic freedom live on average about 15 years longer than those in countries with the least. Such increased life expectancy matters in its own right, but also because of what it reflects: reductions in threats such as disease, physical danger, pollution, and increases in access to health care, sanitation, and so on.[27]

The general empirical trend, then, fits the theoretical argument. The protection of productive rights is positively related to a wide range of measures, reflecting important interests across societies.

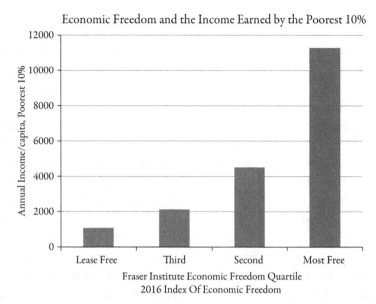

FIGURE 7.3 Economic Freedom and the Income Earned by the Poorest 10%
Source: Gwartney et al. 2016.

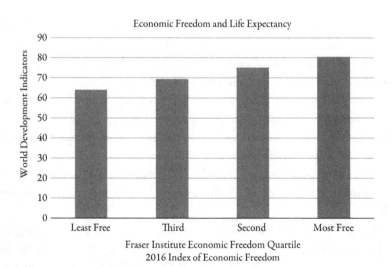

FIGURE 7.4 Economic Freedom Life Expectancy
Source: Gwartney et al. 2016.

Completing the Interest-Based Argument

Interest-theory justifications of rights take two steps. The first shows that rights serve important interests. The second shows that those interests are sufficient for people to have corresponding duties. The arguments above complete the first step. This section addresses the second.

The interests we have been discussing are clearly among the most important we have. Survival and control over our lives are closely related to our ability to exercise agency and live in autonomous, free, and dignified ways. The way these rights help raise standards of living across societies serves to increase welfare, and enables us to pursue important things like education, the arts, and leisure activities.

Since these interests are based on features we share, quite simply, as human beings, they are universally shared around the world. These are not exclusively Western or capitalist interests. We all have important interests in providing for our survival, exercising control over the productive parts of our lives, and being able to do these in ways that help our societies flourish. In fact, we can see the importance and universality of these interests in standard defenses of other rights, like the right to personal integrity, freedom of movement, or education.[28]

A common concern about productive rights is that they do not sufficiently protect, and even threaten, minorities and indigenous groups. But this is a mistake. For one, minorities, women, and other socially marginalized groups are often the main victims of the repression of productive rights. They get barred from certain occupations, their property is most insecure, they are threatened by corrupt officials, and so on. These groups stand to gain at least as much from the universal protection of productive human rights as anyone else. Similarly, when enforcement mechanisms for property rights break down, conflicts break out or intensify. A number of major conflicts around the world are in part resource conflicts, spurred on by disputes over property rights.[29]

Human rights law already affirms the right to property for women, migrant workers, and indigenous peoples.[30] The productive rights serve to further bolster these protections, by extending them to other important economic liberties and by offering them to groups who might not be covered by these protections otherwise.[31] Finally, by protecting and empowering individuals, these rights ensure that group-based rights cannot come at the expense of the productive interests of the individuals who make up those groups.

Should the imposition of the relevant duties not be too burdensome, then, the first step of the argument goes through. Is that the case? Are the burdens imposed by these rights not too burdensome? Given that productive human rights would require that we respect people's exclusive possessions, one might wonder whether compliance with the corresponding duties can be reasonably expected of the world's poor. Hundreds of millions of people live in abject poverty, and the present argument might seem to remove their only way of escape.

But this does not follow. For even though the burdens imposed by productive human rights can be considerable, it's a mistake to infer from this that those duties are too burdensome. To conclude that, we must compare the burdens of productive human rights with the burdens imposed by rival regimes. And second, we should consider the broader institutional landscape within which they are placed.

Judged from this point of view, productive human rights are hard to oppose, perhaps most crucially because the poor stand to gain much themselves from them. They, too, have strong interests in being able to escape conditions of poverty, and productive human rights offer an important avenue for this. These rights provide legal protections in the labor market, protections from bondage, coercion, exploitation, and so on. They protect people's possessions, however inadequate, dirty, and dangerous these may be. And they enable them to borrow and save in order to work their way out of the very worst conditions. Such rights might not always be sufficient for them to escape poverty, but in many cases they are necessary.

Second, even if we suppose that these burdens are indeed too severe, they can be tempered in various ways. One possibility is to couple productive human rights with other protections, such as the consumptive rights mentioned earlier. After all, the case for the former does not imply the denial of the latter. Human rights law already contains numerous such rights and provisions. Rights to basic education, public health measures, and so on all serve to reduce the burdens imposed by these rights, and thus offer further justificatory support to productive human rights as well.[32]

Productivity and Global Justice

Human rights, as we've said, are among the most fundamental and important building blocks of our theories of global justice, indeed of justice in general. When we leave out productive rights, we are leaving out an important piece of the puzzle. It distorts our picture of human rights—and our picture of global justice in the process.

In chapter 5, we discussed John Rawls's and Samuel Freeman's argument against recognizing rights like these as basic liberties. They object that these rights are not strictly speaking necessary for people to develop their basic moral powers. This critique is mistaken, but Rawls and Freeman do raise an important point. What kinds of rights we deem worthy of protection reflects what parts of human life we deem worthy of protection. Our theories of rights and justice track the things that morally matters most about persons.[33]

When theories of human rights or global justice focus almost exclusively on consumptive rights, they give us a certain picture of human life. They presume that what matters most—even exclusively—is what people should be *given*, what they should get.[34] But this picture cannot be right. People matter just as much (if not more) in terms of what they have to *offer*, what they bring to the table. We are producers, as well as consumers. Perhaps we're even producers first.

In the 1990s film version of *Great Expectations*, protagonist Finn, then a young boy, encounters an escaped convict. He decides to feed the convict and gives him tools to remove his bonds. Years later, Finn becomes an artist. Not only do his paintings sell, but he sells every painting he puts in gallery. In the end, Finn learns that his paintings were all purchased by one collector—who turns out to be the escaped convict, now rich. Finn's entire career is just a façade created by the convict to, in a sense, repay a debt.

When Finn learns this, he isn't delighted to discover that he lives in a world of communal reciprocity. He isn't delighted to discover that this his good deeds have been rewarded. On the contrary, when Finn discovers the convict has been buying his art, he thereby learns that he, Finn, is a *failure*. Finn wants other people to want his art not as a *favor* to him, but because they see the art as contributing to their lives. He doesn't want his customers to think, "Finn needs money, so out of a concern for you as an end in yourself, we're buying your art." That attitude expresses respect for Finn as a stomach to be fed, but not as an artist. Finn craves recognition as a producer of art, and he can't get that unless his customers want his art for themselves.

Sure, Finn wants to eat. Perhaps given the choice between being utterly destitute or being paid to make art for people who don't actually like the art, he'd pick the latter. But Finn wants a *good* life, not just a life. For most of us, having a good life means making our own way in the world. We want to be able to produce for others such that, in the end, we can say the world was better off with us than without us.[35]

To leave out productive rights, then, is not just to distort our picture of human rights and global justice. It's to distort our picture of people—including the world's poor. To fully respect people, we must not just make sure that they have enough welfare, happiness, or utility. We must also protect their abilities to provide for themselves, take charge of their lives, and raise their own prospects as well as the prospects of those around them. We must treat them as active and productive agents, as contributors to their own lives and those around them, and not just as consumers or receptacles of goods.

It is worth keeping in mind here just how central the exercise of productive rights is to our lives. Through economic activity we undertake new commitments and plan for the future; we pursue, evaluate, and update complex goals; we make our impact on the external world in ways that our rights to property protect; we take responsibility for others by offering them employment, products, services, and more. These are core exercises of our practical reason.

The productive human rights capture this respect for people as active agents. They express that what matters is not only *that* we avoid poverty, but also *how* we avoid poverty. They reflect the fact that producing and providing for ourselves and those with whom we live are essential to human life, and that this matters from the point of view of justice. They identify us as the recipients of justice, and as the agents who bring about the conditions of justice in the first place. A full theory of global justice captures, respects, and protects these elements of our humanity.

8

Correcting the Past

IMPERIALISM AND COLONIALISM

IN THE FIRST part of this book (chapters 2 through 7), we argued that there are two important dimensions along which the ability of people worldwide to enter into positive-sum or mutually advantageous relations ought to be protected and expanded. Global justice requires that we actively address the plight of the world's poor by opening our borders, letting people move to where they see their skills as most useful, and by opening our markets, letting people sell their goods where they see them most valued. As we will see, doing so offers people the best prospects of actually bettering their situation.

Among philosophers, this is a minority view. Most philosophers defend approaches that are, in one way or another, importantly redistributive in nature. We do not hold out much hope for this. Such approaches are, by their very essence, zero-sum in nature. They seek to make the world's poor better off through taking the resources that others in the world have produced. Our view, by contrast, is that the main way to solve the problems of poverty and global injustice is to better enable the world's poor to become producers themselves.

In this second part of the book, we discuss three ways in which one might defend a more strongly redistributive or zero-sum approach to global justice. These approaches focus, roughly speaking, on purported injustices past, present, and future. More precisely, they defend various large-scale redistributive projects as a response to historical injustices like colonialism (which we will discuss in this chapter),[1] as a response to ongoing injustices perpetrated by the current international economic or legal system (chapter 9), or as a forward-looking response to the fact that we are often in a position to save the lives of people who are in danger of dying (chapter 10). As we'll see, each of these approaches fail to show that large-scale redistribution plays a major part in making the world just.

Let us be absolutely clear. We do *not* hold that there can be no place for redistribution at all. Nor do we oppose all forms of humanitarian or developmental aid. It is no part of our view that people in rich or developed societies have no obligations of assistance to the world's poor. Rather, our point again is this: the core of a theory of global justice should aim at fostering and widening positive-sum relations worldwide. Redistributive measures cannot play or substitute for that role.

The Stolen Watch

One popular view about the causes of global inequality is that rich countries (or their predecessors), through policies of colonialism, imperialism, and resource extraction, victimized and stole from the Third World. For instance, political theorist Seyla Benhabib complains that John Rawls, in devising a theory of global justice, ignores or downplays the African slave trade and global imperialism. She doubts "whether early capitalist accumulation in the West could have been conceivable without colonial expansion."[2] Or, as Thomas Pogge says,

> Existing radical inequality is deeply tainted by how it accumulated through one historical process that was deeply pervaded by enslavement, colonialism, even genocide. The rich are quick to point out that they cannot inherit their ancestor's sins. Indeed. But how can they then be entitled to the fruits of these sins: to their huge inherited advantage in power and wealth over the rest of the world?[3]

According to this view, imperialist resource extraction explains (or helps to explain) why First World countries became wealthy and how people in the developing world became poor. Our wealth is inherited stolen wealth.

Suppose the West's wealth is indeed stolen. What moral upshot might that have? Many think it's obvious. Consider the following thought experiment, as an analogy to Western imperialism:

Stolen Watch
Upon his death, your racist grandfather bequeathed you his prized watch. However, he stole this watch 60 years ago from his

African neighbor, also now dead. Had your grandfather not stolen the watch, your neighbor would have bequeathed it to his oldest grandchild.

Imagine that you find out about this. Should you give the watch to the grandchild? Many people believe that, clearly, you should. For example, in 2017 the Getty Museum agreed to return the 1 B.C. statuette "Zeus Enthroned" to Italy, despite having purchased the piece legitimately, after evidence surfaced that the statuette had been stolen initially. The museum has a policy of returning items if compelling evidence of theft can be produced.

Many people think that the problem of Western Imperialism is just the stolen watch example writ large. They think that the lesson we should draw from this kind of thought experiment is that we, the rich West, should return the wealth stolen by our ancestors to its rightful owners, the people in the developing world.

But the analogy is misleading, at least insofar as it assumes that the reason rich countries are rich is that they extracted wealth from the poor. As we'll see, it is not quite right to say that people living in rich countries, such as England, Spain, or France, are clear beneficiaries of current and past imperialism. On the contrary, the economics literature generally shows that if anything, the typical citizen of an imperial power was harmed, rather than helped, by colonialism and empire building. We'll discuss this further in the following sections.

This is not to say that the analogy with the stolen watch example is wholly powerless. It might indicate, for example, that there is a strong case for forcing King Philippe of Belgium to pay restitution to Congo. But the more important question in the context of the argument in this book is a different one. It's whether the stolen watch example provides a case for thinking that the average Belgian citizen must be made to pay restitution. As we'll see, this doesn't follow. On the contrary, Philippe probably owes the Belgians some restitution too.

The main problem with the stolen watch analogy is that it misdiagnoses the main problems of global justice. Colonialism and imperialism are not the prime reasons why some First World powers are rich. We cannot make a strong case for government-to-government international aid as a means of returning stolen goods.

Imperialism Did Not Make Europe Rich . . .

Starting in the 1400s, European powers engaged in widespread conquest. They claimed large empires for themselves; murdered, enslaved, raped, and subjugated native peoples; stole land from natives; and extracted resources from the conquered lands. They installed colonial regimes and appointed semiprivate monopolies to extract resources, including gold, silver, and raw materials for manufacturing, from the conquered lands.

These are the facts, and they are largely undisputed. What is in contention, though, is what these facts tell us about why some nations are rich and some are poor.

It's tempting to conclude this explains the Great Divergence. This view holds that imperialist exploitation explains why some countries are rich and why others are poor. On this (naïve) view, the imperial powers acted in their citizens' interests. They developed superior weapons or military capabilities, and then used their superior military strength to conquer and steal resources. As a result, the imperial powers got rich at the expense of the colonized peoples.[4]

We've already seen some problems with this story. It offers a thoroughly zero-sum picture of development and poverty around the world, and that picture is false. If it were true, we would expect to see a different kind of divergence than in fact exists. What we would expect to see is that rich countries got richer (in absolute terms) at the same time that poor countries got poorer (in absolute terms). And we would expect to see the rich countries get rich roughly to the same degree the poor countries became poorer. But that's not the case. Instead, over the past 500 years poor countries have generally grown richer, albeit at a much slower rate, while the rich countries grew richer at a much faster rate (see Figure 1.1).

A similarly mistaken (if more sophisticated) view, associated with Marxist economic ideology, is that nineteenth-century European imperialism (if not earlier colonialism) was a symptom of "late capitalism." According to this view, competition among firms caused them to lower wages and immiserate the proletariat. As a result, domestic consumers' purchasing power dropped, and capitalist firms produced more goods than they could sell. The capitalist class then pushed their governments to open up and control foreign markets in order to sell their excess production. Imperialism thus prevented economic collapse in the advanced capitalist economies. On this view, the imperial powers slowed their own demise at the expense of the colonized peoples.

The Marxist theory is, as always, mistaken about how market competition affects wages. In fact, during the Industrial Revolution, workers' wages and the standard of living generally rose. The Marxist view—that competition among firms and workers would lead to lower wages—starts to make sense only if one (mistakenly) assumes that capitalism tends to lead to monopolies. Further, undeveloped poor countries do not make good markets to "dump" excess goods—for it to be profitable to sell to someone, they have to have something to trade back that can be valued more than the goods traded to them. When economists examine flows of goods between imperial powers and their colonies, they don't find any evidence of dumping. The theory is a nonstarter.[5]

The naïve zero-sum view is a starter, but it doesn't withstand rigorous empirical scrutiny. One of its major problems is that there is no clear correlation between economic growth and imperialism. Some of the European countries with large empires, such as Spain and Portugal, remained relatively poor, while others with large empires, such as England, were rich. Some of the richer countries, such as Germany and the United States, acquired empires only after they had already gotten rich. And once rich European powers lost their empires, their supposed sources of wealth, they did not suffer economic setbacks; indeed, they seemed to be better off.[6] Again, the evidence simply doesn't align with the zero-sum story.[7]

All this, however, leaves out the most damning problem with this account. Empires do not appear to have paid for themselves. Economists have meticulously calculated the balance sheets of empires, looking not merely at the value of the raw materials taken but also at profits made from investments in and trade with the colonized lands. They generally find that the European empires *lost* money on their empires.[8] To build and maintain an empire requires outfitting and feeding soldiers, and buying and maintaining ships, weapons, and military bases. Further, Europeans lost money by subsidizing bad investments and paying for (often inefficient) infrastructure and development in their conquered lands.

Modern economics has long been anti-imperialist. One of Adam Smith's major conclusions in the *Wealth of Nations* was that empire-building was a bad deal. Smith carefully surveyed the economic value of the goods Britain and other countries had extracted from the Americas, and then compared the costs these countries incurred to create and maintain the empire. For example, Smith estimated that the Seven Years War (1754–1793) cost Great Britain about 90 million pounds, while the 1739 war with the Spanish cost approximately 40 million pounds.[9] Once the costs of war alone are taken into account, leaving out all other wasteful spending, empire-building already fails the cost-benefit analysis. Smith concluded:

> The rulers of Great Britain have, for more than a century past, amused the people with the imagination that they possessed a great empire on the west side of the Atlantic. This empire, however, has hitherto existed in imagination only. It has hitherto been, not an empire, but the project of an empire; not a gold mine, but the project of a gold mine; a project which has cost, which continues to cost, and which, if pursued in the same way as it has been hitherto, is likely to cost, immense expense, without being likely to bring any profit; for the effects of the monopoly of the colony trade, it has been shown, are, to the great body of the people, mere loss instead of profit.[10]

In fact, Smith thought that this simple calculus (comparing the costs of the war to the value of the raw materials extracted) probably *understates* the loss of empire-building. Part of the problem is that when mother countries monopolize trade with their colonies they thereby encourage inefficient production methods, and thus are likely to drive up the costs of the goods they extract. For instance, Britain got tobacco from Virginia and other colonies at a low price. The colonists were only allowed to trade tobacco to Britain; they couldn't sell to France or Spain.

These trade restrictions were portrayed as being to Britain's advantage. However, Smith argued, this was a mistake. If Virginians could sell their tobacco to more countries, they would have an incentive to invest in better production methods or to invest more land in tobacco production, and thus to produce even more tobacco. Higher levels of tobacco production would lead to a greater economy of scale, and thus Virginians would eventually be able to sell tobacco to everyone, including Britain, for an even lower price. Far from benefiting Britain, colonial trade restriction hurt it, along with everyone else.[11]

The thrust of Smith's views is widely accepted. The general view among economists is that even if we focus narrowly on the economic interests of imperial powers (and ignore the harm they did to those they conquered), empires do not pay for themselves.[12] Of course, as always, not everyone accepts this point. Causality is hard to demonstrate. Nevertheless, in light of the state of the current literature, the burden of proof clearly falls on those who would contend that imperialism was overall beneficial to the imperial countries. And, more importantly, it falls on those who hold that imperialism benefited the majority of people in the imperial countries.

One might object that if empires are such a bad deal, why do so many countries pursue imperialist policies? But the answer isn't too hard to see. It's a mistake to treat a nation as if it were one person pursuing his or her self-interest. Rather, nations are collections of individuals with different interests. And some are better connected than others. In the case of empire-building, the benefits of empire are concentrated among the few, while the costs (which exceed the benefits) are diffused among the many. Weapons manufacturers, trading companies granted monopoly rights, certain generals, and, most importantly, the monarch benefit from empire. They can in turn pass the costs onto taxpayers and consumers, who must pay to finance the war and who suffer from the deadweight loss of inefficient policies.[13] As Smith noted, the average British subject may have been enthralled by and felt pride about the British empire, but he was poorer than he otherwise would have been.

Just why nations engage in imperial conquests is a complicated question. It's probably closer to the truth that the West engaged in imperial expansion not in order to get rich, but *because* it was relatively rich. Having an empire was like having an expensive toy for the political elites of the time—a costly luxury good, not an investment or source of wealth. But there exists a range of competing hypotheses about this.[14] Perhaps leaders wanted to promote their citizens' material self-interest, but mistakenly thought that imperialist exploitation would survive cost-benefit analysis. Or perhaps imperialism is a form of rent-seeking, much as the modern military-industrial complex is a form of rent-seeking.[15] Perhaps some other story is true.

In any case, when one looks at historical data, the zero-sum story is not supported. One does not see Europe getting richer as a result of making the Third World poorer. Rather, the other countries for the most part started off as poor and got only *slightly* richer over time, while the European countries and their offshoots started off as poor and got *much* richer over time. Like Adam Smith, we agree that imperialism was a great evil. But it's a mistake to think that it enriched Europe at the expense of everyone else.

. . . But It Might Help Explain Why Some Countries are Poor

While imperialism appears to have hurt rather than helped most people living in imperialist countries, it may be partly to blame for the persistent economic stagnation of certain former colonies. When imperialist powers established colonies, they replaced existing institutions with institutions of their own design. As Acemoglu, Johnson, and Robinson argue in a famous paper, the kinds of institutions they set up depended heavily on whether Europeans could settle in the colonies.

In places such as North America, where European settlers faced low mortality rates (e.g. because there were low risks of disease) and struggled to bring about successful extractive institutions, imperial powers set up more inclusive institutions.[16] In places such as the Congo, where Europeans faced high mortality rates (again because of disease) and extraction was more easily available, imperial powers set up extractive institutions. After the European powers abandoned or otherwise lost their colonies, these institutions remained behind, and generally morphed into current institutions.

On balance, then, the economic legacy of colonialism in former colonies is mixed. While such counterfactuals are extremely difficult if not impossible to figure out, it's likely that some former colonies (including the non-Europeans living in those colonies) might actually be better off than they would have been without colonization, while others might be worse off.[17] (Let us stress that saying that the economic balance is mixed is *not* to say that the morality of colonialism is mixed. It should be readily apparent that no such policy can be consistent with the views we defend in this book.)

These points significantly complicate questions of global justice. The history of our world is importantly different from the stolen watch thought experiment. In that thought experiment you are richer than you otherwise would have been, and your neighbor's grandkids poorer than they otherwise would have been, because your grandfather stole a watch. Maybe you should return the stolen watch, even though you are an innocent inheritor of a stolen item and your grandfather's evil legacy.

In our world, most people in rich countries are likely not better off than they would have been without colonialism—and they might even be worse off. They, like those who must live in countries that are poor in part because of the history of colonialism, were subjected to the unjust policies of past political elites. While no doubt their plight is much better, and no doubt the injustices perpetrated by those elites are enormous, the story here is not the account depicted by stolen watch experiment.

The Compensation Argument

These facts about how colonialism continues to harm people in the developing world suggests another approach to justifying reparations. The stolen watch experiment is problematic because it focuses on the ill-gotten gains of imperialist countries. A more promising argument would start not with those purported benefits, but with the harms that befall the victims. Instead of saying that reparations are meant to undo unjust gains for the rich, perhaps such payments can be justified as a way of compensating the poor?

In *Should Race Matter?*, philosopher David Boonin offers an argument like this as a justification for reparations for slavery within the United States. The best case for reparations, he argues, is as compensation for the continuing harms experienced by African Americans as a result of slavery.[18] His argument can be amended to the context of colonialism as follows:

The Compensation Argument

1. If persons or governments unjustly harm people, they thereby incur obligations to compensate those people for those harms.
2. Even if the currently existing Western governments did not cause the harms of colonialism, they can nevertheless have obligations to compensate for the harms caused by their predecessors.
3. People in the developing world are harmed as a result of Western colonization.
4. Therefore, currently existing Western governments have obligations to compensate people in the developing world for the continuing harms of colonization.

The compensation argument is hard to reject. As we saw, the empirical claim expressed in premise 3 is true (at least for a number of countries). And the moral principles expressed in premises 1 and 2 are plausible. It does seem right that we owe people compensation for the wrongful harms we cause. And it also seems right that states cannot get out of their duties to make good on historic injustices simply by pointing out that they now have new governments.

Compare an example. When President Bill Clinton apologized on behalf of the United States for President Roosevelt's horrific treatment of Japanese citizens during World War II, most people saw this as fitting and right, even though Clinton wasn't born until after the war. Clinton wasn't apologizing on behalf of white people or even Americans as a whole, but rather apologizing in his capacity as the chief executive of the US government for the behavior of that very government.[19] And the apology came with money attached. The United States allocated $1.25 billion in reparations for the victims of Japanese internment camps and their descendants.[20]

One nice feature of the compensation argument is that it helps justify reparations whether or not people in the West actually benefited from imperialism. And this is as it should be. Consider the following example.

Incompetent Thief

Butch Skassidy buys a pair of diamond-encrusted six-shooters for $250,000 and robs a bank. He kills the bank's armed guards, burns the bank to the ground, and steals everything in the vault. To his chagrin, he discovers that the vault contained only $10,000. During his escape, his prize horse breaks a leg, and it costs Butch another $5,000 to replace his horse. He also drops and loses his pistols during his escape.

In the incompetent thief example, Butch ends up losing $245,000. He would have been much better off staying home than robbing a bank. Nevertheless, Butch still owes compensation to the bank and the families of his victims. That Butch failed to profit from his crime really is neither here nor there. His duty to pay compensation is due to the unjust harms he imposed.

By analogy, then, it seems equally true that even though imperial nations may have lost money by creating and maintaining empires, this does not show that the current governments of those countries are relieved of duties to compensate. The case for reparations doesn't hinge on the economic smarts of former imperialist countries any more than it hinged on Butch Skassidy being a competent thief. Whether or not people in rich countries are better off because of historical injustice, the point remains that some kind of remedy is called for.

One might object that it's still unfair to impose the burdens of such rectification on current innocent subjects of former imperialist countries. After all, *they* never harmed anyone, nor supported, voted for, or were otherwise associated with the governments that caused these unjust harms. Nor did their ancestors live in democracies. They were taxed for, and sometimes forced to fight in, their governments' unjust imperial wars. (Only the United States, a latecomer to imperialism, could plausibly be called democratic, and even then, during the country's period of colonial expansion, more than half the adult population was excluded from voting.)[21]

One popular reply to this objection holds that Western citizens can be made to pay because they are *collectively responsible* for the harms of imperialism. But that idea is troubling. Normally, we don't hold people guilty by association. Normally, we think a person is morally responsible for some wrong only if that person *committed* that wrong, helped or incited someone else to commit it, or had both a duty and the opportunity to stop the wrong from being committed by others. Suppose a black man mugs Bob, and as a result, Bob distrusts all black people and starts saying to every black man he meets, "What's wrong with you people?" We wouldn't normally think, "Oh, well, Bob just believes in collective responsibility," but rather that Bob is a racist.

Larry May, Linda Radzik, and others who are attracted to the idea of collective responsibility say that some of these worries can be assuaged. We don't have to hold that agents are "guilty, blamable, or deserving of punishment" because of what others in their group did, but instead need only hold that they have incurred a debt or grounds for an obligation, or, more weakly, reasons for action.[22] A German born in 1945 should not be punished or blamed for the Holocaust, but might still have some obligation to do something about the Holocaust.

May and Radzik identify a few ways in which they think individuals can incur responsibility for what others in their group did. First, in some cases, we can hold people responsible for the group's behavior because they did not try to stop it. Here, people are responsible for their *omissions*, or for their *complicity*.[23] Second, they can also be responsible if they benefitted from wrongdoing, even if they themselves did not commit those wrongs.[24] Third, they might recognize that "that could have been me"—that is, that while they did not commit the wrongs, in virtue of their group membership, they might well have done so had they been differently situated.

Neither of the first two cases, however plausible they might or might not be, will be of much use in assigning collective responsibility to contemporary people for the sins of the past. After all, none of us could have done anything to have stopped what happened in the past, so we cannot be called complicit. (We will discuss a contemporary variation of the argument from complicity, offered by Thomas Pogge, in the next chapter.) The second avenue relies on the idea of unjust enrichment, and is thus similar to the stolen watch experiment. As we have seen, such arguments fail to support significant redistributive policies from rich countries to poor.

Let's look at the third point then. Suppose Adam shares the hateful attitudes that drive others in his group to harm people in the hated group, but Adam never acts on those attitudes. Still, even though Adam does not harm anyone, he might still think "that could have been me." Perhaps he's right. Had Adam been in the wrong place at the wrong time, or had his circumstances been somewhat different, he might well have perpetrated wrongs as well. Here, the appropriate attitude is *shame* rather than guilt: that is, a feeling of regret over who one *is* rather than what one did.

Radzik and May think feeling shame that "it could have been me" is most plausible if Adam shares the hateful attitudes but didn't act.[25] But this creates some problems for those who would want to use the theory to attribute responsibility for historic injustice to people living today. Most obviously, most people living in former imperial powers today in fact do not share the attitudes of the past. They are not generally in favor if imperialism, of subjugating others, or of exploiting Third World countries. Nor is it clear that "it could have been me" tracks race, nationality, sex, or any other group in the way needed for this argument to succeed. Yes, a German might well have been a Nazi if only he lived in a different era. But, similarly, our black neighbors might also had been Nazis if only they'd lived in a different era and been white. If we're asking "What might you have done if only you'd lived in a different era, and as a result had a different set of attitudes?," then why should we, in imagining this counterfactual, take race, nationality, or some other group characteristic to be essential or constant parts of who we are?

Perhaps most problematically, however, is the fact that the "it could have been me" argument has bizarre implications. We don't hold people responsible for what they might have done. If we know that Bob murdered Charlie, we don't turn to Dan and say, "Well, Dan, you didn't murder Charlie, but had things been different, you would have, so therefore you need to pay Charlie's family compensation." Yes, any one of us might have committed horrific atrocities if we had lived in a different time, had a different set of moral attitudes, and had experienced a different set of opportunities and pressures. But it's bizarre to conclude from these relatively trivial counterfactuals that we are therefore responsible for specific sins of other people from our race, religion, ethnicity, or nationality.

It seems false, then, to say that the current subjects of former imperialist powers are somehow responsible for those crimes. Many of the people now living in the former imperial powers are themselves either descendants of the conquered peoples, or descended from groups that were not part of the imperial power during the time of conquest. It's more than unseemly to suggest that a Filipino American who moved to the United States in the 1980s is somehow responsible for the harms of colonialism the United States caused in the Philippines.

Fortunately, attributing collective responsibility to people isn't really what's most important for the compensation argument to succeed. What matters more is whether current citizens can be held *liable* to bear some of the burden for the compensatory obligations of their governments. After all, irrespective of where the responsibility for colonialism may or may not lie, we have already conceded that those governments do have obligations to compensate those who now suffer as a result of the historical injustices of their predecessors.

One might oppose this idea too, of course. One might think, for instance, that innocent citizens should not be taxed just so their governments can fulfill their financial obligations. Perhaps there is more to be said for this than many people think, but we set it aside here. After all, it is commonly accepted that citizens are tax-liable for the financial obligations of their governments. Most people think they can be legitimately taxed to pay for things like the United Nations or NATO. If governments are going to function and exist at all, such tax liability seems necessary. In any case, our view of global justice does not turn on this point.

Positive-Sum Compensation

Suppose the compensation argument goes through, then. It follows that many Western governments are under obligations of compensation toward many people in the developing world. After all, those people are still worse off as a result of previous Western governments' colonial policies. What are we to make of this?

In his discussion of reparations for slavery, Boonin suggests that one way of measuring whether the US government has fulfilled its duty to compensate the descendants of slavery is by asking whether they are still socially disadvantaged. In general, the way people's lives play out is a product of both their personal choices and environmental factors. When a group of people on average have worse lives, it's plausible that this is the result of their environment containing barriers that others lack.[26] Given that those barriers are the product of the unjust actions of previous governments, the obligation to compensate can be fulfilled by making sure that environment becomes as hospitable to this group as it ought to be. A policy of compensation, in other words, would remove the relevant social disadvantages for the harmed group.

Not anything we might do, then, will count as compensation. And some things that look like compensation will not qualify. Suppose, say, that the US government followed the Clinton administration's precedent and decided to apologize and pay reparations to African Americans. And suppose that after this, African Americans still experienced standards of living not much better than they have today. In that case, even though reparation would in some sense have been paid, we could not say that the US government had carried out its duties of *compensation*. After all, the harms of slavery would still continue, as would the obligations to compensate for them.

The same is true for colonialism. To compensate people for the ongoing harms of colonial rule, we need to remove those environmental factors that are a result of this history and continue to unjustly set back people's lives. As we've seen, that primarily includes removing from their lives the extractive and rights-violating societies to which colonialism gave rise. People now are forced to live under such institutions that continue to harm them, force them to live on zero-sum terms, and be vulnerable to the coercion and theft that this brings. That *is* a continuing injustice. Compensating the victims of colonialism, in other words, means enabling people to leave those institutions behind, becoming free to live on positive-sum terms. Free, as they ought to be.

The theory of compensation, then, is downstream from the broader theory of justice. If we want to know how to compensate people for suffering the bad effects of historical injustice, we first need to know what those people would have been entitled to but for the injustice occurring. Just as the US government paying reparations to African Americans might not really satisfy its obligations of compensation, so too large-scale redistribution from rich to poor might not really satisfy our obligations to people in the developing world. The question is whether such a policy would remove the harmful effects of colonialism.

Unfortunately, such policies carry little promise of actually achieving that goal.[27] As we'll see in chapter 10, the problem is that sending money does nothing to remove the unjust and extractive institutions that continue to harm people. In fact, it may make them worse and more entrenched. When we pour money into an extractive situation, this is good news for those with the power to extract wealth from others. And when extraction remains in place (or, worse, gets reinforced by our actions), the obligations to compensate remain in place as well (or get reinforced, too).

This is obviously a frustrating conclusion. The fact remains that many people possess things that they wouldn't own in a perfectly just world. Anyone who reflects on the enormity of the injustice that exists throughout our history feels the urge to rectify this. And the urge to reach for the most obvious solution—moving possessions from those who have them to those who do not—is understandable as well. At the same time, we cannot undo injustice in our world by ignoring current holdings and redistributing them in accordance with this urge. Doing so might not actually solve things. And just as it's true that many people do not possess things they should, it's also true that many people do possess things they should. We cannot simply hit the proverbial reset button on possessions, at least not with justice on our side.

Justice cannot be about ensuring that no one ever possesses anything with a blemished past. If that were true, justice would be quite literally unattainable in our world. The real issue is how to find a way to live with the fact that our world is deeply marred by injustice. Some might take this as a strike against thinking about justice in historical terms. Justice does not, some will say, consist of only a principle of just acquisition, a principle of just transfer, and a principle of rectification. And that is clearly true. Justice is not exhausted by that. Facing up to historic injustice requires something else beyond merely returning stolen goods to their rightful owners.

At the same time, historic injustices clearly matter; they matter a lot. And we cannot make proper sense of how to deal with them, how to respond to such injustices appropriately, without first recognizing that justice does have an important historic dimension. To find a way of moving forward in a way that does right by victims of the past, we have to look at what that past should have been like in the first place.

In this book we outline a positive-sum conception of justice. That conception helps give content to the historic dimension of justice. It helps us understand what people have a right to when they interact with others. They have a right to engage in what they consider mutually advantageous terms, precisely because this is the way we foster a mutually advantageous world. And they have a right to compensation when they are forced into extractive, zero-sum relations, precisely because such coercion is a departure from that ideal.

Undoing historic injustice must thus be simultaneously backward-looking *and* forward-looking. Rectification or compensation should not only appropriately respond to the wrongness of the past; it should also set us on a path to a more productive future. Punishing the descendants of previous wrongdoers is no good way to make amends. At best, it harms rich people in developed societies to benefit poor people elsewhere. At worst, it harms some without really helping—and maybe even making things worse.

Linda Radzik suggests a better way forward. Historic injustices, she points out, do not only harm people, but also damage the relationships we have with one another. A history of injustice makes it more difficult for us to trust one another, to see each other as respectful cooperators rather than threats or enemies. As a result, a legacy of injustice can make it difficult or impossible for us to go on living and cooperating with one another in peace and prosperity. A good theory of rectifying historic injustice, Radzik argues, must address this as well. Part of the point of making amends is to make it clear that members of the group holding a collective responsibility for past injustice really have broken with the unjust past, and really do not share the same unjust attitudes. Compensation or rectification should repair our relationships, helping us see each other again as fellow inhabitants of a shared world.[28]

Radzik's central idea is that the key to making amends in situations like these is to find a way to repair relationships and move forward. To us, this seems like a call to find positive-sum interactions. We can leave behind the marred past and our mutual suspicions by letting cultures, goods, services, and even people move around the world on mutually agreeable, consensual terms. The key to reconciliation is for us all to see one another not as threats but as partners, and for those who have been harmed by past zero-sum regimes to be welcomed as positive-sum contributors. The way to make good neighbors and create mutual trust isn't to throw food over walls. It's to break down walls that shouldn't be there in the first place.

Our argument is far from a call for inaction or complacency. Compensation does *not* mean doing nothing, even setting aside the major changes required to give people the freedom of movement, freedom of trade, and the world-wide protection of people's productive rights to which they are entitled. It's not clear, for example, why people in the developing world should bear the burdens of escaping the extractive societies in which they are currently trapped. Compensation might require things like the waiving of application fees for immigrants, setting up language courses for newcomers, or even sponsoring travel from the developing world to ours. And, even more importantly, former imperial countries have an obligation to organize their societies in ways that make it as easy as possible for immigrants to become productive citizens themselves. They should, as we have said, foster welcoming institutions.

All of this means putting our money where our mouths are. Making amends—really showing that one has distanced oneself from the historic injustice—requires incurring some costs. None of that is in question here. However, the form of reparation, rectification, and compensation that is appropriate depends on what will actually bring the ongoing victims of our colonial past back to relations of justice. This depends on how we can enable them to interact with people around the world on positive-sum terms. We are no closer to justifying the large-scale redistributive programs with which we began.

9

Improving the Present

JUSTICE AND THE GLOBAL ORDER

WHILE SOME WHO seek to justify large-scale redistributive responses to global poverty focus on past injustices, others focus on the current state of the world. Like us, the proponents of these arguments hold that coercive political institutions and rules stand in need of justification. Unlike us, they hold that the key to making these rules and institutions legitimate is significant global redistribution. This chapter discusses three versions of this argument.

Pogge on the Resource and Borrowing Privileges

The most influential version of this argument comes from Thomas Pogge. In *World Poverty and Human Rights* and a number of related publications, Pogge has argued that the global economic order is deeply unjust. His starting point in this argument is similar to ours, namely that the use of force requires moral justification. Since the global economic order is coercively imposed on the world's poor, it needs to be justified.

As Pogge points out, the existing economic order fails spectacularly at this. In fact, it's unable to pass even the most minimal of justificatory tests: that an order is unjust if it is both (a) imposed by a small minority on a large majority, and (b) contributing to the majority being in avoidable life-threatening poverty.[1] Since the world's existing economic rules are largely imposed by a few powerful Western governments and actively contribute to poverty in the developing world, Pogge argues, both these clauses are in fact violated. Our current world can't even pass this test.

Pogge's diagnosis is correct. In fact, this test is so minimal as to be implausible as a necessary condition for injustice. For the world to become just, it probably needs to improve a lot more than merely what would be needed to pass this test. It's true that the rules of international law, and especially the coercive restrictions put on international economic freedom, harm the world's poor in devastating ways. And that alone is enough to make it unjust.

We have already discussed several ways in which the current state of the world unjustly harms poor people around the world. Pogge adds a number of other harms. One of these is the so-called international resource privilege, which allows whomever controls the state of a country, no matter how corrupt, to sell off a country's natural resources. Another is the borrowing privilege, which allows regimes that control countries to take out loans in those countries' names.[2]

The problem with privileges like these is that they enable corrupt rulers to funnel money into their private accounts, fund their cronies, and thus prop up their extractive and abusive regimes. Worse, they incentivize corrupt leaders to seize power by making available great financial reward to whomever ends up being the de facto leader of a country. Since these rewards are, under current international law, available to leaders no matter how violent or corrupt they may be, these privileges incentivize the creation and maintenance of abusive and extractive regimes. As we have seen, the creation of such institutions typically has terrible results.[3]

Pogge's argument is a helpful reminder of the fact that the creation and maintenance of harmful and extractive domestic institutions does not happen in a vacuum. It is also a response to the international environment in which those institutions exist. And that environment, to say the least, is toxic. To the extent that governments, institutions, rules, or people contribute to it, they are contributing to deep and serious injustices. The international legal rules that empower crooks to sell off their countries' natural resources and take out loans in their countries' name are unjust and ought to be reformed.

So far, so good, then. But what might follow from this? Pogge argues that if the rules of the international order are to be acceptable to everyone, no one should face the kind of crushing poverty of the developing world. And the redistributive policies he favors can be justly imposed on rich countries. He offers several arguments in defense of this conclusion. One of them invokes an idea we have seen before, namely that people in developed nations are responsible for their governments' creating or supporting harmful international rules. Or, as he puts it, they are *complicit* in these injustices.[4]

We can summarize Pogge's version of this argument as follows:

1. When people facilitate injustice, they become complicit in injustice.
2. The governments of developed nations contribute to the injustice of our current global order.

3. The citizens of developed nations facilitate the actions of their governments.
4. Therefore, citizens of developed nations are complicit in global injustice.

In light of this complicity, Pogge argues, those citizens might be justly taxed to fund his favored redistributionist proposals.

In effect, this argument is a variation of the compensation argument we discussed in the previous chapter. Instead of focusing on the obligation to compensate for historic injustices, Pogge focuses on the currently ongoing harms imposed by the global order.

At times, it can be difficult to distinguish the presently existing order from those historical injustices. Much of international law that Pogge discusses, including the resource and borrowing privileges, is very old, tracing back to the Peace of Westphalia of 1648. These rules are part of what is often called the international legal rule of "effectiveness," by which those who effectively control the state apparatus that governs over a territory with a fixed population are considered, from the point of view of international law, members in good standing of the international community (as long as they comply with the other requirements of international law, such as the prohibition on aggressive war).[5]

As with the remnants of historical injustices, it is difficult to see how the citizens of currently existing governments can plausibly be said to be complicit in the existence of the resource and borrowing privileges. Citizens alive today simply do not stand in any morally meaningful relation of responsibility to those legal principles, rules that have come down since the Peace of Westphalia and through subsequent international law. Today's citizens never voted for these rules, few actively support them, and many probably do not even know of their existence. This is not a promising route for justifying imposing significant tax burdens.

Pogge responds to worries like these that rich countries' governments have the ability to change these rules. Or at least some of them do. And since he thinks that citizens facilitate their governments, this still means that those citizens are failing to stop the injustice of the global order. This is enough to make them complicit in that injustice, and therefore tax-liable in the way he wants.

This further idea, however, highly questionable. Consider a simple case:

Jason and Bas Hire a Thug
Jason and Bas pay a thug to set fire to Pogge's house. The thug goes over and burns the house down. As a result, Pogge faces significant financial burdens.

Here, it's clear that Jason and Bas owe Pogge compensation. And this is true even though neither of them directly caused the fire themselves. By paying the thug, they are indeed responsible for, and complicit in, the harm that befell Pogge. As such, they can properly be made to compensate him.

Compare this with a similar, slightly different case:

Jason and Bas Fail to Stop a Thug

Suppose the same thug burns down Pogge's house on his own accord (or on somebody else's orders). Jason and Bas could have stopped him from doing so, for example by hiring him to mow their lawns, but they didn't. The thug burns down the house, again costing Pogge lots of money.

Contrary to before, saying that Jason and Bas owe Pogge compensation in this second case seems far-fetched, to say the least. In general, we do not come to owe people for failing to prevent harms that befall them. And so it seems false to say that Jason and Bas owe Pogge for the thug's damage, merely because they did not prevent him from setting fire to Pogge's house.

Note that we are not saying that's it's never true that people can be liable or responsible for failing to prevent others from doing things that are wrong. If a police officer knows about the thug's plans and does nothing, for example, we will plausibly think quite differently about that. The same seems true when our government fails to prevent crime from getting out of control. The government, too, is responsible in the sense that is relevant here. Perhaps it might even be said that Jason and Bas have a moral obligation to prevent the thug from committing his wrong if doing so was very easy for them. They might be obligated to call the police, for example.

But all of these cases are very different from the one Pogge discusses. Police officers and governments are obligated to prevent wrongs from happening because it's their job. They have a *special* obligation to prevent wrongs from being committed, obligations that the rest of us do not share. Doing so is the reason they exist in the first place. But the same is not true of us as citizens. It's not our job to prevent every wrong from occurring. And we can't dismantle the current global order by doing something as easy as calling the police.

For the citizens of rich countries to be generally complicit or responsible for wrongs their governments fail to prevent, they would have to be in some sense connected to those injustices. They would have to actively support or vote for them, to be in a position that creates a special moral duty to make sure these wrong don't happen, or something similar. And none of that is true, at least with respect to the parts of international law that Pogge discusses. As a result, this particular defense of global redistribution fails.

To say this is not to dismiss Pogge's general insight, of course. His point remains that the international order causes real and severe harms for innocent people across the developing world. And some of these policies do enjoy broad popular support. Immigration and trade restrictions are popular (in developed countries and elsewhere), and cause tremendous poverty and suffering. However, as we have seen, the appropriate response to these policies is not the creation of yet another coercive policy in the form of global redistribution. The correct response is to end coercive interference with people's lives in the first place, to make sure that people around the world can exercise their rightful freedoms. The cure, in other words, is moving toward a more open world.

Pogge on Economic Globalization

Pogge would disagree. When he offers his arguments against the international resource and borrowing privileges, he blends these with a much more ambitious and encompassing critique of economic globalization. According to Pogge, the West has strongly contributed to world poverty by furthering economic globalization, thus "greatly increasing international interdependence." And, again, he thinks this contribution justifies holding Western citizens liable to redistributive taxation.

Among the more pressing issues, he thinks, is the way institutions such as the World Trade Organization (WTO) and the consequent legal rules of trade and property help to structure the international economy. Unfortunately, in this case (and contrary to his correct criticisms of the resource and borrowing privileges), Pogge has his facts backward. As a number of scholars, including Mathias Risse, Loren Lomasky, and Fernando Tesón have pointed out, this assertion relies on heterodox views of what the WTO has done and what the effects of these policies are.[6]

It's true, of course, that the WTO has contributed to liberalizing international trade. However, it's not true that this has significantly harmed poor people around the world. Developing economies often have a comparative advantage in agriculture or labor-intensive, low-skill work. And as we've seen, people living in these countries are greatly harmed by the wide range of tariffs and subsidies in place in many developed countries. Those subsidies aim to protect farmers and industries in rich societies from competition by the developing world. By preventing poor farmers and workers from competing, rich societies deny them jobs, income, and opportunities they would otherwise have had. The WTO thus largely benefits (or better: has reduced the harms to) people in the developing world.

No doubt much remains that is problematic. As critics of the WTO like to point out, rich countries enjoy relatively strong bargaining positions at international institutions like these. And they often use this position to negotiate trade deals that are advantageous to them. Such deals can require the partial removal of tariffs in sectors where rich economies have competitive advantages, while keeping other tariffs in place in sectors where the poor would otherwise have an advantage.

Of course, saying that rich countries keep in place tariffs that are advantageous to them is not quite right. A more accurate statement would be that those tariffs are advantageous to certain groups within rich countries, usually groups that are politically well-connected. But while protectionist policies benefit these groups, they hurt many others. As we've seen before, this includes not only people in poor countries, but also most of the people in the rest of the world. They *also* have these rules imposed on them, and they also are forced to purchase goods at higher prices than they should. Tariffs enrich the few at the expense of the many, both the many in the developed world and the developing world.

We do not deny that such trade deals are unfair. They plainly are. But the widespread nature of these harms reveals the true nature of the problem. It's not the *removal* of tariffs that is unjust, but the keeping intact of others. Those tariffs are the things that unjustly harm people, both in the developing and the developed world. And those are the things that prevent them from entering in mutually advantageous deals with willing others. There is no injustice in opening global markets and giving people better access to foreign trading partners. But there is injustice in doing this only partially, while keeping in place barriers to prevent people from bettering themselves on positive-sum terms.

The Resource Ownership Argument

Even though tariffs continue to hurt people around the world, it's hard to maintain that they are a *major* reason for poverty around the world. As we have seen in chapter 5, the deadweight loss from protectionism (excluding labor mobility restrictions) is usually estimated to be around 1 to 3% of world product.[7] That's real harm, but a much bigger part of the story lies somewhere else. The main culprit is the quality of developing countries' institutions.

Pogge's main contribution is that those institutions do not arise in a vacuum. They are the result, at least in part, of an unjust international system. The international resource and borrowing privileges contribute to—indeed they encourage—the creation and maintenance of extractive institutions. And to the extent that they do, the international system of which they are a part is unjust.

In his recent book *Blood Oil*, Leif Wenar has developed this idea into an intriguing argument. As he points out, the idea that whoever has "coercive control over a population" also has "legal control over that population's resources" is clearly problematic. Consider an example. Suppose Bas is trying to sell Jason a barrel of oil, but Jason knows Bas obtained it by killing or enslaving people in the Niger delta. Jason wouldn't buy the barrel even if it were cheaper than other barrels on the market. He wouldn't want to have the blood on his hands. Jason is willing to incur some costs in order to avoid supporting the oppression and killing of innocent people. As he should.

Here's how Wenar puts it:

> From a market perspective, effectiveness for foreign resources looks wrong. If bandits take over a warehouse, after all, no one thinks they gain the legal right to sell off the merchandise and keep the money. Yet effectiveness is the international rule for resources, and it creates incentives for coercion and crime in resource-rich regions.[8]

Wenar holds that it's wrong to continue buying the "blood oil." However, he does not think that simple measures like instituting a boycott will be very effective. The production of virtually every product we consume involves petrochemical products at some point, whether it be through the manufacturing of plastics; transport by boat, plane, or automobile; or myriad of ways in which our purchases may involve, way down the production line, oil sold by rapacious governments. Thus, even if country A boycotts country B and refuses to buy oil from it, A may still end up buying B's oil when country C uses B's oil to produce plastic, and sells that to A.

This a general problem with doing commerce. When we buy or sell, or make loans, we do not just affect the immediate person or corporation with whom we do business. We also affect millions of others indirectly. Even a simple number 2 pencil takes tens of millions of people around the world to produce, so by buying a pencil, we're affecting tens of millions of people indirectly.[9] The people with whom we do business might use their profits for good or for evil, or for something of no moral valence. In general, we don't know what will happen, and we aren't expected to know. But sometimes, we know that if we buy something from someone, the profits will be used to hurt people. Perhaps in some such cases we should refuse to trade.

Wenar suggests that in order to disengage from commerce with extractive regimes (and thus remove the perverse incentives created by the resource privilege), countries ought to not only implement a boycott on buying resources directly from those regimes,[10] but also start what he calls a "clean hands trust." This trust is designed to deal with the problem above. When countries buy goods that are produced with resources from boycotted countries they put an additional duty on the product, the revenue of which is collected in the clean hands trust. This money—which should approximate the difference between the (now) lower price the goods commanded on the market *because* they involve prohibited resources and the price they would have commanded but for being sold by an abusive regime—would then become available to the boycotted country once "a minimally accountable government is in place."[11]

The organizing idea behind Wenar's argument is that natural resources belong to "the people." His proposal, simplifying greatly, is for governments to commercially disengage as much as possible with countries in which the resources are not controlled by the people, but are being sold by governments for private gain. Wenar offers an ingenious idea about whether the people actually control their resources. The people control natural resources when they have a free and informed vote on how the government is run (where free and informed means they can access the relevant information, have the right to dissent, and are not coerced to vote one way or another).[12]

There is much to like here. Most importantly, it removes the pernicious incentives created by the rule of effectiveness. Whereas now natural resources encourage domestic violence, extraction, and civil war—as means to seize the power to sell them abroad—Wenar's alternative requires "a minimally accountable government" for the resource funds to become available. Only once a country protects basic civil liberties, such as freedom of the press and political rights, do the resource funds become available. No doubt this would be much better than the doctrine of effectiveness.

Despite these advantages, Wenar's proposal faces serious problems of its own. If we are to replace ownership by effective governments with ownership by "the people," we need to know who the people are. In some cases, this might seem an easy question to answer. For example, in the Netherlands the people are Dutch citizens. And so the natural gas reserves under Dutch soil would belong to the citizens of that country. In other cases, circumstances are a little more complex. Perhaps we might say with confidence that the oil found off the coast of Norway belongs to the Norwegian people, or the citizens of Norway. Still, we should recognize that a little over a century ago, we would have said with equal confidence that the oil belonged to the Swedish people.

Sometimes, the question can be even more complex. Sometimes, there simply is no clear or uncontested answer whatsoever to the question who the people are in a given geographic location. Many societies have violent histories, including colonialism. And as a result, they contain different groups that may identify as different peoples, with different cultures, languages, and ethnicities. They may see themselves as having very different (and separate) histories, customs, and religions. And even though they live together in a state, this may be more a reflection of force than of unity.

This includes some of the conflict-ridden countries where Wenar's proposal is supposed to help. Are the persons who live in such countries a "people"? Wenar doesn't say,[13] but we do need an answer. Consider the following case:

Oil in Duoland
Imagine a country called Duoland, containing two ethnic groups, the Alphas and the Betas. They have different cultures and speak different languages, but have long lived together peacefully in Duoland. One day, rich oil reserves are discovered under the part of Duoland that is majority Alpha. A debate breaks out about who owns the oil. The Alphas claim that they are clearly "a people" and that therefore they (and not the Betas) own the oil. The Betas disagree, pointing out that Betas have long lived among the Alphas, and that they're all Duolanders, making them a single "people." To them, "the people" are the citizens of Duoland, at least insofar as the oil is concerned.

Neither the Alphas nor the Betas are clearly wrong in this case. In one sense, perhaps an ethnic or linguistic sense, the Alphas are right that they form a people. In another sense, call it a civic sense, the Betas are right that they all form a people together. If the oil is to belong to "the people," we need to know which of these senses of people (and others) is the relevant one.

Clearly, no one would seriously entertain the idea that natural resources belong to the members of specific ethnic groups, such that all and only "pure" Alphas have a claim to a share of the revenues from the sale of the oil. Needless to say, such a proposal would have disastrous effects. Soon, fights would break out about who counts as pure, how many Alpha-ancestors one needs to qualify, and so on. Setting aside the questionable idea that ethnicity as such is a morally relevant category, people's membership in ethnic groups is as much a matter of social construction as it is biologically determined (if not more). This is not stable enough to be the cornerstone of a theory of resource ownership.

We might say that the Betas are right, then, and opt for the civic sense of "a people." However, this civic sense is not very stable either. Countries are formed by the drawing and redrawing of borders. And the way those borders are drawn is often a reflection of force, violence, and conflict. The American people, Wenar confidently asserts, own the oil found within US territory.[14] Yet much of that oil is found in what used to be Mexican territory. Had the US government not waged an aggressive war to annex this land, one might say with equal confidence that the oil belongs to the Mexican people. But it's bizarre for a theory of justice to treat aggressive war as legitimizing ownership. As Wenar puts it, "rewarding violence with rights makes a nonsense of property."[15]

The case of Duoland is relatively peaceful. But it's not hard to see how the discovery of oil can lead to tensions within societies, tensions over exactly who does (and who does not) count as a member of "the people," even using a civic conception. Consider the following scenario:

Secession from Duoland
After months of rising tensions, the Alphas decide to secede from Duoland. The Betas are none too pleased about this idea, as it would mean missing out on the oil revenue. The Betas threaten the Alphas that any move to secede will be met with force. The Alphas cite their desire for national self-determination and begin to arm militias.

It's not difficult to see that scenarios like these may lead to violence.

One might think here that Wenar's theory has a way to avoid outcomes like these. After all, the funds from the clean hands trust won't become available unless a democratic government is established. And democracies, one might think, offer protections against such violence. Unfortunately, this is simply not true. While it's true that virtually all countries that have strong protections against violence are democratic, it's not true that all democracies have strong protections against violence. In fact, such protections exist mainly in highly developed democratic societies. At low and intermediate levels of democracy (which are to be expected in those places currently marred by conflicts over resources), violence, violations of minority rights, and even extreme violations such as state-sponsored killings and genocide are just as likely as they are in nondemocracies.[16]

Perhaps Wenar might propose that we add a nonaggression rule to his theory. Perhaps the truth is that the people own resources only if they didn't get them by violence. But surely the Mexican people will have some questions at this point. For why should the rule of nonaggression begin today or a few decades ago and not, say, in 1845, before the Mexican-American War? Why should the American people get to keep "their" violently gotten oil, while the Alphas do not?[17]

The problem with Wenar's approach, then, is that it retains a crucial part of the effectiveness rule—this time located at the level of the people. The difference is whose effectiveness gets counted. Where right now resource funds are available to whoever manages to be counted as a sovereign, Wenar's proposal would make resource funds available to whoever manages to be counted as a people. But while replacing one kind of effectiveness with another might mitigate the problem, it cannot solve it.

The way out, then, is quite simply to abandon effectiveness altogether. If we need an account of the people capable of showing why particular agents have legitimate claims on resources, and this account needs to rely on something else than mere presence, ethnicity, or legal control, there really is only one answer available that has proven to help avoid conflict and allow for resources to be used productively. The answer is the classical one: ownership of natural resources is similar to the ownership of things in general. The people who own them are, quite simply, people, the private owners.

Hassoun on International Institutions

In *Globalization and Global Justice*, Nicole Hassoun attempts to provide a new justification for international redistribution. She, too, thinks that such transfers are necessary to ensure that current coercive international institutions are legitimate. A coercive institution,[18] Hassoun writes, "can only be legitimate if it ensures that its subjects secure sufficient autonomy to consent to its rules."[19] This in turn requires that "coercive international institutions must ensure that people secure . . . basic food, water, shelter, and so forth," because doing so is necessary "to secure sufficient autonomy."[20]

Hassoun thinks libertarians in particular should find this line of argument compelling. Libertarians, she says, are likely committed to the view that coercive institutions are legitimate only if those people subject to them actually consented to them. However, she claims, people cannot genuinely consent to be subject to coercive institutions unless they have sufficient autonomy, and they can't have sufficient autonomy unless their basic needs are met. Thus, to make sure people have "sufficiently good reasoning and planning ability to consent to, or dissent from, the rule of their coercive institutions," these basic needs must be addressed.[21] Given that those needs aren't met for many people around the world, there is a requirement for international redistribution.

Hassoun's argument can be summarized as follows:

1. Coercive institutions must be legitimate.
2. For a coercive institution to be legitimate, it must ensure that its subjects secure sufficient autonomy to autonomously consent to, or dissent from, its rules.
3. Everyone, to secure this autonomy, must secure some food and water, and most require some shelter, education, health care, social support, and emotional goods.
4. There are many coercive international institutions.
5. So, these institutions must ensure that their subjects secure food, water, and whatever else they need for sufficient autonomy.

Despite relying upon some plausible background ideas, Hassoun's argument is unsound. In particular, premise 2 can't be right. Or more precisely, what's right about premise 2 won't get us to Hassoun's conclusion that rich states have to give money to poor states. However plausible this principle might sound at first, upon further reflection it has some deeply counterintuitive implications, and thus ought to be rejected.

Consider an example. Suppose that for whatever reason, Bob is not sufficiently autonomous. Say he lacks the external resources Hassoun claims one needs to be autonomous. Now, suppose nonautonomous Bob turns violent, attempts to harm our children, and the only way to stop him is to use coercion (that is, violence). It seems obvious that we can coerce Bob to defend our children. We don't need to first supply him with the resources necessary to ensure he is sufficiently autonomous to *consent* to our coercive interference. We don't need his consent. We can just coerce him to stop him from hurting our children.

The fact that Bob is nonautonomous can make a difference, of course. For example, if Bob doesn't count as autonomous, then this may mean that he is less than fully blameworthy for his actions. And perhaps that might even mean that the appropriate response to his aggression is not to punish, but to help him. But none of that bears on the question we're asking here, which is whether we may use coercion against him. And the answer to that question is clearly yes. We don't first have to give Bob sandwiches and education before we can protect our kids.

Hassoun might respond that she's only talking about what it takes to justify using coercion to enforce institutions, not coercion as such. But now repeat the thought experiment with a few modifications. Suppose we want to protect our private property when nonautonomous Bob is looking to smash up our cars.[22] Again, even if Bob still lacks sufficient resources to count as autonomous, it is obvious that we don't first have to worry about whether he is sufficiently autonomous before we can use coercion to stop him. Perhaps someone somewhere owes Bob the resources he supposedly needs to count as autonomous, but this has no bearing on whether we can exercise that coercion.

Perhaps Hassoun would claim that we're misinterpreting her. She's not talking about institutions in the economists' sense, in which an institution is just a set of rules that govern social life. Rather, she means that *organizations* can coerce people only if they ensure that those people have sufficient autonomy. The emendation seems ad hoc: after all, isn't it something about the coercion that calls for justification, rather than the party that uses it? But even if it does make sense, this won't save her argument.

Consider another example. Former Zimbabwean president Robert Mugabe oppressed his subjects and kept many of them desperately poor. Imagine now that the WTO had worked out a deal with Mugabe, using their carrots and sticks, to get him to lower trade barriers a bit. And suppose that this helped to make the poorest Zimbabweans a little better off, but not well-off enough to qualify as sufficiently autonomous in Hassoun's theory. By Hassoun's account, the WTO's actions would remain illegitimate or morally impermissible, unless more resources are first provided to the Zimbabweans.

That is a bizarre result. It places the burden of fixing injustice in the hands of the wrong people, and it instead imposes a high moral tax on doing things that actually help the very people Hassoun wants to help. Her theory implies that in many cases we cannot enforce rules that would make people's lives go better, unless we first get rice and houses to everyone those rules affect. That's to discourage people (or institutions) from doing things that actually make people's lives better.

The problem, quite simply, is that the justification of coercion does not always require consent. There is a large range of cases in which it is permissible for anyone, be it a person, an institution, or an organization, to coerce others in order to protect people's rights or to prevent a person (or group or organization) from harming others. And this is true even if the people being coerced lack sufficient autonomy. It looks as if Hassoun's premise—that an organization may coerce others only if it ensures they have sufficient autonomy—is simply false.

Hassoun tries to hook liberals and libertarians into her theory by arguing that they are committed to taking consent very seriously. According to Hassoun, liberals and especially libertarians should be most attracted to "actual consent" theories of legitimacy. Actual consent theories of legitimacy hold that the reason that coercive institutions (such as governments) have the right to impose rules on people and enforce them through coercion is that the people subject to those rules in fact consent to them. And in general, that idea is very plausible. Our mortgage lenders, for example, can coerce us into repaying our debts to them because we consented to be bound by the terms of our mortgage contracts.

But these consent-based theories of political legitimacy are notoriously difficult to satisfy. Consider: we (Jason and Bas) recently had dinner together at Guglhupf Artisanal Bakery and Café in Durham, North Carolina. We consented to exchange our money in return for their food. All of the following were true:

1. We performed an act that signified our willingness to pay. In this case, we asked for a table and ordered food, knowing that by convention in the United States, this signaled consent. Had we *not* performed this act, for instance, had we not gone to that restaurant, they could not have charged us.
2. We were not forced to perform that act. No one put a gun to our head and told us to go there.
3. Had we explicitly said, "We're here to tell you that we refuse to buy your food; we think schnitzels and sausages are disgusting," they would not have brought us food or charged us.
4. Had we paid them first, but they failed to deliver the food, they would have had to repay us. They were not entitled to take our money without doing their half of the bargain.

These are the kinds of facts and counterfactuals that hold in examples of real, valid consent. Removing any one of these features would have made the exchange or the interaction nonconsensual. For instance, had they just sent us food and then taken money out of our bank accounts without first asking us, that would have been theft. Had they forced us to buy the food, that would have been theft. Had they given us the food anyway, despite us repeatedly telling them we don't want it, that would have been an unwelcome gift. Or had we ordered and paid for the food, but they never served us, that would have been fraud.

Now consider our relationship to typical political institutions, such as governments and their laws. As A. John Simmons and others have long pointed out,[23] in our relationships with our governments *none* of the conditions of consent obtain. Governments do what they want without our explicit consent, and continue to do it even when we do explicitly dissent. Most of us have no reasonable way to opt out of the rule of the particular government we are born under. And finally, most governments do no regard themselves as having a contract with individual citizens. If you call the police because there's an intruder in your house, and the police never dispatch someone to help you, you will still be required to pay taxes for the protection services the government chose not to deploy on your behalf.[24]

In short, for many of us, our relationship to our government lacks *any* of the features of a consensual relationship. For many of us, whether one has sufficient resources to be sufficiently autonomous or not, one cannot consent to one's government. Deeply impoverished citizens of developing countries do not consent to their government. But neither do the sufficiently autonomous citizens receiving welfare payments from their First World social democracies. At most, a few highly mobile and extremely rich people, who have the resources and permission to choose which country they will live in, might said to consent to their governments.

Perhaps Hassoun is right in that we ought to believe that consent is necessary for coercive institutions to be legitimate. However, relying on this theory plainly does not lead to the conclusions she wants. The correct implication is not that liberals and libertarians must now demand that governments and institutions guarantee a minimal level of welfare to people around the world. The correct implication, instead, is that existing governments and institutions are simply illegitimate.[25]

How to End Unjust Coercion

Pogge, Wenar, and Hassoun all object to the ways in which the world's coercive rules and institutions harm poor people around the world. We do, too.

The world is rife with governments and other institutions coercively interfering with people's freedom, rights, and possessions in ways that harm them and those around them. These authors have done a great service in drawing attention to these injustices.

At the same time, however, there is somewhat of an odd fit between the initial starting points of these authors' arguments and their relentless focus on *inequality* at the global level.[26] They begin with the very plausible claim that the global order unjustly harms people in developing countries, and then takes this point in the direction of strongly redistributive global policies. But these are two very different things. Ending unjust coercion does not necessarily require redistribution, and redistribution does not necessarily end unjust coercion.

Consider an example. Suppose that after reading Pogge's and Hassoun's books, the world's rich countries responded in a different way than they hope. Rather than reforming the global order and imposing their preferred redistributive schemes, these countries might simply withdraw from interacting with the developing world altogether. They might dismantle the global order and sever all economic ties with the developing world, trading and cooperating only among themselves.

In that world, it would no longer be possible to claim that the world's rich governments are coercively imposing a global order on the poor.[27] But clearly, there is little to recommend this kind of response. When the rich withdraw from interacting with the poor, nothing is done to advance their plight. (In fact, they will likely be even worse off.) The poor do not need autarky and isolation; they need the ability to interact with people around the world on mutually advantageous and consensual terms.

It's not clear whether authors like Pogge and Hassoun can agree. Given their premises, if the rich did radically withdraw from imposing rules on the poor, that should end the problems of global injustice—or at least the ones with which they are concerned. Where nothing is being done, no harm can be done, either. But this result is not only bizarre on its face, it also does not match Pogge's and Hassoun's complaints about global justice as an issue of inequality. After all, the rich radically disengaging from the poor would not end global inequality. It would very likely worsen it.

In the end, the truth is much more straightforward. The way to end unjust coercion is to do just that: end unjust coercion. We cannot fight it by simply redistributing resources, moving money from here to there. Perhaps such policies would undo the material harms people experience as a result of unjust coercion. But they won't remove the injustice itself. If Jane accepts a job across the country, one that pays much better than her current employment, but is forcibly prevented by Jim from going before she can move, clearly Jim commits an injustice. And clearly Jane has been harmed financially as a result. If a philosopher suggested that in order to make Jim's treatment of Jane just, Jim needs to pay Jane some money, we would not take that very seriously. Of course, the redistribution would make Jane better off and perhaps even undo her financial loss. But the injustice remains: Jim should respect Jane's freedom to move where she wants.

The purported solutions from Pogge and Hassoun fail in the same way. At best, they would undo the financial losses people experience as a result of global injustice (although it's questionable whether they would even do that). But they cannot remove the injustice itself. To do that, only one thing will suffice: remove the wrongful coercion of border controls, trade restrictions, and the like.

10

Toward a Better Future

INTERNATIONAL AID AND GLOBAL CHARITY

A THIRD ARGUMENT for why global justice might have a strongly redistributive component is forward-looking. Even if past injustices or the current harms imposed by the global order do little to justify redistributive efforts, one might still say that redistribution is justified because of the good it would do moving forward. On this approach, the point of redistribution isn't to fix to past, but to fix the future.

The intuition here is straightforward. The persistence of absolute poverty in our world is bad in the face of wealth elsewhere. And this is so even if the wealthy did not grow wealthy at the expense of the poor, and even if the wealthy did not cause the poor to be that way. People in the developed world can do something about it—they can give money to the poor—and so they should.

The most famous of these arguments, of course, comes from Peter Singer. According to Singer, morality demands that people who live in a world of poverty and are in a position to help, ought to help the poor. (Singer doesn't say that "justice" per se demands it.)

We agree with Singer that well-off people (i.e., almost everyone in the West) should give *something* to charity. But here we'll argue that our duties of charity are not as stringent as Singer thinks. Further, if we take the empirical facts about development seriously, we should recognize that a duty to help the poor is not merely a duty to donate to them, but a duty to welcome them as trading partners.

Singer's Argument

Peter Singer argues that relatively well-off people—by which he means al-most every adult living in the developed world—are morally *required* to give away most of their income and wealth to very poor people around the world. Singer argues that this is a basic moral duty rather than a supererogatory or admirable action.

According to Singer, most of us are already implicitly committed to certain principles and ideas that force us to agree with him. To show this, Singer has a simple, clear, and seemingly powerful argument for the con-clusion that each of us should give away significantly more than we do. The argument comes in a stronger and a weaker version.[1] Here's how the strong version goes:

1. "Suffering, and death from a lack of food, shelter, and medical care are bad."[2]
2. *The Singer principle (strong version):* "If it is in our power to prevent some-thing bad from happening, without thereby sacrificing anything of com-parable moral importance, we ought, morally, to do it."[3]
3. *The empirical claim:* By donating to certain charities, we prevent suffering and death from a lack of food, shelter, and medical care without thereby sacrificing anything of comparable moral importance.
4. Therefore, morally we ought to donate money to charity.

This argument has extremely demanding implications. If sound, we are *required* to spend our money (and time) helping people, as long as there are people who need help and we would otherwise spend it on less important things. It means we cannot buy things like a cup of coffee at Starbucks or an iPhone, subscribe to Netflix, or really buy anything else that's nonessential. If that money can be used to help people elsewhere, we have to send it there. More precisely, the requirement stops at the point where the marginal disutility of giving is larger than its marginal utility for others.[4]

Of course, virtually no one really lives that way. And to many, the demandingness of this conclusion, which itself depends on the demandingness of the strong version, seems too much to accept. In response, Singer gives a second version of his argument, which replaces premise 2 with a weaker principle:

2. *The Singer principle (weak version)*: If it is in our power to prevent something bad from happening without sacrificing anything of moral significance, then we ought, morally, to do it.

This weaker version allows us to forgo helping others if doing so means we must sacrifice something of "moral significance." Singer largely leaves it up to his readers to assess what has moral significance. Perhaps buying our kids one small present on their birthdays has some significance, though surely buying them $500 worth of presents does not. The stronger version of Singer's argument does not allow us to buy our children any birthday presents—it's more important to feed the starving than to give our children some new toys. But the weaker version can allow for such things. Bonding with one's children is morally significant, even if not quite as important as fighting global poverty.

The Argument for the Singer Principle

At least until they read Singer's work, most people think that Singer's conclusions cannot be true. Most people think their obligations to help others are limited. Sure, we should help people who have less than us, but at some point, we've done enough. At some point, we are allowed to get on with our life. Perhaps we could do more, but doing more goes above and beyond the call of duty.

Singer thinks that this is mistaken. True, many people find the idea that our obligations are limited intuitive, but on reflection that intuition cannot be sustained. For one, it conflicts with another, much more powerful intuition,[5] captured by a famous thought experiment:

> If I am walking past a shallow pond and see a child drowning in it, I ought to wade in and pull the child out. This will mean getting my clothes muddy, but this is insignificant, while the death of the child would presumably be a very bad thing.[6]

Saving the child means incurring some personal cost. We might need to throw out those muddy clothes, for example. Still, almost everyone agrees that we are obligated to help the child in this case. It would be wrong—a violation of *duty*, and not just uncharitable—to walk away, even though rescuing will cost us something valuable.

Here is a variation of this thought experiment, one that puts an exact price on the cost of saving the child's life:

One Drowning Child

You are walking along one day when you see a child drowning in a pond. You can reach in and save the child, though doing so will cause you to drop $500, which will blow away in the wind. Are you obligated to save the child?

In this case, too, most people say yes, you are required to save the child. They might make an exception for you if you desperately need the $500, for instance to feed your own kids. But if the money will be spent on things you don't strictly speaking need, then you should drop it and save the child.

The intuition in the one drowning child example, Singer argues, is best explained by the Singer principle (on either its weak or strong version). And the Singer principle clearly denies that we are only required to save a few people, but not a lot. To see this, consider what you would say about the following case:

Two Drowning Children

You are walking along one day when you see a child drowning in a pond. You can reach in and save the child, though doing so will cause you to drop $500, which will blow away in the wind. Nevertheless, you save the child. When you continue on your walk, you see another child drowning in a pond. Again, you can save the child, at a cost of $500.

Are you obligated to save the second child? Unless the second $500 represents a very significant moral loss to you, Singer thinks the answer is again clearly yes. We already agreed that you should perform the first rescue. And the second case of rescue, it seems, is similar to the first. So it seems that you again are required to save the child.

The two drowning children scenario presents a repeated version of one drowning child, then. But given that each repeating case of rescue is similar to the first, and given that we believe there is an obligation to rescue in that first instance, the obligation too seems to repeat. After all, we ought to treat like cases alike.

Obviously, there is nothing magical about the number two. Presumably, if the obligation to rescue extends from one to two persons, it also extends from two to three persons, from three to four, and so on. In principle, the logic of this argument extends until we either (happily) run out of people who need saving or (unhappily) out of the ability to save, at least without serious cost.

And this, of course, is precisely the Singer principle: we must help others in need, until the costs of doing so become too great.

There are many important differences between these examples and sending money to developing countries across the world. However, Singer argues that none of these make much of a *moral* difference. For example, people in the developing world live far away from us, while the children in the pond were right in front of us. But that difference cannot explain why there might be an obligation to save in one case but not the other. Mere distance or geographic location isn't a morally meaningful fact. Where we live doesn't change our moral worth, the value of life, or our basic rights.

We can see this in the following case, concerning a child that lives far away.

One Distant Child

You are sitting at home one day when you get a call from an old friend you trust very much. He is a humanitarian worker on the other side of the world, and tells you he's come across a child in grave danger. Saving the child will cost $500. Unfortunately, your friend is all out of money—having spent it saving other children—and asks you to help. Are you obligated to send the $500 to save the child?

Most would agree that the intuition that we are required to sacrifice $500 to rescue the child's life remains intact. Of course, it's much *easier* (psychologically speaking) to ignore this last child than it is to walk away from a child drowning right in front of your eyes. After all, we don't have to look this last child in the eyes when we refuse to save it. But while it may be easier, it's clearly not the right thing to do. Morality doesn't have to be convenient or easy. Doing the right thing can be difficult.

So too, then, with sending money abroad, Singer holds. As the cases show, the Singer principle is true in cases like that of the one drowning child, and it repeats in cases where there are many people who need rescuing. Nor does the fact that these people are far away make much of a difference. In the end, he holds, the conclusion is inescapable—we ought to send much more abroad than nearly all of us actually do.

Feedback Loops in Morality

One way—perhaps the most obvious way—to resist Singer's argument is to question whether the empirical premise is true. Perhaps preventing suffering on the other side of the world isn't quite as easy as Singer seems to think.

(It's definitely not as easy as rescuing a drowning child who's right on front of us.) We turn to this in the next section. First, let's look a little closer at the Singer principle itself. A key step in that argument is that when cases like one drowning child repeat, the obligation to rescue also repeats. Is that true?

Singer's point is that merely increasing the *number* of people who need saving cannot lessen our obligation. And that does seem true. If anything, when more people need rescuing, there is more, not less, pressure on us to perform rescues. When lots of people are in need, the problem may seem overwhelming. But that's no good reason for inaction.

At the same time, sometimes when the numbers increase more can change than *only* the number of people that need rescue. Often, when lots of people are in danger, the situation is not one in which many people just happen, one by one, to be in danger, with no relation or connection between their respective situations. The threats people are facing can be related. Sometimes they are related in such a way that the dangers some of them are facing can influence the dangers others may face as well. At other times, they can be related to our actions, so that what *we* do may improve or worsen the situation of others.

This includes our actions of rescue. Sometimes performing a rescue in one case can lead to greater dangers for others. In such situations, the Singer principle can no longer apply in the same way. When our actions may create harm down the line, we cannot act as if we are simply facing a string of unrelated rescues. We need to think about not just the person in front of us, but also the situation of the other people who will be affected by what we will do.

Situations like this can arise in a variety of ways. Consider, for instance, yet another example, this one a variation on an example originally offered by David Schmidtz.[7]

Iterated Drowning Children
A baby is drowning in the pool beside you. You can save the baby by a process that involves giving the man who threw the baby in the pool a hundred dollars. If you do not save the baby, the baby will die. You save the baby. A crowd begins to gather, including more men, carrying more babies. Seeing what you have done, a few throw their babies into the pool. The babies will drown unless you give each of the men a hundred dollars. More men begin to gather, waiting to see what you do.

In the iterated drowning children case there is a relationship—let's call it a *moral feedback loop*—between the various cases. How we act in one case of need affects others, including whether other cases of need arise in the first place. When this is true, we should no longer act the way Singer wants us to. By continuing to rescue babies, we'll only be causing more babies to need rescuing. And that cannot be right.

The iterated drowning children case is not exactly a counterexample to the Singer principle. After all, the principle only holds that we have an obligation to rescue if doing so means avoiding something (much) worse. And that's not the case here. So Singer might well say that his principle applies only when there are no negative feedback loops in place.[8]

Nevertheless, the example does make an important point. When lots of people are in need of rescuing, we should be very careful about making sure there are no negative feedback loops in place. If there are, we cannot act the way Singer wants us to. Unfortunately, there often are feedback loops in place in cases where Singer wants us to act as if his principle applies. When warlords or abusive political leaders become able to make money from making or keeping others in need, for example, the problem of poverty is not mainly a lack of donations.

Charity and Aid or Development and Growth?

In his book *The Life You Can Save*, Singer writes that if everyone made "quite a modest contribution," we would actually stop the world's poor from dying.[9] Singer praises the effectiveness of NGOs in saving lives by distributing bed nets, immunization, and other measures. Another example is the prevention of malaria, one of the cheaper ways to save lives, which costs somewhere between $623 to $2,367 per person according to the aid-monitoring website GiveWell.[10]

Nobel laureate economist Angus Deaton is skeptical of foreign aid. Nevertheless, he notes something very similar:

> One of the stunning facts about global poverty is how little it would take to fix it, at least if we could magically transfer money into the bank accounts of the world's poor. In 2008, there were about 800 million people in the world living on less than $1.00 a day. On average, each of these people is "short" about $0.28 a day; their average daily expenditure is $0.72 instead of the $1.00 it would take to life them out of [extreme] poverty. We could make up that shortfall with less than a quarter billion dollars a day ... Taking ... into account [differences in purchasing power in poor countries], ... world poverty could be eliminated if every American adult donated $0.30 a day; or, if we could

build a coalition of the willing from all the adults of Britain, France, Germany, and Japan, each would need to give only $0.15 a day.[11]

Deaton says that simple calculations like this make it seem that ending world poverty is *easy*. It seems that we Westerners could, if only we wanted to, end world poverty by paying a tiny tax, less than what many pay in sales taxes for our daily Starbucks fix. On this view, international aid really is analogous to the one drowning child case: "Fixing world poverty and saving the lives of dying children is seen as an engineering problem, like fixing the plumbing or repairing a broken car."[12]

However, and despite the success stories on which Singer likes to focus, these sorts of calculations are misleading, Deaton contends:

> These calculations . . . are examples of what I call the *aid illusion*, the erroneous belief that global poverty could be eliminated if only rich people or rich countries were to give more money to poor people or to poor counties. . . . far from being a prescription for eliminating poverty, the aid illusion is actually an obstacle to improving the lives of the poor.[13]

In the past 50 years, hundreds of billions of dollars have been spent on government-to-government and other forms of international aid. In just the past decade, between 2000 and 2010, governments provided $128 billion in foreign aid.[14] As a fraction of their total budgets, the amount governments spend on foreign aid is quite small. Nevertheless, $128 billion spent on foreign aid is real money. We should hope that it would do a lot of good.

The evidence is not encouraging. Looking at Africa over the past 50 years, Deaton finds an inverse relationship between growth and aid:

> Growth *decreased* steadily while aid *increased* steadily. When aid fell off, after the end of the Cold War, growth picked up; the end of the Cold War took away one of the main rationales for aid to Africa, and African growth rebounded . . . [A] more accurate punchline would be "the Cold War is over, and Africa won," because the West reduced aid.[15]

Of course, this simplifies things greatly. Many different factors are at play here, and it's not at all clear how they might interact. But at least as an initial observation, the point is not encouraging. "The record of aid," Deaton concludes, "shows no evidence of any overall beneficial effect."[16]

Of course, others have disputed these findings. Overall, the research on whether aid works is mixed.[17] Nevertheless, even taking the dissenting voices into account, the weight of the evidence offers little reason to think that international aid has a good chance of ending poverty or spurring economic growth. In a comprehensive survey of the existing literature, Hristos Doucouliagos and Martin Paldam conclude that overall, "after 40 years of years of development aid, the evidence indicates that aid has not been effective."[18]

In their book *Why Nations Fail*, Daron Acemoglu and James Robinson explore this problem in some detail. After reviewing the depressing history of foreign aid, they write:

> Despite this unflattering track record of "development aid," foreign aid is one of the most popular policies that Western governments, international organizations such as the United Nations, and NGOs of different ilk recommend as a way of combating poverty around the world. And of course, the cycle of the failure of foreign aid repeats itself over and over again. The idea that rich Western countries should provide large amounts of "development aid" in order to solve the problem of [world] poverty . . . is based on an incorrect understanding of what causes poverty. Countries such as Afghanistan are poor because of their extractive institutions—which result in a lack of property rights, law and order, or well-functioning legal systems and the stifling domination of national and, more often, local elites over political and economic life. The same institutional problems mean that foreign aid will be ineffective, as it will be plundered and is unlikely to be delivered where it is supposed to go. In the worst-case scenario, it will prop up the regimes that are the very root of the problems of those societies.[19]

Deaton calls this problem the "central dilemma" of aid. When countries have good institutions, and meet the "conditions for development," then the need for aid is typically not as great. After all, such countries will be growing and developing on their own. However, when "local conditions are hostile to development, and the need for help exists, "aid is not useful, and it will do harm if it perpetuates those conditions."[20]

Countries that are poor, in other words, are mired in negative feedback loops. They are governed by abusive elites, people who make a living (and stay in power) by extracting resources from their countries and people. In such conditions, to pour more money into a country may well mean lining the pockets of the abusive regime, not feeding the people who need it the most.

Stronger yet, sending money to places governed by such extractive institutions may do further harm down the line. When rulers make a living by taking resources from their societies, sending more money effectively means increasing the rewards of being in power. The availability of foreign aid can make bad governments continue to thrive without the support of their citizens; encourage factions within those countries (different agencies, bureaucracies, strongmen) to compete for power in order to gain control of the incoming resources; and end up subsidizing corruption, escalating conflicts, inciting civil wars, and causing human rights violations. A policy of aid may incentivize the continuation, even the entrenching of extractive and abusive institutions. Rather than move a society onto a path of development and growth, aid can prolong and worsen the conditions that create poverty and need in the first place.

There is a difference between *aid* and *development*. We deliver aid when we send food, money, or medicine to places where people lack access to these resources. Development happens when a society begins to grow economically, and the conditions that cause people's poverty begin to disappear. No one denies that aid can do good. Christopher Coyne, no great supporter of foreign aid, has shown that aid seems to be most effective in increasing predetermined outputs in response to immediate humanitarian crises.[21] We see homeless people after an earthquake, and humanitarian agencies buy and distribute tents and food; people survive. Foreign aid is at its most effective when it aims to stop the worst problems associated with poverty, such as disease and starvation (though as Coyne documents, if can also fail at that, and sometimes even makes things worse).[22]

The problem with Singer's approach to global poverty is that it approaches things as if this is where our focus should be. But this is a mistake. Development is at least as important—and probably even more so. It's development that really helps people leave behind the circumstances in which they need aid. And unfortunately, there is no known way of spurring sustained, poverty-ending development by focusing primarily on aid. It may be that there simply is no way for aid to accomplish this, period, even though it's easy for philosophers to imagine it doing so. If Deaton and Acemoglu and Robinson are right, aid may even make this problem worse.

At times, Singer seems to deny this. In *The Life You Can Save*, he addresses the objection that aid doesn't lead to growth. His response is that "our focus should not be growth for its own sake, but the goals that lie behind our desire for growth: saving lives, reducing misery, and meeting people's basic needs."[23] We agree, of course, but putting things this way overlooks the most important thing. Growth *is* what actually saves lives, actually reduces misery, and actually meets people's basic needs over time. Past economic growth is why Bas, Jason, Peter Singer, and our readers are debating how much a duty we have to rescue distant strangers, rather than ourselves jostling for the best position in a breadline. Future growth is our best bet—possibly our only bet—to lift the millions who are suffering today out of poverty.

Limits to the Obligation of Rescue

When Singer first offered his argument, he presented it as a challenge to ordinary moral thinking. Most people believe that they should do things to help others, but that this requirement is limited. They believe that something like the following is true:

> *The Kant-Ross principle:* We all have duties to help others who need it. However, after a certain point, you have "done your part," and any additional help you give is good but no longer obligatory.[24]

The Kant-Ross principle is intuitively attractive, but directly conflicts with the Singer principle. And the arguments we discussed give credence to the idea that something like the Singer principle is more likely to be true. At least if there are no negative feedback loops, Singer would argue, we should continue to help until the cost of doing so becomes too high. After all, even if we've already helped four, five, or however many children, if the next child is someone we could save, it seems that we should do so. We might still be able to avoid something very bad without giving up too much.

Why does the Kant-Ross principle seem intuitive, then? One reason is the thought that we don't have to spend our entire lives helping others. At some point, we get to think of ourselves, too, and move on with our day. The Singer principle doesn't leave much (if any) room for that. As long as there is suffering in the world we could prevent, we cannot go play a game of tennis, spend some time with our friends, learn to play the guitar, and so on. This does seem overly demanding.

Singer notes that people seem to be unwilling to donate even a small part of their incomes to help people in need. In some ways, he's right. Many of us don't give as much as we can (and maybe should). To Singer, this is part of an unflattering explanation for why people find the Kant-Ross principle attractive. We like to let ourselves off the hook, and the Kant-Ross principle can help with that.

However, Singer seems to underestimate people's willingness to give. Sometimes people do give in extraordinary ways to help others. When disasters strike, impressive amounts of money are raised for relief efforts. After an earthquake devastated Haiti in 2010, for instance, the American Red Cross alone raised around half a billion dollars for its relief efforts. People aren't always as unwilling to give as Singer suggests.

In the iterated drowning children case, we saw that sometimes people can stand to gain from others' misery. The point of the example is not to suggest that our world always works like this. We do not believe that every donation and all aid serve only to line the pockets of oppressive regimes. Again, we do not deny that there is a place for aid; we make donations ourselves.

The point, rather, is that our willingness to rescue *itself* can negatively affect the problems around the world. People respond to how we behave, and that includes when we decide to try and help others. When we announce that the money starts flowing as soon as problems appear, and stops flowing as soon as they are solved, we shouldn't necessarily expect to see fewer problems in our world. We ought to reject moral principles that move our world closer to the scenario of iterated drowning children.[25]

Intuitively, we know that a world in which our duties of assistance are unlimited is not a good world to live in. Intuitively, we know that we can't treat other people's problems as things that we must always solve, and then expect the world to become a better place for everyone. Intuitively, we know that at some point we really do get to move on with our day. Unless we treat our obligations of rescue as limited in some way, such as the limitations captured by the Kant-Ross principle, we will end up encouraging bad people to immiserate others just so they can capture the aid.

Perhaps, then, it is no coincidence that people are willing to donate rather large amounts in response to natural disasters, but not in response to poverty caused by social and political dysfunction. When natural disasters strike, we can be relatively confident that we are dealing with an isolated case, a situation in which our willingness to aid will not induce others to oppress so they get to live off the aid. But this is not true in cases of systemic poverty. There, as we have seen, negative feedback loops are rife. And in those cases, tragically, we have to recognize that our obligations of assistance are limited, or else we may become part of the problem.

Of course, this is tough pill to swallow in any real situation, for it remains true that there are people in real need whom we might be able to help. But this difficulty is an unavoidable result of the two points of view we've been discussing so far. Each separate case is genuinely a case of need. And so each separate case really does call on us to help. But in cases of systemic poverty, we are not just dealing with isolated cases. We are also dealing with an iterated set containing negative feedback loops. And this calls on us *not* to act, at least not in ways that deepen the problem.

None of this means that we cannot do anything to help people in poverty. But sometimes there's a difference between doing things that show a *desire* to help, and doing things that *actually* help. Sometimes we do things because we want to help, and end up making things worse. At other times, we do things for other reasons and actually end up helping others along the way.

Seventy years ago Japan, Taiwan, South Korea, Singapore, and Hong Kong were poor. Now they are rich. It wasn't out of any desire to help these countries that we bought their products and actually helped them develop. The main way people in developed societies have contributed to ending poverty abroad has been through buying Made in China products. It was only when Americans, Europeans, and others started buying so many goods from China that the country finally started to escape extreme poverty.

Singer thinks we should stop buying things like Blu-ray players and iPhones, and instead donate this money to charity. Twenty years ago, he would have advised us not to buy VCRs and video game systems; 40 years ago, he would have advised us to stop buying stereos or import cars. But the willingness of people in developed countries to buy Blu-rays, VCRs, video games, stereos, and cars they don't really need makes a *huge* difference in fighting poverty abroad. We may not buy these products because we're trying to aid those who need jobs or income. But we may end up providing just that.

In reality, the policy of buying stuff we don't need does a much better job of rescuing people from extreme poverty than the policy of giving money away. Giving away money is not even a close second. Historically, the thing that eradicates destitution is not throwing money at destitution, but throwing money at the very forms of commerce Singer advises us to avoid.[26] So far, *no* country has been lifted out of poverty by aid alone. So far, no country has even been lifted out of poverty primarily because of aid. Aid and trade both have their places, but aid is no substitute for trade. If we care about development, Singer offers us the wrong advice.

Conclusion

The images we choose in thinking about global justice matter. They frame our thinking, and they express in which respects we take people to be of moral significance. Despite the arguments presented in this chapter, perhaps the most important mistake in Singer's argument is this disanalogy between global poverty and the case of the one drowning child. Even under the most crushing conditions of poverty, violence, persecution, and corruption, circumstances almost perfectly designed to stamp out their energy and spirit, the world's poor continue to find ways to make ends meet, help themselves and their loved ones survive, and make whatever they can out of their daily lives. They are not helpless children, thrust in a pool, waiting for *us* to save them.

When we begin to think about people in developing countries this way, and not as helpless children in a pool, different solutions come to mind. As anyone who's ever visited a developing country knows, these are bustling places bursting with entrepreneurship, exchange, and productivity. What people in those societies need is for the barriers that prevent their hard work from being really productive to be removed. They need the fruits of their labor to end up in their pockets. That's a call not for aid alone, but for a chance at genuine development. Much of that development they'll do themselves, if only given a chance.

If we're going to have an analogy, perhaps the following would be better: the world's poor are not like children in a pond, and they do not need to be pulled out by nobly motivated Westerners. They are people, perfectly capable of swimming and rescuing themselves, who are trapped in in a pond surrounded by fences keeping them from escaping on their own initiative. What they need, what they really need, is for those fences to be taken down. They need the removal of the barriers that keep them in a position where they *need* help. Such an analogy would recommend protecting people's productive rights, improving their access to markets around the world, and freeing their ability to migrate.

The point we have been making throughout this book is that the focus of a theory of global justice should be squarely on creating those positive cycles, and ending the negative ones. The key to a more just world is to transform the former set of circumstances into the latter. It's to free up the movement of people and goods in ways that enable and encourage them to seek positive-sum interactions, and create growth for themselves and those around them. And, paradoxically perhaps, this can mean that sometimes the right thing to do when facing poverty is *not* to donate money. We don't say that lightly. But when donating more means fueling the negative cycle of extraction and poverty, the right thing to do is to break the cycle.

I I

The Climate Change Objection to Economic Growth

OUR CENTRAL THESIS in this book has been that global justice is as much about creating conditions that are, as much as reasonably possible, conducive to productive or positive-sum relations between people across the globe. Those relations are the engine of growth, which in turn is what ultimately makes humanity capable of addressing the gravest injustices around the world, most notably—but not limited to—extreme poverty. The policies we recommend, in short, are ones that will lead to real and lasting economic growth, and enable the world's poor to take advantage of it.

This view exposes us to an objection. For now, and for the foreseeable future, continued economic growth requires the emission of carbon dioxide. But as we all know, the atmosphere is heating up; industrialization and the increased carbon emissions that go with rising living standards are what's heating the earth. If we get our way, it seems, there would be not only significant economic growth but also, and as a result, an even further increase in our collective carbon footprint.

This may seem too dangerous to accept. Standard models predict that more carbon in the atmosphere means a warmer earth, and a warmer earth means more droughts, heat waves, and other extreme weather events, along with melting ice caps and rising sea levels.[1] By cranking up the engines of the global market economy, we could end sacrificing the environment upon which we depend.

There are many important and complicated questions and problems surrounding the prospect of further climate change. We cannot address all of these here. Instead, we'll focus primarily on whether this prospect should make one rethink the conclusions of this book. While we are very concerned about climate change—any reasonable person would be—and accept the need for certain mitigating measures (such as a carbon tax), we ultimately do not believe it undercuts this book's thesis to any serious degree. In fact, we think a stronger claim is true: because dangerous climate change is coming, it is imperative that we have further growth.

A Comparative Approach

The United Nations Framework Convention on Climate Change has as its central objective the "stabilization of greenhouse gas concentrations in the atmosphere at a level that would prevent dangerous anthropogenic interference with the climate system." Taken at face value, this goal is impossible. Global temperatures will continue to rise for at least 50 more years no matter what we do. Even if emissions went down to zero tomorrow, the world would continue to heat up. The levels of carbon currently in the atmosphere will make that happen.

We might take the Convention's demand to be that no *more* heating is acceptable than has been caused already. That is at least a possible goal. Is it also a desirable one? The world's carbon emissions are still growing. To prevent further warming we would need to not only stop those increases, we would have to *decrease* emissions. Even stabilizing current levels of emissions would mean continued heating. For even at current levels, the world continues to add carbon to the atmosphere at a level sufficient for further warming. Our question is *how*, not *whether*, we are going to live in a warming world.

Much of the current growth in the world's emissions is due to economic growth in the developing world. With increased development comes increased energy use. And indeed, the availability of increased energy to the developing world is precisely why we insist that global justice *must* be focused on fostering growth. Things such as infrastructure, health care, education, transport, and leisure, as well as the availability of refrigerators, washing machines, and air conditioning, are all essential to solving the problems of world poverty. But none of these are possible without expending significant levels of energy.

Consider three ways in which one might say that emissions are to be decreased. The first option would be to demand that economic growth in the developing world stop (or perhaps even be rolled back), and insist that the developed world reduce its emissions. The second would be to let the developing world grow, but insist that the developed world greatly reduce its emissions so as to offset the increases elsewhere. The third would be to invest in noncarbon based energy production so as to allow further increases in energy use while decreasing carbon emissions.

Each option for mitigating climate change has its costs. Reducing emissions comes, at least under current conditions, at the expense of further growth and the benefits it brings. Options one and two aim to impose those costs on different populations, while option three will have its own, different costs.[2] And whatever one's view on what the correct trade-offs might be, it follows that thinking about climate change has to be *comparative* in nature. That is, we cannot endorse a certain policy without asking whether the costs it imposes are acceptable in light of the available alternatives.

Some of these costs will be relatively obvious. We need to take into account the damage further warming will do to the environment. We need to take into account the harm that reduced growth will do to the world's poor. And we need to take into account the harm that reduced growth will do to the rest of the world.

But some costs are must less obvious. We here focus on two. First, we need to take seriously the fact that the world will continue to heat up for the coming 50 years regardless of what we do. It's a given that this will impose very serious dangers on people around the world, and especially the world's poor. This means that any acceptable policy will have to take into account not only the reasons we have to avoid further warming, but also the need to mitigate the dangers that will result from the warming that's already been caused. Second, we need to take seriously the fact that some of these costs are connected. The cost we impose on one side may increase the cost on another.

The Cost of Foregoing Growth

The question we face, then, is what sorts of policies will *overall* lead to people around the world leading prosperous, safe, and happy lives surrounded by an environment that is hospitable for human life. And, in particular, we should look for policies that will tend to alleviate severe, life-threatening, crippling poverty in our world.

Darrel Moellendorf argues that it's unreasonable for the world's poor to bear the costs of climate change mitigation to the extent that this perpetuates their poverty. He proposes the following principle as a condition for any morally acceptable energy policy:

> *Policies and institutions should not impose any costs of climate change or climate change policy (such as mitigation and adaptation) on the global*

poor, of the present or future generations, when those costs make the
prospects for poverty eradication worse than they would be absent them, if
there are alternative policies that would prevent the poor from assuming
those costs.[3]

We think that Moellendorf is mistaken about the practical implications of this principle. But his point is important nonetheless. The harm of global poverty is the greatest humanitarian disaster of our world. And while that in no way diminishes the severity of the problem of climate change, any acceptable mitigation strategy cannot imply the continuation of this disaster.

Many people who haven't thought deeply about environmental issues subscribe to a simple but mistaken view: the earth naturally provides a good climate and environment for humans, but thanks to industrialization, we are now ruining that. That's not quite right.

We won't dwell on this point, but it needs to be stressed. Absent technology, most of the Earth is a lousy place for human beings to live most of the time. Water is unclean and filled with parasites. Dangerous, disease-carrying ticks, mosquitoes, and other insects abound. Without technology, many places are too cold for us. Many places are too hot. Without technology, we would die of hypothermia or exposure if we tried living in North Carolina or Washington, DC. Hurricanes and floods would kill us—we wouldn't be able to escape quickly to safety. And so on.[4]

Consider the typical yearly weather pattern in your city or town and ask yourself whether if you somehow had a guaranteed food source, could you last the year without any technology, such as rudimentary shelter and clothing? Probably not. What makes Earth livable (outside of a narrow range) is technology. Even our pre-homo sapiens ancestors were able to spread out as much as they did because of (polluting) technology, such as the control of fire. Our ability to live all over the world is technology-driven. Our current population is unsustainable without advanced technology.

When people are poor, not only are they more likely to suffer from starvation or disease, but their ability to cope with bad weather and weather disasters is also much worse. We often hear that climate change may lead to more frequent and more severe superstorms. It may indeed, even if the United Nations recently released a report arguing that so far, it has not.[5] But it's worth noting that weather-related deaths have declined dramatically over the past century. Despite a much larger population, the absolute (not just relative) number of yearly weather-related deaths are only about one-fiftieth now what they were 80 years ago.[6]

According to the EM-DAT International Disaster Database at the Université Catholique de Louvain, while the total number of natural disasters and the absolute monetary costs of disasters has risen over the past 80 years (though some of this is increase is likely due to better record-keeping and reporting in recent years), the total number of deaths from natural disasters is much lower now than in the past.[7] (Keep in mind that the natural disasters include earthquakes, tsunamis, and volcanic eruptions unrelated to weather or climate.) See Figures 11.1, 11.2 and 11.3.

Figure 11.2 requires some explanation, as it may make things seem worse than they are. Note that the EM-DAT database only has data on the economic costs of disasters from 1960 onward. We did not truncate the data. In Figure 11.2, the large peak in 2011 is to a significant degree the result of the massive earthquake and tsunami that devastated Fukushima, Japan. There were also serious droughts, floods, cyclones, and tornados; unlike the earthquake, these latter disasters could have been the result of global warming.

Note also that increased wealth can make the weather disasters more destructive in absolute terms simply because wealthier people have more stuff, and more valuable stuff, to destroy. To illustrate, suppose three people live next to each other. The first, P-22, has the wealth and income that a person like Jason or Bas had at age twenty-two. The second, P-28, has the wealth

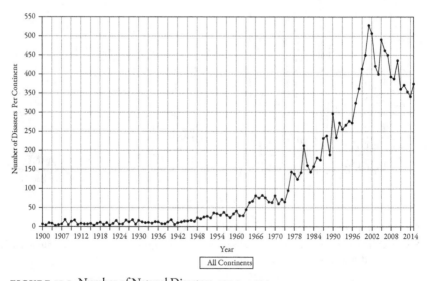

FIGURE 11.1 Number of Natural Disasters, 1900–2014

Source: OFDA/CRED International Disaster Database, www.emdat.be, Universite Catholique de Louvain, Brussels.

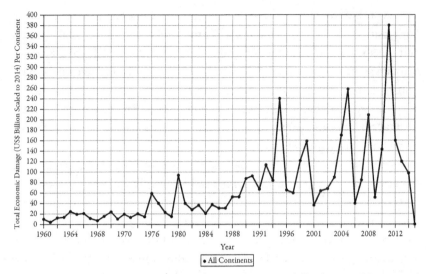

FIGURE II.2 Total Economic Damage (in constant 2014 dollars) Caused by Natural Disasters, 1960–2014

Source: OFDA/CRED International Disaster Database, www.emdat.be, Universite Catholique de Louvain, Brussels.

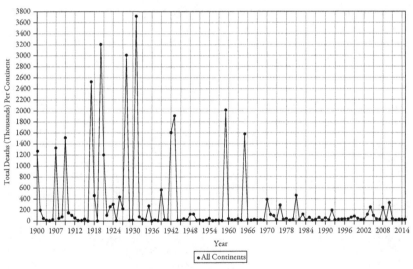

FIGURE II.3 Total Deaths from Natural Disasters, 1900–2014

Source: OFDA/CRED International Disaster Database, www.emdat.be, Universite Catholique de Louvain, Brussels.

and income that this person had at age twenty-eight. The third, P-36, has the wealth and income of this person at age thirty-six. Now suppose a tornado hits. Suppose it destroys everything P-22 owns, half of what P-28 owns, and a quarter of what P-36 owns. In monetary terms, P-36 would suffer the most damage, even though in some sense he's the least affected. P-36 simply has more and better stuff.

A similar point is true to countries. The fire that destroyed almost every house in London in 1666 produced only about £1.5 billion of damage in 2016 pounds.[8] A well-motived terrorist or a finely aimed natural disaster could do equivalent economic damage by destroying the Shard and two or three other large buildings in London today. In an experiential or humanitarian sense, the 1666 disaster would be far worse. But destroying the Shard and two other major buildings in London would register as greater total economic destruction.

As countries get wealthier, the economic costs of disasters tends to go up. But it's much better, of course, to be rich and have your mansion damaged than to be poor and have your shack destroyed, even if the latter shows up as a smaller economic loss. Since gross world product in 2011 was approximately $95 trillion in 2014 dollars,[9] the massive disaster peak in 2011 amounted to less than one half a percent of world product. The $100 billion in damage shown for the year 2014 amounts to less than one-tenth of a percent of world product in 2014, while the $260 billion in damage in 2004 amounts to less than four-tenths of a percent of 2004 world product.

Figure 11.4 plots the damage from all natural disasters as a percent of world product. The trend line indicates the five-year moving average. As the world gets richer, this will naturally bias the absolute damage from natural disasters upward for the reasons we discussed. (And data on the economic costs of natural disasters in the 1960s is not as good as data for more recent years.) Nevertheless, the total economic damage done by natural disasters, as a *percentage* of world product, remains roughly the same. Note that we're using US Consumer Price Index (CPI) as a conversion tool, which is only a rough approximation of global inflation, though EM-DAT represents its data in 2014 USD.[10] Thus, take Figure 11.4 with a few grains of salt.

Figure 11.4 seems to show a very slight increase. Other calculations show no increase in disaster damage as a percent of world product.[11] The upshot is that while the total damage from disasters is increasing, it's increasing at a rate roughly proportional to economic growth.

Perhaps more importantly, wealth allows us to better deal with storms and earthquakes. Wealthy people may have fancier cars, but they are also more likely to survive disasters. They are better able to avoid disasters, they live in

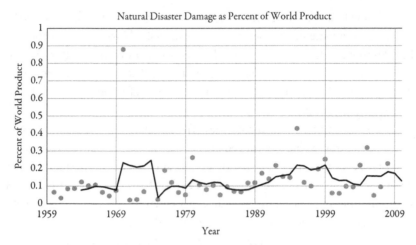

FIGURE II.4 Natural Disaster Damage as Percent of World Product, 1960–2008

Source: https://www.rug.nl/ggdc/historicaldevelopment/maddison/releases/maddison-project-database-2018, OFDA/CRED International Disaster Database, www.emdat.be, Universite Catholique de Louvain, Brussels; Maddison Project Dataset; authors' calculations.

stronger houses, they have better warning systems, and get better help afterward. As Figure 11.5 shows, the risk of death from environmental factors is *much higher* in poor countries than in rich countries.

In some ways, graphs like this understate how wealth helps us deal with changes in climate. It's not just that when people get wealthier they can afford better homes, medicine, and sanitation, and so are less likely to be killed by earthquakes, hurricanes, or climate-related disease. A wealthier world is also a world in which more human minds can be dedicated to high-level problem-solving rather than meeting basic needs. There are poor children in the developing world who would be scientists and engineers working on technologies that may mitigate the harms of climate change, if only they'd been born in wealthier societies.

William Nordhaus, perhaps the leading economist working on climate change, takes a line that's roughly similar to ours.[12] He notes that there is the possibility of serious disaster, and he thinks it is important to invest in alternative energy-generating technologies. Nevertheless, he asks readers to imagine what would happen if we take no steps to reduce greenhouse gas emissions: "To give an idea of the estimated damages in the uncontrolled (baseline) case, those damages in 2095 are $12 trillion, or 2.8% of global output, for a global temperature increase of 3.4 °C above 1900 levels."[13] Nordhaus thus estimates that world product in 2095 will be $450 trillion in 2010 dollars, which means he's assuming a modest 2.5% annual growth rate. By contrast,

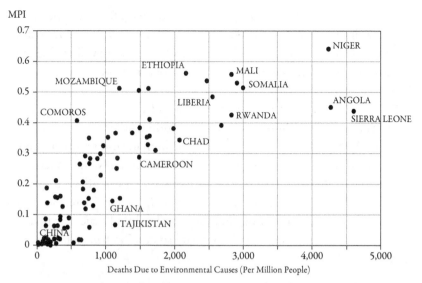

FIGURE 11.5 Deaths Attributable to Environmental Risks Associated with High Multidimensional Poverty (MPI) Levels

Source: http://hdr.undp.org/sites/default/files/reports/271/hdr_2011_en_complete.pdf, Figure 3.5, p. 51.

stopping growth in order to save the climate would condemn billions of people to "poverty and disease for the indefinite future."[14]

Climate change makes us worse off. Growth makes us better off. What we should do depends on the relative strength of these effects and the trade-offs we face. On Nordhaus's estimate, even if we do *nothing* to reduce climate change, we'll probably be vastly better off in 2095 than we are now. If the world continues to grow at a 2.5% rate (a rate that we hope is fairly conservative), and given the UN's projection that world population will be about 11.2 billion,[15] the average person worldwide by 2095 will be as rich as the average German or Canadian right now. (Note that this uses the UN's median projection. Since richer people have fewer children, it's possible that world population will peak in a few decades and then start to fall, in which case world product per capita would be even higher.)[16]

The 2006 *Stern Review on the Economics of Climate Change* provides far more pessimistic estimates.[17] Stern believes that by 2100, climate change will reduce economic output by 20%. But Stern does not mean that in 2100 world product will be 20% lower than it was in 2006. Rather, this means that climate change will reduce world product in 2100 by 20% compared to a hypothetical baseline in which carbon emissions and temperatures had not risen.

A *conservative* estimate is that by the year 2100 world product per capita will be well over $40,000 in today's dollars, while world product will be over $400 trillion. Stern's estimate is that global warming will reduce these numbers by 20%. If he's right, that's a real loss. But the people living then will live better than we live now.

The choice, then, is largely between a world much better equipped to deal with poverty *and* climate change and a world that's much worse in both respects. The Netherlands and Bangladesh are both in large parts beneath sea level. But we need not worry about rising sea levels in the Netherlands nearly as much as we do in Bangladesh, because the Dutch can afford to protect themselves. They can build dikes, they can anticipate and guard themselves against increased disease vectors, they can afford to build structures that will withstand changing weather conditions, and so on. The Bangladeshi mostly cannot.[18]

The Case for Growth Revisited

The case for growth survives the threat of climate change, then. Better, it survives in part *because* of the threat of climate change. Given that we face at least 50 years of rising temperatures, and given that we already face the enormous disaster of world poverty, the case for growth remains. Indeed, it is even stronger. The just thing for us to do is to implement policies that lead to growth and in turn outweigh the negative effects of climate change.

Some who think that more growth is not needed think that we already have the economic output to solve world poverty. In their minds, the world already produces enough to ensure that everyone has a decent life. If that's so, we don't need growth. We just need to re-allocate consumption in order to spread the world's output more equally. What remains can then be focused on mitigating climate change.

This will not do, however. For one, as we've seen, freezing world output at current levels will not in fact stop global warming. At current levels of emissions, the world will continue to heat up even beyond the 50-year point where current concentrations in the atmosphere will have had their effect. Those coming harms, including the further harms this proposal will itself inflict, will require a response. And even if current output is enough for our world today, it may not be enough for the world this proposal will bring about.

At the same time, however, it's questionable whether current output is enough to end world poverty. World product per capita in 2015 was roughly $16,000 in current USD.[19] This is about on par with the US poverty line, and on par with per capita income in the poorest towns in the US Appalachian region. Getting everyone in the world up to $16,000 a year would be wonderful, of course, and a gigantic improvement for much of the world's poor. But it would not mean the end of poverty or the injustices that result.

What's more, the existence of a $16,000 per capita world product does not mean that it is currently possible to provide everyone in the world with a $16,000 income. Not all economic production occurs in a form that could, in principle, be converted to income and transferred or redistributed to individuals. As we've seen, large-scale redistribution from developed to developing nations does not have a track record of success. And even at the best of times, much of what the developed world produces cannot be reallocated without significant loss. In reality, the proposal to halt growth in the name of climate change would mean a significantly lower standard of living.

It's important to realize here that the implications of this proposal are more than merely economic in kind. As we've seen before, allowing the world's poor to migrate to richer countries will itself cause growth, simply by freeing up the supply of labor to meet higher-valued uses around the world. But that is precisely what this proposal rules out. As a result, the price of climate change, in this view, is not just a per capita standard of living well below Appalachia. The price will be that the world's poor are morally required to remain as they are—left to deal with their climate (and other challenges) on a sub-Appalachian budget.

Of course, we find this unacceptable. And we suspect that you the reader will find it unacceptable as well. The challenge, then, is not whether we *should* encourage growth in light of climate change, but to what extent and where to encourage growth.[20]

Connections Part I: Innovation and the Environment

Consider an alternative response to climate change. Perhaps we should not stop overall economic growth, but reduce it. (Proponents of this view would hope to reduce it only in the developed world. The next section looks at whether that's realistic.) But this runs into the first of two important connections between the costs imposed by mitigation efforts: the relation between growth and our ability to avoid harming the environment.

This may sound paradoxical. Wouldn't greater economic output mean greater damage to the environment? Initially, the answer to that question is yes. Worldwide, as countries develop and industrialize, they do more damage to their environment for every dollar's worth of output. However, there seems to exist a certain turning point, around $9,000 GDP/capita, at which countries typically start to pollute less per additional dollars' worth of output.[21] Economists call this the "environmental Kuznets curve," which we show in Figure 11.6.

Consider the United States as an example of this trend. Carbon emissions in 1900 were 1.8 tons per $1,000/GDP in $2005 USD. Emissions peaked in the 1930s at about 2.8 tons per $1,000/GDP. Since then they have fallen steadily, to about .4 tons per $1,000/GDP today.[22] As Nordhaus summarizes, "Since 1930, the CO_2-gross domestic product (GDP) ratio has fallen at an average rate of 1.8% per year."[23]

One likely explanation for this trend is that environmental quality functions like a "superior good," a good that is pursued more strongly by those with higher incomes.[24] When people are desperately poor, they have little incentive to think long-term. Instead, they are forced to focus on meeting their immediate needs: food, shelter, heat. And we have to get these things any way we can. To cook our food or warm our dwellings, we might thus burn whatever fuel we can find, generating energy in very inefficient and polluting ways. Poverty means one cannot forego these things without great sacrifice.

However, as people become richer, they become more willing and able to make the kinds of trade-offs required to improve environmental quality. People become more willing to forego additional material benefits to instead enjoy a cleaner environment. Few people are willing to let their children starve to keep the air clean, but most people are willing to pay a little extra for

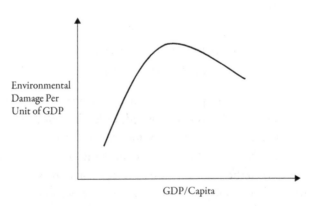

FIGURE 11.6 Environmental Kuznets Curve
Source: Authors.

catalytic converters in their cars to keep the air clean. Few people are willing to chance hypothermia during the night, but many are happy to choose more expensive solar energy to power their flat screen TVs.

If this trend holds, this is grounds for optimism. The point is that we need to get the world over the hump so that we become able to afford spending resources on protecting the environment. If the world becomes rich enough that people believe their children are safe and secure, we'll all become more likely to support the needed environmental protections.

It's possible of course that the trend won't continue (and we're not resting our argument on it).[25] But even if the theory of the environmental Kuznets curve ultimately rests on a mistake, one thing remains. The ability of mankind to deal with the current and already caused harmful effects of global warming, as well as the ability to live with future growth, strongly depends on the development of better technology. Only by developing more efficient means of energy consumption, and less carbon-intensive means of energy production, can we live with climate change. Such innovation will enable the developing (and the developed) world to move up in its living standards without thereby also significantly increasing its harmful impact on the environment.

Such innovation does not fall out of the air. It requires the sustained and significant investment of resources. And here the intuition behind the environmental Kuznets curve remains sound. For the world to be able to afford the kind of investment needed, further growth is required.

Connections Part II: The Ability to Pay Principle

A different possible response would aim to reduce growth overall, while redirecting its negative effects away from the world's poor. The correct response to climate change is to reduce economic growth and thus to swallow some of the setbacks this implies, but also to distribute these setbacks to rich countries, those who are best placed to bear them.

Darrel Moellendorf has proposed a version of this approach. According to him, the anti-poverty principle we cited above implies an ability-to-pay policy.[26] Such a policy requires assigning "states responsibility for mitigation in accordance with their ability to pay measured broadly in terms of their level of human development."[27] The idea is relatively straightforward: since mitigating climate change should not harm the development of the world's poor, the world's developed countries should bear the burdens of reduced energy consumption.

We accept Moellendorf's anti-poverty principle. However, that principle does not imply an ability-to-pay policy. Indeed, the principle may well advocate *against* such a policy. The main reason is that countries aren't autarkic economies, such that what happens in one does not affect the others. Economies are deeply interconnected, and increasingly so. As a result, reducing growth in one society can seriously impact the possibility of growth in another. And to the extent that reducing energy consumption in a rich country comes at the expense of growth in a poor one, Moellendorf's principle will argue against reducing emissions in the rich country.

Consider a case similar to the one we discussed in chapter 6. Suppose a rich country's economy consists of 10% manufacturing. And suppose that reducing emissions means that its manufacturing sector will end up 10% smaller than it would have been. Suppose further that about 50% of a developing country's economy consists of selling resources and materials to the rich country for its manufacturing sector. The net impact of the emissions reduction in the rich country will then be a 1% reduction in its economic activity. However, this reduction diminishes the rich country's imports of resources for manufacturing as well. Assuming for the sake of ease that the reduction on imports is proportional to the total reduction in activity (which is not a given, as the impact may be amplified), the net impact for the poor nation will be a 5% reduction in its economy.

The poor country thus suffers proportionally more *even though it was not subject to any emissions reduction*. And while 5% of a smaller economy may represent a smaller dollar amount than 1% of a large economy, this 5% will typically hurt a lot more. It will represent a much more harmful impact on its people's standards of living.

Effects like this can be compounded. Developed societies have access to more efficient forms of technology, both on the energy consumption and energy production side. That's what it means to be developed. However, the result of this is that reducing emissions by a single unit in a developing society will have a much bigger impact on its economic output than reducing it in a developed nation. Because developed nations are more efficient energy users, reducing energy use by the same amount has a bigger economic impact overall.

If we take seriously that climate change mitigation must not harm the ability of the world's poor to escape their dire circumstances, it follows that such mitigation efforts cannot be directed at developed nations in ways that harms the developing nations' prospects to export (and import) goods to (and from) there. And this directly contradicts the ability-to-pay principle.

That principle looks only at levels of human development, but it takes no account of how reductions in its economic activity might harm other countries.[28]

Climate Change in a World of Incentives

Reducing growth and reducing emissions are not the same thing. Our hope is for a world in which we can reduce emissions while continuing growth. But to accept that is precisely to accept our thesis—global justice requires continued, indeed accelerated, attention to unleashing humanity's productive and innovative forces.

Taking the anti-poverty principle seriously argues in favor of two related proposals. The first should be obvious, even if it's rarely really mentioned. Fossil fuel subsidies around the world amount to about $500 billion per year. Most of these occur in developing countries, especially in oil-rich ones like Venezuela or Saudi Arabia. Such subsidies more than cancel out even the most ambitious existing schemes of taxing carbon emissions. Worldwide, fossil fuel subsidies amount to about $15 per ton of carbon emitted. India has a $1 tax per ton of coal. It also hands out about $45 billion in annual fossil fuel subsidies.[29] Such subsidies are indefensible. They are unjust in themselves. And they're among the more destructive things people (and their governments) are doing to our planet.

The second is more familiar: a carbon tax. Such a tax has many benefits. It fits with the general moral principle that polluters ought to be taxed for the negative externalities they impose. But more importantly, such a tax has two further related benefits. It will incentivize the development of precisely those new and less-polluting technologies on which the world's ability to deal with climate change may well hang. And it will help reduce emissions in those places where they will cost the least.

The final and perhaps most important thing, however, is a further emphasis on one of our central conclusions. In order to get the incentives right, we must give people the option to act on them. And this means freeing the world from the enormous barriers that exist against free movement. Perhaps the easiest mitigation strategy for harmful climate change is to let people who live in places that will be badly affected move to places where this is less so, or where mitigation is more of an option (because of geography, wealth, or both).

Postscript

TOWARD A MORE OPEN WORLD

WE BEGAN THIS book by drawing attention to the pockets of prosperity that exist around the world. The overarching theme of this book has been that global justice is about giving people the opportunities to enjoy and help produce such prosperity. Doing that requires that they have the right to work and trade with willing others, move around the world, and then to reap its rewards. A world that gives people these opportunities will be much freer than it is today. It will be a world of open borders, free trade, and economic liberty.

Our world today is very far from this idea. Not only are borders around the globe hermetically sealed, voters and politicians increasingly reject openness. More and more, people see the world as if it consists of several separate societies, each with their own identity, people, and rules of justice. In order to do right by "their own" people, voters seem to believe they should ramp up—not bring down—the boundaries that divide us.

We've been arguing that thinking about the world, and thinking about justice, in this way is arbitrary, unacceptable, even morally callous. When we close off societies from one another, we are not only respecting their separate affairs or rights to self-determination. We are actively harming people who might want to interact with others across borders. Doing so is, quite simply, unjust. It may be the greatest evil we inflict upon each other. When free people choose to interact in mutually advantageous ways, justice demands that we leave them be.

We do not know how to change the trajectory of the world toward more openness. Nor do we know how to turn poor and dysfunctional societies into better, more productive ones. We know that extraction and oppression are things that make societies poor. And we know that productivity and innovation are things that make them rich. Exactly how to turn the former into the latter, well, no one really knows.

Still, there are easy steps we can take in the right direction. Countries around the world have erected walls and barriers that stop free people from being productive. Our world actively prevents people from doing the things that actually abolish poverty. It interferes with their productive activities, it stops them from working where their services are most needed, and it makes it difficult to sell their products to others who want them.

What we owe people around the world is *openness*. We owe them to remove the constraints on human freedom that keep people from helping make this a better and more prosperous world. Immigration restrictions, quotas, tariffs, and protectionist regulations should be abolished. And we should welcome newcomers into our societies, encouraging them to be productive citizens, just like they want to be.

The poor around the world have much to offer us, if only we *let* them. And we have much to offer them. A just world is not one consisting of some societies that have and others that have not—where the haves get stuck feeding the have-nots. It's a world in we can welcome each new person, no matter from where they come, as someone with talents, someone who is a blessing to have in our midst. And it's a world in which those people will feel welcome, because they can contribute and benefit from doing so themselves.

Notes

PREFACE

1. Ezra Klein, "Bernie Sanders: The Vox Conversation," July 28, 2015, http://www.vox. com/2015/7/28/9014491/bernie-sanders-vox-conversation.
2. It's worth noting just how odd Sanders's message would be even if we granted him his alternative facts: Sanders—an avowed left-wing socialist and supposed champion of social justice and equality—wants to maintain policies which keep the world's most vulnerable people mired in poverty and oppression, in order to protect the income of the top 10% of income-earners in the world.
3. Economist Brad DeLong commented on this sad affair: "The political truthiness has been flying thick and fast on this subject for decades now. Politicians are taking claims that have a very tenuous connection to economic reality—claims that *feel true*—and running with them, sometimes out of ignorance, sometimes because of cynical calculation." http://www.vox.com/the-big-idea/2017/1/24/14363148/ trade-deals-nafta-wto-china-job-loss-trump.
4. Caplan 2007.

CHAPTER 1

1. Roser and Ortiz-Ospina 2017.
2. Using Angus Maddison's data, the Netherlands in 1750 A.D. had a GDP/capita (in 1990 Gheary-Khamis dollars) of $2,355. England in 1750 had a GDP/capita of $1,695. Spain had GDP/capita of $783. Maddison doesn't have data for France in 1750, but by 1820, France had a GDP/capita of only $1,135, and didn't match the Netherlands' 1750 standard of living until about 1889. In contrast, total world product per capita in 1750 was well under $700. (The Maddison-Project, http:// www.ggdc.net/maddison/maddison-project/home.htm, 2013 version.)
3. From $130 constant 2000 US dollars in 5000 B.C. to $250 constant 2000 US dollars in 1800 A.D. according to Delong 2002, 120. Angus Maddison gives different numbers: $467 world GDP/capita in 1990 dollars in 1 A.D. up to $6,516 world GDP/capita in 2003 A.D., according to Maddison 2007, 70.

4. World per capita income as of 2014 is approximately $16,100 in 2014 US dollars, up from under $500 in 1800. https://www.cia.gov/library/publications/the-world-factbook/fields/2004.html.

5. Maddison 2007, 70.

6. Maddison 2007, 382, Table A.7.

7. Rawls 1971, 280–290.

8. By contrast, as we'll see, the evidence that global redistribution would do much good is weak, and there is strong evidence that it often hurts at least as much as it helps. Economists such as Jeffrey Sachs, who claim otherwise, are in the minority, and even Sachs recommends much more economic freedom than philosophers of global justice would accept. Sachs wants economic liberalization, robust market economies, *and* redistribution, not just redistribution, and certainly not redistribution plus the destruction of the market.

9. We say "at their best" because, technically speaking, interactions can be positive-sum in different ways. For instance, cases in which one party gains more than the other loses are different from what we have in mind here, but are not zero-sum. After all, the interaction does create a net gain. Alternatively, interactions can be nonzero-sum when at least one party gains and no parties are made worse off. Some textbooks will define the former as a positive-sum interaction, while others restrict the term to the latter. In any case, and to be absolutely clear, what we have in mind here is that it's best to find institutions that avoid win-lose or lose-lose interactions in favor of win-win interactions. When we say zero-sum, we mean lose-win, and when we say positive-sum, we mean win-win.

10. While there is clear overlap in terms of our conclusions, in this respect our argument is significantly different from Lomasky and Tesón 2015.

11. Collins, Morduch, Rutherford, and Ruthven 2010.

12. DeLong 2002, 120.

13. Maddison 2007, 70; The Maddison-Project, http://www.ggdc.net/maddison/maddison-project/home.htm, 2013 version.

14. Maddison defines the Western offshoots as the United States, Canada, New Zealand, and Australia.

15. John Maynard Keynes, "Economic Possibilities for Our Grandchildren," reprinted in Keynes 1972.

16. World per capita income as of 2014 is approximately $16,100 in 2014 US dollars, up from under $500 in 1800. https://www.cia.gov/library/publications/the-world-factbook/fields/2004.html.

17. http://data.worldbank.org/indicator/NY.GDP.PCAP.PP.CD.

18. http://data.worldbank.org/indicator/NY.GDP.PCAP.PP.CD.

19. Maddison-Project,   http://www.ggdc.net/maddison/maddison-project/home.htm, 2013 version; Landes 1999, xx.

20. As economist Angus Maddison summarizes the trends (Maddison 2007, 70–71):

In the year 1000 the inter-regional spread was very narrow indeed. By 2003 all regions had increased their incomes, but there was an 18:1 gap between the richest and poorest region, and a much wider inter-country spread.

One can also see the divergence between the West (Western Europe, the United States, Canada, Australia, New Zealand) and the rest of the world economy. Real per capita income in the West increased 2.8-fold between the year 1000 and 1820, and 20-fold from 1820 to 2003. In the rest of the world income rose much more slowly—slightly more than a quarter from 1000 to 1820 and seven-fold since then.

21. Pogge 2001, 65.
22. This may not be Pogge's intended point. As we'll see, Pogge draws attention to the damaging dynamics of what he calls the resource privilege. We agree with Pogge that the international system disastrously incentivizes violence and oppression in the pursuit of de facto ownership of natural resources, although we disagree with him on the moral implications of this fact. One possible interpretation is that Pogge is merely using this argument to defend his conclusions, even though those conclusions are not clearly connected to these supposed injustices.

   Another interpretation might be this. Perhaps Pogge means that the rich are using more natural resources because the production and consumption of their wealth involves the use of resources, and all resources ultimately rely on natural ones. On this option, a rich person, *in virtue of being rich*, uses more natural resources than a poor person. And Pogge's account would then imply that anytime someone gets rich, she owes others compensation for her use, in virtue of being rich, of natural resources. We find this version of the thought bizarre, but we can safely set it aside for now. For given that in many places around the world rich people live side-by-side other reasonably well-off people, this first version, even if sound, can have little to do with the extreme poverty we find around the globe.

23. Weil 2013, 453.
24. Weil 2013, 450.
25. Weil 2013, 450–451.
26. Acemoglu, Johnson, and Robinson 2005; Acemoglu and Robinson 2013; Cowen and Tabarrok 2010, 92–106; North 1990; North, Wallis, and Weingast 2012; Rodrick, Subramanian, and Trebbi 2004.
27. North 1990, 3.
28. Roland 2014, 108.
29. Rodrik, Subramanian, and Trebbi 2004, 13; Risse 2005. Similarly, Cowen and Tabarrok 2010, 101 state that "the key to producing and organizing the factors of production [in ways that lead to prosperity] are *institutions* that create appropriate *incentives*."
30. Acemoglu and Robison 2005; Acemoglu, Johnson, and Robinson 2001, 2002; Hall and Jones 1999; Hall and Lawson 2014; De Soto 2000.
31. Acemoglu and Robinson 2005, 403.

32. Gwartney, Lawson, and Hall 2015; Gwartney, Lawson, and Hall 2017.

33. http://www.heritage.org/index/.

34. Author calculations, using data from Gwartney, Lawson, and Hall 2015, and World Bank World Development Indicators, http://data.worldbank.org/products/wdi, last accessed 8/21/15.

35. Gwartney, Lawson, and Hall 2015, 24.

36. World Justice Project Rule of Law Index, 2015, http://worldjusticeproject.org/sites/default/files/roli_2015_0.pdf.

37. Rodrik, Subramanian, and Trebbi 2004 suggest that institutional quality is the main explanatory variable of growth. See also Acemoglu and Robison 2005; Acemoglu, Johnson, and Robinson 2001, 2002; Hall and Jones 1999; Hall and Lawson 2014; De Soto 2000; Easterly and Ross 2003.

38. Leeson 2010, 227–233.

39. Acemoglu and Robinson 2012, 74–75.

40. Acemoglu and Robinson 2012, 372–373.

41. As we have said, these rights will not be *sufficient* for development. If they are to have any chance, these rights will have to be embedded in a broader set of political institutions, such as the rule of law, as well as basic civil and political liberties. In what follows, we spend little time defending these, as they are uncontroversial. We simply insist that philosophers offer their economic counterparts the same kind of support.

42. For a useful discussion and defense of a similar methodological approach, see Huemer 2016.

43. Lomasky and Tesón 2015.

CHAPTER 2

1. See http://www.oecdbetterlifeindex.org/topics/income/. The US Census Bureau offers a significantly higher estimate of US median household income of $53,657. See http://www.census.gov/content/dam/Census/library/publications/2015/demo/p60-252.pdf. There is a more extended discussion of Nogales, as well as other cases, in Acemoglu and Robinson 2013.

2. http://www.state.gov/e/eb/rls/othr/ics/2013/204729.htm.

3. http://www.who.int/countries/sle/en/.

4. See Deaton 2013.

5. Or, as Joseph Carens (1987) put it, the modern equivalent of feudal birthright.

6. Moreover, as we will see later, the existence of bad institutions not only harms life prospects directly, it also takes some of the ways we might (otherwise) address global poverty off the table. While financial aid can have good effects, it has proven highly ineffective as a developmental strategy. Aid in extractive regimes often disproportionally benefits the extractors—and sometimes even strengthens their

extractive positions. As a result, aid is mainly a tool for fighting the symptoms of extreme poverty; it rarely cures the disease.

7. See Collier 2009. Compare to Collier 2007, 130. For similar views, see Lal 2005.

8. See Van der Vossen's half of Tesón and Van der Vossen 2017.

9. http://www.iom.int/files/live/sites/iom/files/pbn/docs/Fatal-Journeys-Tracking-Lives-Lost-during-Migration-2014.pdf.

10. Clemens 2011, 85.

11. https://www.cia.gov/library/publications/the-world-factbook/geos/xx.html.

12. Moreover, many of those who did move stayed only temporarily. As we'll discuss in the next chapter, this is a more general trend.

13. Oddly, the importance of this is often overlooked, in particular by philosophers. For example, Joseph Carens (2013, 233), himself an advocate of open borders, oddly says, "I agree that eliminating extreme inequalities, and, especially, eliminating extreme poverty, are more urgent and fundamental tasks than opening borders." That reads perilously close to saying that eliminating smallpox is a more urgent and fundamental task than distributing smallpox vaccines.

14. By comparison, US federal, state, and local governments spent a combined $416 billion on infrastructure and transportation in 2014. https://www.cbo.gov/publication/49910.

15. This paraphrases Huemer 2010.

16. As Liberia did in 2015, quarantining part of the country to contain an outbreak of Ebola, for example. http://www.bbc.com/news/world-africa-33323664.

17. Although it's far more controversial among academics than it is among people in general. Approximately one-fifth to one-third of Americans are broadly libertarian. See Brennan 2012, 171–172.

18. Gaus 2004, 207.

19. Miller 2005.

20. Miller 2005, 196.

21. Miller 2005, 199–202.

CHAPTER 3

1. Kerr and Kerr 2011, 12; Friedberg and Hunt 1995; Longhi, Nijkamp, and Poot 2005, 2006; Longhi et al. 2010; Okkerse 2008.

2. Ottaviano and Peri 2008; Peri and Sparber 2009, 162; D'Amuri and Peri 2011.

3. Friedberg and Hunt 1995.

4. See, e.g., OECD 2013; Dustmann and Frattini 2013.

5. We get this phrasing from Nowrasteh and Cole 2013.

6. In any case, it's difficult to generalize from examples like this. For one, the loss of welfare here is not large. And we're only willing to forego giving the toy because our children are too young to understand the obvious fair solution: that we should

distribute it via lottery, or have the children share. Or, failing that, even ask one kid to just accept that the other got lucky this time.

7. Would it still be wrong to give kids *unequal* amounts of toys, even if doing so meant more toys for everyone? Perhaps kids just can't help feeling envious as a result. Fair enough, but at some point we need to recognize the difference between treating people as kids and treating people as citizens.

8. Caldwell 2009, 136. Similar numbers are available for other countries such as Sweden.

9. *The Economist*, "An Edgy Inquiry: Ethnic Minorities in France," April 4, 2015.

10. See Caldwell 2009, 140ff. and chapter 6. Of course, this is heavily disputed. Others say that the crime numbers may be due to selective or discriminatory law enforcement, that Western military involvement in the Middle East is causing hostility among Islamic immigrant groups, and so on.

11. As Paul Collier (2013, 68) puts it, "migrants bring their culture with them."

12. Collier also invokes another claim. In addition to the worry that immigrants might bring their bad norms along, Collier asserts that there is a negative relationship between the "distance" of cultures that live together and social trust that exists between them. Thus, whether or not the cultures in question are dysfunctional, the more diverse a population, the less trust there will be. This, too, is a reason for limiting immigration.

We here ignore this argument, as it is plainly unacceptable. Collier bases this argument on research by political scientist Robert Putnam, who found that in racially diverse US neighborhoods people trust each other less than in more homogenous ones. This raises a similar problem to what we have seen. If Collier's view that increased diversity lowers social trust can justify excluding people from other nationalities at the borders, presumably it is also good enough to exclude co-citizens from parts of the country. Indeed, it would seem good enough to justify excluding people from different races from moving into certain neighborhoods. This conclusion is a *reductio*.

As an aside, it's worth noting that Putnam's results have become increasingly questioned. For instance, the finding that social trust is negatively affected by cultural diversity seems mostly due to nonwhite people in predominantly white societies generally reporting lower social trust (which in turn is mostly because of their residential instability, socio-economic status, etc.), and being overrepresented in culturally heterogeneous communities. See Abascal and Baldassarri 2015.

13. See chapter 2 and the references therein. In the context of immigration, Ryan Pevnick (2009) suggests a pure institutionalist view. Clark et al. (2015) find that allowing immigration generally has beneficial effects on institutions.

14. The purported relation goes back far: countries populated by people who descend from places that were early adopters of agriculture during Neolithic times, among other things, tend to do better than those populated by the descendants of those who switched later. See, e.g., Glaeser, La Porta, Lopez-de-Silanes, and Shleifer

2004; Enrico Spolaore and Wacziarg 2013; Putterman and Weil 2010; Comin and Hobijn 2010; Easterly and Levine 2016.

15. Collier 2013, 68.

16. There is little reason to think that the dynamics of economic productivity are importantly different from other valuable parts of human life. After all, productivity does not occur in a vacuum. As the institutionalists point out, economic productivity requires and happens against a background of (and in that sense presupposes) rich social, cultural, and institutional support. And if we cannot realistically have the former without the latter, it seems safe to assume that these conclusions generalize.

17. In fact, these norms seem to transfer home to the immigrants' families even if they themselves do not return, presumably via visits, conversations, and so on. Collier recognizes this, incidentally, citing Beine, Docquier, and Schiff 2013.

18. The Manhattan Institute tracks integration in the United States along a variety of dimensions, and writes that "immigrants are now more assimilated, on average, than at any point since the 1980s." See http://www.manhattan-institute.org/html/cr_76.htm#.VgcXALSFbww. For discussion, see Clemens and Sandefur 2014.

19. See the discussion of "critical junctures" in Acemoglu and Robinson 2013.

20. This is not to say we can never use force to stop crime. Clearly, we can. If the police catch people en route to committing a crime, there is no problem with stopping and apprehending them. But this is significantly different than what we're considering here. For this argument justifies only restricting the freedom of specific persons in specific cases, based on the evidence that they are, in fact, about to commit a crime. It does not justify preventing entire groups or populations from exercising their right to move freely on the grounds that people in their demographic commit crimes more frequently than people in other demographics.

CHAPTER 4

1. Miller 2005, 198.

2. Pogge 1997, 14–15. Pace Pogge, there is evidence that, e.g., the very poorest Haitians benefit significantly from migration. See Clemens and Pritchett 2008.

3. Easterly and Nyarko 2009.

4. Kapur 2013.

5. For a general study of this relation, see Docquier et al. 2016. For results about Mexico, see Pfutze 2012. See also Easterly and Nyarko 2009.

6. Among many other studies, see Acosta et al. 2008; Clemens and Bazzi 2008; de Haas 2005, 2006; Gupta, Pattillo, and Wagh 2009; López-Córdova, Tokman, and Verhoogen 2005; Pritchett 2006; Taylor 1999. Richard Adams and John Page (2005) find that a 10% increase in a country's share of emigrants leading to a 2.1% decline of people living on less than $1 a day, and a 10% increase in remittances leading to a 3.5% decrease in the poverty rate.

7. See Stark, Taylor, and Yitzhaki 1986; Koechlin and Leon 2007; McKenzie and Rapoport 2007.

8. Pogge 1997, 14, emphasis in original. No less bizarre, Pogge and Brock simply get the facts wrong, claiming that since remittances are sent, again, by the "most privileged" they will not help the poorest. See Pogge 1997, 14–15; Brock 2009, 205–206.

9. As Gillian Brock argues in Brock and Blake 2015.

10. Brock and Blake 2015, 5.

11. Oberman 2013.

12. Brock and Blake 2015, 14.

13. This section builds on arguments initially developed in van der Vossen 2015.

14. We suspect people reason, roughly, as follows: just as individuals have the right to lead a life of their choosing, so states have a right to determine their own path. But states aren't like people. Governments govern collections of individuals with different goals and paths. As Achen and Bartels 2016 and Brennan 2016b show, there is no "will of the people" and democratic governments are not "the people choosing for themselves." Politics is a matter of justice.

15. Wellman has developed this view in several pieces, including Wellman 2008; Altman and Wellman 2011; Wellman and Cole 2011.

16. Note that Wellman uses the slightly different example of one state annexing the other. I choose the present example for two reasons: (a) it adequately expresses the intuitive appeal of Wellman's view (if the view is sound, it ought to work for this example as much as for his chosen case of annexation), and (b) the example of annexation invites confusion for reasons to be explained.

17. This conception of self-determination is suggested by Kershnar 2000, in particular the "contract" argument on 142–145.

18. See Altman and Wellman 2011, 6. See also Waldron 2010 and van der Vossen 2016.

19. Buchanan 1999.

20. For a more detailed version of this argument, see Huemer 2010. Unfortunately, however, Huemer fails to address the collectivist conception of self-determination, which animates most of the proponents of this view. Huemer (correctly) adds that if states really were self-determining in the way voluntary associations are, it becomes unclear why, say, sexist or inegalitarian societies are unjust. Thus, insofar as one thinks that substantive demands of justice apply to states, they are not self-determining in the same way as free associations of individuals.

21. The first two quotes are from Wellman 2005, 41 and 42, respectively, emphasis in original; the latter is from Altman and Wellman 2011, 7.

22. Wellman wrongly thinks that such incorporation actually supports his case. He writes that if the United States were to annex Canada, this would violate Canadian self-determination. That's true, of course, but is importantly disanalogous to the case of immigration. In the case of annexation, it's the *incorporated party* whose self-determination is violated. In the case of immigration, it is the *incorporating party* whose self-determination is supposedly violated.

23. Of course, we are aware that Wellman has offered reasons why states may exercise self-determination one way but not the other, such as a requirement of equal treatment for citizens. But this is precarious business, as these kinds of reasons are far less straightforward and less intuitive than the original argument itself.

24. For a more detailed exploration of this line of thought, see Van der Vossen 2015.

25. Macedo, 2007, 64.

26. Macedo 2007, 74.

27. Macedo 2007, 64.

28. Macedo asserts that his theory is "politically liberal" and that he is a "philosopher on the Left." See Macedo 2007, 65.

29. See Blake 2005.

30. Compare Blake 2001.

31. See Clemens and Postel 2017.

32. Del Carpio and Wagner 2015.

CHAPTER 5

1. Caplan 2007.

2. Mueller, 2003, 349–354.

3. Caplan 2007.

4. Or buy. Who buys and who sells makes no difference, of course. In fact, strictly speaking, each party to a trade is *simultaneously* a seller and a buyer. When the rich buy goods from the poor, paying with their dollars, the poor "buy money" from the rich, paying with their goods.

5. Nozick 1974, 237.

6. Krugman 1993.

7. http://www.igmchicago.org/igm-economic-experts-panel/poll-results?SurveyID=SV_odfr9yjnDcLh17m.

8. http://www.chicagobooth.edu/about/newsroom/news/2013/2013-05-03-igm-survey.

9. https://kaiserfamilyfoundation.files.wordpress.com/1996/09/1199-t.pdf.

10. This section incorporates and revises material from Brennan and Jaworski 2016, 172–175.

11. For more discussion of these and related objections, see Lomasky and Tesón 2015, chapter 6.

12. Mueller 2003, 349–354.

13. Clemens 2008, 85; Wall 1999; Hufbauer and Elliott 1999. However, if we include the associated welfare losses from the rent-seeking that produces many trade restrictions, the number may be far higher. See Mueller 2003, 355.

14. Irwin 2007.

15. This section incorporates and revises material from Brennan 2016b.

16. Rawls 1996, 5–6.

17. Freeman 2007, 54.
18. Freeman 2007, 54.
19. Freeman 2007, 55 (emphasis in original).
20. As Freeman writes: "Rawls holds that classical liberal property rights and the enforcement of the traditional doctrine of laissez-faire are not conditions of free and equal persons' adequate development and full exercise of their moral powers and their achievement of their rational autonomy, and so are not an essential social basis of self-respect." See Freeman 2011, 54. See also http://bleedingheartlibertarians.com/2012/06/can-economic-liberties-be-basic-liberties/. Rawls, when discussing what he considered "wider conceptions" of property than only "personal property," wrote: "They cannot, I think, be accounted for as necessary for the development and exercise of the moral powers." See Rawls 1996, 298.
21. Tomasi 2012. For another compelling defense of economic freedoms on "high liberal" grounds, see Queralt 2017.
22. Freeman (2011, 32): "Rawls implies that, while ownership of one's residence and personal belongings is necessary for individual independence and privacy, laissez-faire rights of ownership of means of production and near-absolute freedom of economic contract are not necessary for these general purposes—however much certain individuals might want to enjoy these rights given their specific life-plans (to be wealthy, for example)."
23. See Rawls 1996, 315–329; Rawls 2001, 18–26.

CHAPTER 6

1. Zwolinski 2007.
2. Powell and Skarbek 2006.
3. Zwolinski 2007, 707.
4. http://www.nytimes.com/1997/06/22/weekinreview/in-principle-a-case-for-more-sweatshops.html.
5. http://www.bls.gov/oes/current/oes_nat.htm#00-0000.
6. Maybe Ana will hire María, perhaps to help her clean the house. Question: what should *she* pay María?
7. Hassoun 2012, 147.
8. Hassoun 2012, 143–168.
9. Lest the reader think we're being unfair, Hassoun literally describes her chapter as "critiquing the simplest version of the Argument from Comparative Advantage." See Hassoun 2012, 144. Fernando Téson (2014) has a similar worry:

> In this vein, Professor Hassoun claims, first, that the assumptions of the comparative advantages model are unrealistic. Yet the comparative advantage model has been adapted by many to show that the basic result continues to hold even if you relax assumptions about full employment, worker homogeneity, worker mobility, and other factors. *The only way* one can get to the conclusion that trade is bad from

a total national wealth standpoint is if one is willing to *assume* that the models of "returns to scale," "infant industry," or "learning by doing" hold in some cases. *Professor Hassoun does not discuss these. . . .* You need one of these models to yield a negative result and even then, a defense of protectionism requires that you believe that these bad regimes who can't even manage to feed their people somehow have the great insight to determine what industries to protect to reap these gains, and the strength and honesty to stand up to rent-seeking interests (emphasis added).

10. Hassoun 2012, 167–168.
11. Hassoun 2012, 176–184.
12. For example, while all libertarians are free traders, some reject the idea intellectual property, while others accept it. Some who accept intellectual property think that intellectual property laws are too strict and are creating a tragic anti-commons, while others think the laws are fine, and yet others think they need to be stricter.
13. James 2012, 61–62.
14. The phrase "an *international market reliance practice*" appears in James 2012, 37 (emphasis in original).
15. James 2012, 60ff.
16. James 2012, 41 (emphasis in original).
17. James 2012, 42. We note but do not dwell on the fact that these claims have obvious counterexamples in the extensive black markets that exist all over and across the world. (At times, James puts some stock in the claim that this would no longer be *international* trade. See, e.g., James 2012, 42–43. Fine.) For a robust empirical critique of James's empirical presuppositions, see Stringham 2015.
18. James 2012, 37–38. James separates (3) into two separate conditions. We keep it as one here for ease of exposition.
19. James 2012, 40 (emphasis added).
20. James does not tell us how exactly we might measure gains from trade. See, e.g., James 2012, 169.
21. If this strikes you as odd, imagine that B is a much larger country than A. In what follows, we continue to assume that the countries are of equal size.
22. Pre-trade per capita income in A: .9*1,000+.1*10,000= $1,900. Pre-trade per capita income in B: .1*1,000+.9*10,000= $9,100. Post-trade per capita income in A: .9*2,000+.1*10,000= $2,800 (+$900). Post-trade per capita income in B: .1*2,000+.9*10,000= $9,200 (+$100).
23. His principle of "international relative gains" requires that "the gains to each trading society, adjusted according to their respective national endowments (e.g., population size, resource base, level of development) are to be distributed equally, unless unequal gains flow (e.g., via special trade privileges) to poor countries." James 2012, 18.
24. James 2012, 61–62.
25. James 2012, 61–62.
26. See James 2012, chapter 5, and the references therein.

27. Gilens 2012; Achen and Bartels 2016.

28. Question: If those who benefited from unjust coercion do not deserve to be compensated, might they be required to compensate those that were harmed by the restrictions?

29. Risse 2012, 267–268.

30. Question: Can the fact that slavery is *much* more unjust than a tariff be sufficient to explain the difference?

CHAPTER 7

1. For examples, see the recent special issue of the *Journal of Applied Philosophy* 30 (2012); Brownlee 2013.

2. Nor is it meant to be exhaustive. The best justification for a number of standard civil and political rights may refer to the need to restrict state power, for example. And clearly there can be productive human rights beyond the narrow economic list.

3. See Nickel 2005.

4. See, e.g., Article 29 of the UDHR.

5. For similar approaches, see Christiano 2011, and Buchanan 2013, 107–172.

6. See Morsink, 1999, chapters 4–6. See also Malfliet 2002, 163.

7. We say "limited" because (a) the European Convention on Human Rights excluded the right from the main Convention and relegated to the optional First Protocol (because several European nations at the time were engaged in nationalizing industries); and (b) this court, like others, gives the widest interpretation to national prerogative to regulate and curtail private property. See Janis, Kay, and Bradley 2008, 519–520.

8. Morsink (1999, 133) writes, "to Humphrey 'socialism . . . [was] a religion.'"

9. See Morsink 1999, 139.

10. For discussion, see Buchanan 2013, 167–168.

11. See Morsink 1999, 147.

12. Examples where the Human Rights Committee refrained from enforcing the right to property are *Oló Bahamonde v. Equatorial Guinea, Ackla v. Togo, Diergaardt of Rehoboth Baster Community* et al. *v. Namibia*, and *Adam, Blazek and Marik v. The Czech Republic*. For an excellent resource, see the entry on property of the Icelandic Human Rights Centre: http://www.humanrights.is/the-human-rights-project/humanrightscasesandmaterials/humanrightsconceptsideasandfora/substantivehumanrights/therighttoproperty/.

13. See Cruft 2006. A sampling of works in which property rights are debunked or ignored are Beitz 2011; Gilabert 2012; Griffin 2009; Bilchitz 2007. John Rawls (1999, 79–80) following the tradition from Humphreys, includes only a right to personal property in his list of human rights.

14. The only sustained defense is Nickel 2007, chapter 8.

15. For the classical statement of this as a general theory of rights, see Raz 1986, chapter 7.

16. For defense of this second approach, see Raz, 1986, 179, 247–248.

17. One need not assert, then, that each of the productive rights is inextricably linked to productive activities. Even if some of their exercises do not count as directly productive, this does not impugn their justification, as long as their inclusion reliably makes the legal system of human rights better serve its function.

18. As Nickel (2007, 128) points out, this is most clearly visible in the duress imposed on people by involuntary unemployment.

19. For similar arguments about the moral importance of private property, see Nickel 2007, chapter 8; Tomasi 2012; Wadron 1988.

20. We set aside here that productive rights also serve interests that are not easily labeled *individual* interests. As will become clear, productive human rights are crucial to people's abilities to form and run churches, unions, associations, and other communal organizations. In this way, they serve our interests qua group members as well.

21. Acemolgu and Robinson 2013, 75; see also 9, 71–74, and throughout. Economist Dani Rodrik (2003, 10) makes a similar point, writing: "Institutions that provide dependable property rights, manage conflict, maintain law and order, and align economic incentives with social costs and benefits are the foundation of long-term growth." See also Freeman and Lindauer 1999; van de Walle and Johnston 1996.

22. These points are widely recognized in economic history and development. See, e.g., North 2012; Acemoglu and Robinson 2013, 9, 71–75, and throughout; Acemoglu and Johnson, 2005; de Soto 1989, 2000; Rodrik, 2003.

23. Acemolgu, Johnson, and Robinson 2001, 2002, 2005.

24. Available at http://www.freetheworld.com.

25. See Acemoglu and Robinson 2013, 71.

26. See in general Dollar and Kraay 2002, 2004; Bergh and Nilsson 2014.

27. Deaton 2013, chapters 2–4.

28. Again, we are not claiming that the productive rights will be sufficient for particular person or group's protection. Rather, our point is that without these rights, key protections remain foreclosed, despite us having important and universal interests.

29. Boudreaux, 2006.

30. See the International Convention on the Protection of the Rights of All Migrant Workers and Members of Their Families, the Convention on the Elimination of All Forms of Discrimination Against Women, and the United Nations Declaration on the Rights of Indigenous Peoples. http://www.ohchr.org/EN/ProfessionalInterest/Pages/CMW.aspx.

31. For more on the role of property rights and economic freedom in the protection of minorities, see *Mayagna (Sumo) Awas Tingni Community v. Nicaragua*. See also Nickel 2007.

32. Some might worry about distributional effects. Obviously, this issue cannot be discussed in full here, but we note the following. First, again, nothing in the argument rules out forms of just taxation, regulation, and the like. The productive human rights are no more absolute than any other human right. Of course, a robust affirmation of these rights does rule out certain things, including strongly socialist regimes. But if the arguments are sound, these regimes fail to serve people's important interests as well as productive human rights. As such, they ought not to be consistent with human rights protections.

33. See, e.g., John Rawls 1996; Freeman 2011.

34. As Darrel Moellendorf puts it: "Theories of justice give accounts of who is owed what; they are accounts of the moral creditors" (Moellendorf 2014, 7).

35. Cohen (2009, 39) claims that utopian, if not realistic, socialism realizes what he calls the "the principle of communal reciprocity," which is "the antimarket principle in which I serve you not because of what I can get in return by doing so, but because you need or want my service, and you, for the same reason, serve me." Cohen doesn't imagine utopian socialists to be selfless, so he means here a principle in which one person serves another not *simply* out of self-interest but also out of a desire to serve others. Cohen provides no philosophical argument that this principle is somehow incompatible with markets or capitalism, and he provides no empirical evidence that this attitude is found less in market society than in socialist or nonmarket societies. (On the contrary, as Jason has pointed out, it appears this attitude is more prevalent in market societies than elsewhere. See Brennan 2013, 2014; Brennan and Jaworski 2016.) We invoke Cohen here to illustrate that the personal value of being a contributor is not a value unique to capitalist or market ideologies. See also Miller 2002.

CHAPTER 8

1. While there are relevant differences between colonialism and imperialism, the difference doesn't matter much for our purposes. As a result, we will treat the two as more or less interchangeable here.

2. Benhabib, 2004, 100. She cites no economics literature to back up her doubts.

3. http://www2.ohchr.org/english/issues/poverty/expert/docs/Thomas_Pogge_Summary.pdf.

4. For example, see Cardoso and Faletto 1979.

5. Rosenberg and Birdzell 1986, 17–18; Landes 1999, 429, concludes the Marxist view is "nonsense."

6. As Landes summarizes, "To the disappointment of the anticolonialist doctrinaires, the ex-imperial nations suffered not a whit by the loss of these territories; on the contrary" (1999, 439).

7. Rosenberg and Birdzell 1986, 18.

8. Landes 1999, 423; Davis and Huttenback 1987; Rosenberg and Birdzell 1986; Kimura, 1995; O'Brien 1988; Offer 1993; Davis and Huttenback 1982; Ferguson 2003; Edelstein 1982; Foreman-Peck 1989; Coelho 1973; McDonald 2009; Fieldhouse 1961.

9. Smith WN V.3.92.

10. Smith WN V.3.92.

11. Smith WN IV.vii.c.17.

12. Landes 1999, 423; Davis and Huttenback 1987; Rosenberg and Birdzell 1986; Kimura 1995; O'Brien 1988; Offer 1993; Davis and Huttenback 1982; Ferguson 2003; Edelstein 1982; Foreman-Peck 1989; Coelho 1973; McDonald 2009; Fieldhouse 1961.

13. Davis and Huttenback 1987 bears this out. A small subset of upper-class individuals with political connections made out well, but as Davis and Huttenback note, "the British as a whole certainly did not benefit economically from the Empire" (306).

14. Davis and Huttenback 1987, 3–6, list a number of different theories from the academic literature.

15. Davis and Huttenback 1987 stay silent on this issue, but their accounting of differential costs and benefits suggests that it is the most plausible story.

16. Or better, ended up being forced to set up inclusive institutions. See Acemoglu, Johnson, and Robinson 2001; Acemoglu and Robinson 2013.

17. Others have found similar results. For example, Robert Grier argues that the current economic performance of former colonies is strongly correlated with how long European powers held those colonies. See Grier 1999.

18. Boonin 2011, chapters 1 and 2. For a similar, earlier argument, see Kukathas 2003, 183.

19. Thanks to Mike Huemer for this point.

20. Schmidtz 2006, 214.

21. It's true that many Europeans were in favor of their empires, even though the empires hurt them. Probably most Europeans accepted what Adam Smith called mercantilist economic policies. They mistakenly believed empire was good for them. Imperialism was also source of national pride. British subjects felt superior to French subjects because Britain had a bigger empire, and they felt superior to the colonized and conquered peoples. Had the former imperialist powers put their imperialist policies to a popular vote, the population might well have voted on behalf of the very policies that depleted their pocketbooks and sent their sons off to die. Nevertheless, the Imperialist European powers *did not* put such policies to anything like a real democratic vote. So, while Europeans might well have voted for such policies had they gotten the chance, and even if such a vote would have been enough to make them responsible in the way needed for claims of compensation, nevertheless, the truth is that imperialism was imposed upon the subjects of imperialist as well as upon the conquered peoples. It may well be that given the

opportunity, you the reader would burgle our houses, but that doesn't mean you owe us compensation for when some other person burgles our houses.

22. Radzik 2001, 459.

23. Beerbohm 2012.

24. Radzik 2001, 458.

25. Radzik 2001, 460. Might this be a mistake? It's easy for people who have never had the opportunity to act on their hate to believe that they would not do so if given the chance. And when someone has the opportunity to act on their hate, and yet does not, that might reveal something *good* about that person's character (even if that person is also deficient for being hateful). Why not hold that the anti-Semite German who, during the years before WWII, didn't act on his racism, is revealed to be better than we thought precisely because he didn't act when given the chance to hurt others?

26. Assuming, as seems safe, that there are no significant innate differences between the groups. For good discussion of this, see Boonin 2011, 94ff.

27. We say "unfortunately" not as a rhetorical device; we wish the problem of global poverty was that easy to solve. Unfortunately, it isn't.

28. Radzik 2009.

CHAPTER 9

1. Pogge 2002, 106–107.

2. Pogge 2002, chapter 6.

3. Pogge 2002, 112–123; see also 139–144.

4. See Pogge 2011.

5. Wenar 2015, 142–145. See also the conditions of statehood outlined in Article 1 of the 1933 Montevideo Convention on the Rights and Duties of States. https://www.ilsa.org/jessup/jessup15/Montevideo%20Convention.pdf.

6. Risse 2005b; Lomasky and Tesón 2015.

7. Clemens 2011, 85.

8. Wenar 2015, xlv.

9. http://www.econlib.org/library/Essays/rdPncl1.html.

10. Wenar 2015, 284.

11. Wenar 2015, 289–291. The quoted passage is on 290.

12. Wenar 2015, 227–228.

13. Unfortunately, Wenar says little on the topic other than that a "people" is not the same as a state or the regime that controls it. Wenar 2015, 212–245.

14. Wenar 2015, 204.

15. Wenar 2015, 73.

16. Easterly, Gatti, and Kurlat 2006. One problem: the more ethnically heterogeneous a democracy, the less likely it will have significant checks on its executive power. See Aghion, Alesina, and Trebbi 2004; also Easterly 2006, 106.

17. Add a statute of limitations, then? But that will not help to solve the problem with which Wenar is concerned, for it would fail to incentivize the *transition* from extractive regimes to democratic and peaceful ones. The longer countries will have to wait to get the funds from the Clean Hands Trust, the less it will help to create stable democracies.

18. Hassoun understands as coercive any institution capable of imposing sanctions (2012, 7). She does not specify whether such sanctions must be enforced or imposed by violence.

19. Hassoun 2012, 18.

20. Hassoun 2012, 18.

21. Hassoun 2012, 28.

22. Many economists and philosophers, from widely different ideological backgrounds, conceive of rules of private property as a set of coercive institutions; e.g., Schmidtz 1994; Cohen 2011.

23. Simmons 1979; Huemer 2013; Brennan 2016a.

24. As Michael Huemer notes, the US Supreme Court has repeatedly ruled that the government has no duty to protect individual citizens. Huemer 2013, 32–33. Huemer cites three separate recent cases in which the Supreme Court held that the government has no duties to individual citizens, but only to the public at large.

25. Might Hassoun say that if actual consent is the standard for which we're shooting, then we should at least try to come *closer* to meeting that standard? In that case, having a generous welfare program ensures everyone is autonomous, and so guarantees we better approximate the standard of consent. Still, if actual consent is necessary, then taking steps to ensure autonomy is no substitute. Suppose a would-be rapist abducts a poor woman, a woman so poor that she lacks sufficient autonomy in Hassoun's sense. Suppose he first provides her with a large amount of resources, enough to make her sufficiently autonomous on Hassoun's theory. Afterward, he rapes her. Here, that he took steps to ensure she is sufficiently autonomous does *nothing* to legitimate him in coercing her. Sure, a rapist that feeds his victims is better than one that lets them starve, but this does not somewhat or partially legitimate the rape. See Tesón 2014.

26. The argument in this section is primarily directed against Pogge and Hassoun.

27. The reader might object here that unless the rich allowed poor people to immigrate or trade with their subjects, they would *still* be imposing unjust coercion on the poor. Clearly, that's right. However, this objection is not available to people like Pogge and Hassoun. Pogge explicitly opposes open borders, arguing that justice does not require freedom of movement. And both hold that free trade is inconsistent with justice. Whatever coercion might be present here, then, they cannot condemn it as unjust.

CHAPTER 10

1. See Singer 1972. For a more recent version of essentially the same argument, see Singer 2010.
2. Singer 1972, 231.
3. Singer 1972, 231.
4. For a similar argument, see Unger 1996.
5. It is not quite right that Singer thinks we should reject this because it conflicts with another intuition. In fact, Singer rejects arguments on the basis of intuitions. He thinks such intuitions and judgments are unreliable, while our thinking about abstract moral principles is far more reliable. Still, we focus here on the intuitions since almost all of Singer's readers find the example of the drowning child the most persuasive part of his argument. See Singer 2005, 350–351.
6. Singer 1972, 231.
7. Schmidtz 2008, 148.
8. We labeled the example *iterated* drowning children. We're following terminology from the theory of rational choice. There is a difference between merely repeated cases of one-shot interactions, and what we're calling iterated cases. For example, in a one-shot prisoner's dilemma situation, the rational thing to do for each party is to cheat or defect. That's what maximizes their expected payoff. And when we repeat prisoner's dilemma situations, it remains true that in each individual case, cheating is what maximizes in that isolated situation. The same is not true, however, in an iterated series of such choices. When we interact repeatedly with the same person, for example, the rational thing to do is not to cheat, but to find a way to cooperate. Even though, in each individual instance, one can do better by cheating, doing so forecloses opportunities for future cooperation. And the rewards of repeated cooperation strongly outweigh the rewards of one-off cheating.
9. Singer 2010, 39.
10. Singer 2010, 88.
11. Deaton 2013, 268–269.
12. Deaton 2013, 272.
13. Deaton 2013, 270.
14. Coyne 2013, 47.
15. Deaton 2013, 285.
16. Deaton 2013, 306.
17. Here, we draw from Coyne 2013, 51. See also Banerjee and Duflo 2011; Collier 2007; Easterly 2002; Easterly 2006; Sachs 2005, Moyo 2009; Hubbard and Duggan 2009; Karlan and Appel 2011. Some studies claim to find that aid often has a positive effective on growth, but only on the condition that the recipient country already has good institutions, such as strong protections of private property and the rule of law (Burnside and Dollar 2000). These studies corroborate the "institutions trump everything else" story: aid is helpful only if the right institutions are in place.

Other studies claim to find that aid always has *some* positive effect, even without good background institutions. (Hanson and Tarp 2001.) But many other studies claim to find no effect, or, even worse, that aid has a negative effect (Brumm 2003; Rajan and Subramanian 2008; Bauer 2000; Easterly, Levine, and Roodman 2004; Doucouliagos and Paldam 2009a; Doucouliagos and Paldam 2009b).

18. Doucouliagos and Paldam 2009a; Doucouliagos and Paldam 2009b; Elbadawi 1999; Lensink and White 2001, 42–65.

19. Acemoglu and Robinson 2012, 452–453.

20. Deaton 2013, 273.

21. Coyne 2013, 17.

22. Coyne 2013.

23. Coyne 2013, 115.

24. We name this after Immanuel Kant and W. D. Ross, who endorsed this view of beneficence. We take it this is the commonsense view of beneficence, at least among Westerners.

25. For more on this theme, see Schmidtz 2008, 145–164.

26. If you think "destroy" is too strong, consider the following passage from Singer's original article. After admitting that his prescriptions may very well undo the fabric of modern prosperity, Singer asserts that "from the moral point of view, the prevention of the starvation of millions of people outside our society must be considered at least as pressing as the upholding of property norms within our society." See Singer 1972, 237.

CHAPTER 11

1. Although we do not make anything of the point, it's worth noting that the link between increased carbon emissions and these effects is more tenuous than the link between them and rising temperatures.

2. A fourth option—not to do anything at all—also has it costs, of course. We don't discuss this option, since we think it's clear that the costs to this option are unacceptable.

3. Moellendorf 2014, 22 (emphasis in original).

4. Nordhaus 2013, 71, makes a similar point.

5. The fifth IPCC report argues there is little evidence that global warming is thus far causing spikes in extreme weather events, such as floods, droughts, tornados, and hurricanes. See https://www.ipcc.ch/report/ar5/wg1/.

6. Goklany 2011.

7. http://www.emdat.be/disaster_trends/index.html.

8. Reddaway 1940, 26, calculation to current value made using https://www.measuringworth.com/calculators/ukcompare/relativevalue.php.

9. https://www.cia.gov/library/publications/the-world-factbook/geos/xx.html.

10. Another important caveat: the EM-DAT data is approximate.

11. Environmental studies professor Eric Pielke Jr., using damage estimates from Munich Re, a large reinsurance companies whose publically available data sets are widely used, finds that since 1990, disaster damage as a percentage of world product has decline slightly, but remained nearly constant at about 0.3. (Pielke uses the UN's GDP estimates, while we used Maddison Project estimates.) See https:// fivethirtyeight.com/features/disasters-cost-more-than-ever-but-not-because-of-climate-change/.

12. Nordhaus 2010, 2013.

13. Nordhaus 2010.

14. Nordhaus 2013, 82.

15. United Nations 2015, 1.

16. Economists Gernot Wagner and Martin Weitzman (2015, 63), who defend much stronger mitigation policies than we do, agree:

> At a 3% annual growth rate, global economic output will increase almost twenty-fold in a hundred years. Subtracting 10%, 30%, or even 50% for climate damages after a hundred years will still leave the world many times richer than it is today. Climate change, in short, may be bad, but even the worst seems to leave the world much better off so long as economic growth remains robust.

17. Stern 2007. To our knowledge, the Stern Review is largely seen as too pessimistic and as using improper methods. See Carter et al. 2006.

18. For a similar reading of the disagreement between Nordhaus and Stern, see Heath 2016.

19. https://www.cia.gov/library/publications/the-world-factbook/geos/xx.html.

20. Wagner and Weitzman 2015, 64, admit: "Human ingenuity has seemingly outpaced environmental degradation in the past. Things always seem to be getting cheaper, smaller, faster, better. Technology will win the day once again." But they're skeptical. Or perhaps afraid, asking: "Maybe. But what if there are limits?" However, there's no evidence that if there are limits, we'll hit these in the period for which we're considering. Trying to be careful may well mean being overly careful.

21. Grossman and Krueger 1995.

22. Nordhaus 2013, 22.

23. Nordhaus 2013, 23.

24. Frankel 2002.

25. See Stern 2005 for a critique of the Environmental Kuznets Curve.

26. Moellendor 2014, 173–177.

27. Moellendorf 2014, 176.

28. It's worth mentioning that some of the assumptions behind Moellendorf's proposal can be—and should be—questioned. Even if we want to direct the harms of climate change mitigation, it's quite problematic to take societies or countries as the

relevant unit of analysis. Such mitigation strategies will harm people across those societies, irrespective of whether they themselves have actually contributed much to climate change. (The same will be true for various attempts to impose the costs of climate change mitigation on grounds of responsibility for warming. See, e.g., Caney 2011.)

29. Wagner and Weitzman 2015, 22.

Bibliography

Abascal, Maria, and Baldassarri, Delia. 2015. "Love Thy Neighbor? Ethnoracial Diversity and Trust Reexamined," *American Journal of Sociology* 121: 722–782.

Acemoglu, Daron, Johnson, Simon, and Robinson, James A. 2001. "The Colonial Origins of Comparative Development: An Empirical Investigation," *American Economic Review* 91: 1369–1401.

Acemoglu, Daron, Johnson, Simon, and Robinson, James A. 2002. "Reversal of Fortune: Geography and Institutions in the Making of World Income Distribution," *Quarterly Journal of Economics* 117: 1231–1294.

Acemoglu, Daron, Johnson, Simon, and Robinson, James A. 2005. "Institutions as a Fundamental Cause of Long-Run Growth," in *Handbook of Economic Growth, Vol 1A*, ed. Philippe Aghion and Steven N. Darlauf, 386–472. Amsterdam: Elsevier.

Acemoglu, Daron, and Robinson, James A. 2005. "Unbundling Institutions," *Journal of Political Economy* 113: 949–995.

Acemoglu, Daron, and Robinson, James A. 2013. *Why Nations Fail*. New York: Crown Business.

Achen, Christopher, and Bartels, Larry. 2016. *Democracy for Realists*. Princeton, NJ: Princeton University Press.

Acosta, Pablo, Calderon, Cesar, Fajnzylber, Pablo, and Lopez, Humberto. 2008. "What Is the Impact of International Remittances on Poverty and Inequality in Latin America?," *World Development* 36: 89–114.

Adams Jr., Richard H., and Page, John. 2005. "Do International Migration and Remittances Reduce Poverty in Developing Countries?," *World Development* 33: 1645–1669.

Aghion, Philippe, Alesina, Alberto, and Trebbi, Francesco. 2004. "Endogenous Political Institutions," *Quarterly Journal of Economics* 119: 565–611.

Altman, Andrew, and Wellman, Christopher H. 2011. *A Liberal Theory of International Justice*. New York: Oxford University Press.

Banerjee, Abhijit, and Duflo, Esther. 2011. *Poor Economics*. New York: Public Affairs.

Bauer, Peter T. 2000. *From Subsistence to Exchange*. Princeton, NJ: Princeton University Press.

Beerbohm, Eric. 2012. *In Our Name*. Princeton, NJ: Princeton University Press.

Beine, M., Docquier, F., and Schiff, M. 2013. "International Migration, Transfers of Norms and Home Country Fertility," *Canadian Journal of Economics* 46: 1406–1430.

Beitz, Charles. 2011. *The Idea of Human Rights*. New York: Oxford University Press.

Benhabib, Seyla. 2004. *The Rights of Others*. New York: Cambridge University Press.

Bergh, Andreas, and Nilsson, Therese. 2014. "Is Globalization Reducing Absolute Poverty?," *World Development* 62: 42–61.

Bilchitz, David. 2007. *Poverty and Fundamental Rights: The Justification and Enforcement of Socio-Economic Rights*. New York: Oxford University Press.

Blake, Michael. 2001. "Distributive Justice, State Coercion, and Autonomy," *Philosophy and Public Affairs* 30: 257–296.

Blake, Michael. 2005. "Immigration," in *A Companion to Applied Ethics*, ed. R. G. Frey and Christopher H. Wellman, 224–257. Oxford: Wiley-Blackwell.

Boonin, David. 2011. *Should Race Matter? Unusual Answers to the Usual Questions*. New York: Cambridge University Press.

Boudreaux, Karol. 2006. "Property Rights and Resource Conflict in the Sudan," in *Realizing Property Rights*, ed. Hernando de Soto and Francis Cheneval, 68–73. New York: Ruffer & Rub.

Bourguignon, François, and Morrisson, Christian. 2002. "Inequality Among World Citizens: 1820–1992," *American Economic Review* 92: 727–744.

Brennan, Jason. 2007. "Rawls's Paradox," *Constitutional Political Economy* 18: 287–299.

Brennan, Jason. 2012. *Libertarianism: What Everyone Needs to Know*. New York: Oxford University Press.

Brennan, Jason. 2013. "Is Market Society Intrinsically Repugnant?," *Journal of Business Ethics* 112: 271–282.

Brennan, Jason. 2014. *Why Not Capitalism?* New York: Routledge.

Brennan, Jason. 2016a. "Do Markets Corrupt?," in *Economics and the Virtues*, ed. Jennifer Baker and Mark White, 236–256. New York: Oxford University Press.

Brennan, Jason. 2016b. *Against Democracy*. Princeton, NJ: Princeton University Press.

Brennan, Jason, and Jaworski, Peter. 2016. *Markets without Limits*. New York: Routledge.

Brock, Gillian. 2009. *Global Justice: A Cosmopolitan Account*. Oxford: Oxford University Press.

Brock, Gillian, and Blake, Michael. 2015. *Debating Brain Drain*. New York: Oxford University Press.

Brownlee, Kimberley. 2013. "A Human Right Against Social Deprivation," *Philosophical Quarterly* 63: 199–222.

Brumm, Harold J. 2003. "Aid, Policies, and Growth: Bauer Was Right," *Cato Journal* 23: 167–174.

Buchanan, Allen. 1999. "Democracy and Secession," in *National Self-Determination and Secession*, ed. Margaret Moore, 14–33. New York: Oxford University Press.

Buchanan, Allen. 2013. *The Heart of Human Rights.* New York: Oxford University Press.

Burnside, Craig, and Dollar, David. 2000. "Aid, Policies, and Growth," *American Economic Review* 90: 847–868.

Caldwell, Christopher. 2009. *Reflections on the Revolution in Europe.* New York: Doubleday.

Caney, Simon. 2011. "Human Rights, Responsibilities, and Climate Change," in *Global Basic Rights*, ed. Charles R. Beitz and Robert E. Goodin, 227–247. New York: Oxford University Press.

Caplan, Bryan. 2007. *The Myth of the Rational Voter.* Princeton, NJ: Princeton University Press.

Cardoso, Fernando, and Faletto, Enzo. 1979. *Dependency and Development in Latin America.* Berkeley: University of California Press.

Carens, Joseph. 1987. "Aliens and Citizens: The Case for Open Borders," *The Review of Politics* 49: 251–273.

Carens, Joseph. 2013. *The Ethics of Immigration.* New York: Oxford University Press.

Carter, Robert M., de Freitas, C. R., Golanky, Indur, Holland, David, Lindzen, Richard, Byatt, Ian, Castles, Ian, Henderson, David, Lawson, Nigel, McKitrick, Ross, Morris, Julian, Peacock, Alan, Robinson, Colin, and Skildesky, Robert. 2006. "The Stern Review: A Dual Critique," *World Economics* 7: 165–232.

Christiano, Thomas. 2011. "An Instrumental Argument for a Human Right to Democracy," *Philosophy & Public Affairs* 39: 142–176.

Clark, J. R., Lawson, Robert, Nowrasteh, Alex, Powell, Benjamin, and Murphy, Ryan. 2015. "Does Immigration Impact Institutions?," *Public Choice* 163: 321–335.

Clemens, Michael. 2011. "Economics and Emigration: Trillion-Dollar Bills on the Sidewalk?," *Journal of Economic Perspectives* 23: 83–106.

Clemens, Michael, and Bazzi, Sami. 2008. "Don't Close the Golden Door: Making Immigration Policy Work for Development," in *The White House and the World: A Global Development Agenda for the Next U.S. President*, ed. N. Birdsall, 241–272. Washington, DC: Center for Global Development.

Clemens, Michael, and Postel, Hannah. 2017. "Shared Harvest: Temporary Work Visas as US- Haiti Development Cooperation," *Center for Global Development Briefs.* www.cgdev.org/shared-harvest-temporary-work-visas-us-haiti-development-cooperation.

Clemens, Michael, and Pritchett, Lant. 2008. "Income per Natural: Measuring Development for People Rather Than Places," *Population and Development Review* 34: 395–434.

Clemens, Michael, and Sandefur, Justin. 2013. "Let the People Go: The Problem with Strict Migration Limits," *Foreign Affairs.* https://www.foreignaffairs.com/reviews/review-essay/2013-12-16/let-people-go.

Coelho, Philip R. P. 1973. "The Profitability of Imperialism: The British Experience in the West Indies," *Explorations in Economic History* 10: 253–280.

Cohen, G. A. 2009. *Why Not Socialism?* Princeton, NJ: Princeton University Press.

Cohen, G. A. 2011. "Freedom and Money," in *On the Currency of Egalitarian Justice, and Other Essays in Political Philosophy*, ed. M. Otsuka, 166–192. Princeton, NJ: Princeton University Press.

Collier, Paul. 2007. *The Bottom Billion: Why the Poorest Countries Are Failing and What Can Be Done About It*. New York: Oxford University Press.

Collier, Paul. 2009. "In Praise of the Coup," *The Modern Humanist*. http://rationalist. org.uk/articles/1997/in-praise-of-the-coup.

Collier, Paul. 2013. *Exodus: How Migration Is Changing Our World*. Oxford University Press.

Collins, Daryl, Morduch, Jonathan, Rutherford, Stuart and Ruthven, Orlanda. 2010. *Portfolios of the Poor*. Princeton, NJ: Princeton University Press.

Comin, Diego, and Hobijn, Bart. 2010. "An Exploration of Technology Diffusion," *American Economic Review* 100: 2031–2059.

Cowen, Tyler, and Tabarrok, Alex. 2010. *Modern Principles of Economics*. New York: Worth.

Coyne, Christopher. 2013. *Doing Bad by Doing Good: Why Humanitarian Action Fails*. Stanford, CA: Stanford University Press.

Cunningham, John Wood. 1983. *British Economists and the Empire*. New York: St. Martin's Press.

Cruft, R. 2006. "Against Individualistic Justifications of Property Rights," *Utilitas* 18: 154–172.

D'Amuri, Francesco, and Peri, Giovanni. 2011. *Immigration, Jobs, and Employment Protection: Evidence from Europe*. No. w17139. Cambridge, MA: National Bureau of Economic Research.

Davis, Lance E., and Huttenback, Robert A. 1982. "The Political Economy of British Imperialism: Measures of Benefits and Support," *Journal of Economic History* 42: 119–130.

Davis, Lance E., and Huttenback, Robert A. 1987. *Mammon and Empire*. New York: Cambridge University Press.

Deaton, Angus. 2013. *The Great Escape*. Princeton, NJ: Princeton University Press.

de Haas, Hein. 2005. "International Migration, Remittances and Development: Myths and Facts," *Third World Quarterly* 26: 1269–1284.

de Haas, Hein. 2006. "Migration, Remittances and Regional Development in Southern Morocco," *Geoforum* 37: 565–580.

de Soto, Hernando, 1989. *The Other Path: The Invisible Revolution in the Third World*. New York: Harper Collins.

de Soto, Hernando. 2000. *The Mystery of Capital*. New York: Basic Books.

Del Carpio, X. V., and Wagner, M. C. 2015. "The Impact of Syrians Refugees on the Turkish Labor Market," Policy Research Working Paper no. WPS 7402. Washington, DC: World Bank.

DeLong, Brad. 2002. *Macroeconomics*. New York: McGraw Hill.

Docquier, Frédéric, Lodigiani, Elisabetta, Rapoport, Hillel, and Schiff, Maurice. 2016. "Emigration and Democracy," *Journal of Development Economics* 120: 209–223.

Dollar, David, and Kraay, Aart. 2002. "Growth Is Good for the Poor," *Journal of Economic Growth* 7: 195–225.

Dollar, David, and Kraay, Aart. 2004. "Trade, Growth, and Poverty," *Economic Journal* 114 (2004): F22–F49.

Doucouliagos, Hristos, and Paldam, Martin. 2009a. "Aid Effectiveness on Accumulation. A Meta Study," *Kyklos* 59: 227–254.

Doucouliagos, Hristos, and Paldam, Martin. 2009b. "The Aid Effectiveness Literature: The Sad Results of 40 Years of Research," *Journal of Economic Surveys* 23: 433–461.

Doyle, Michael. 1983. "Kant, Liberal Legacies, and Foreign Affairs, Part I," *Philosophy and Public Affairs* 12: 205–235.

Dustmann, Christian, and Frattini, Tommaso. 2013. "The Fiscal Effects of Immigration to the UK," Centre for Research and Analysis of Migration. http://www.cream-migration.org/publ_uploads/CDP_22_13.pdf

Easterly, William. 2002. *The Elusive Quest for Growth*. Cambridge, MA: MIT Press.

Easterly, William. 2006. *The White Man's Burden*. New York: Oxford University Press.

Easterly, William, Gatti, Roberta, and Kurlat, Sergio. 2006. "Development, Democracy, and Mass Killings," *Journal of Economic Growth* 11: 129–156.

Easterly, William, and Levine, Ross. 2003. "Tropics, Germs, and Crops: How Endowments Influence Economic Development," *Journal of Monetary Economics* 50: 3–39.

Easterly, William, and Levine, Ross. 2016. "The European Origins of Economic Development," *Journal of Economic Growth* 21: 225–271.

Easterly, William, Levine, Ross, and Roodman, David. 2004. "Aid, Policies, and Growth: Comment," *American Economic Review* 94: 774–780.

Easterly, William, and Nyarko, Yaw. 2009. "Is the Brain Drain Good for Africa?," in *Skilled Immigration Today: Prospects, Problems, and Policies*, ed. Jagdish Bhagwati and Gordon Hanson, 316–361. New York: Oxford University Press.

Edelstein, Michael. 1982. *Overseas Investment in the Age of High Imperialism: The United Kingdom, 1850–1914*. New York: Columbia University Press.

Elbadawi, I. A. 1999. "External Aid: Help or Hindrance to Export Orientation in Africa," *Journal of African Economics* 8: 578–616.

Ferguson, Niall. 2003. "British Imperialism Revisited: The Costs and Benefits of 'Angloglobalization,'" *Historically Speaking* 4: 21–27.

Fieldhouse, D. K. 1961. "'Imperialism': A Historiographical Revision," *Economic History Review* 14: 187–209.

Foreman-Peck, J. 1989. "Foreign Investment and Imperial Exploitation: Balance of Payments Reconstruction for Nineteenth-Century Britain and India," *Economic History Review* 42: 354–374.

Frankel, Jeffrey. 2002. "The Environment and Economic Globalization," in *Globalization: What's New*, ed. Michael Weinstein, 129–169. New York: Council on Foreign Relations.

Freeman, Richard, and Lindauer, David. 1999. "Why Not Africa?," Working Paper 6942. Cambridge, MA: National Bureau of Economic Research.

Freeman, Samuel. 2007. *Rawls*. New York: Routledge.

Freeman, Samuel. 2011. "Capitalism in The Classical and High Liberal Traditions," *Social Philosophy and Policy* 28: 19–55.

Freiman, Christopher. 2017. *Unequivocal Justice*. New York: Routledge.

Friedberg, Rachel, and Hunt, Jennifer. 1995. "The Impact of Immigrants on Host Wages," *Journal of Economic Perspectives* 9: 23–44.

Gaus, Gerald. 2004. *Contemporary Theories of Liberalism*. Thousand Oaks, CA: Sage.

Gilabert, Pablo. 2012. *From Global Poverty to Global Equality*. New York: Oxford University Press.

Gilens, Martin. 2012. *Affluence and Influence*. Princeton, NJ: Princeton University Press.

Glaeser, Edward L., La Porta, Rafael, Lopez-de-Silanes, Florencio, and Shleifer, Andrei. 2004. "Do Institutions Cause Growth?" *Journal of Economic Growth* 9: 272–303.

Goklany, Indur M. 2011. "Wealth and Safety: The Amazing Decline in Deaths from Extreme Weather in an Era of Global Warming, 1900–2010," Policy Study 393. Washington, DC: Reason Foundation. https://reason.org/files/deaths_from_extreme_weather_1900_2010.pdf.

Grier, Robert. 1999. "Colonial Legacies and Economic Growth," *Public Choice* 98: 317–335.

Griffin, James. 2009. *On Human Rights*. New York: Oxford University Press.

Grossman, Gene M., and Krueger, Alan B. 1995. "Economic Growth and the Environment," *Quarterly Journal of Economics* 110: 353–378.

Gupta, Sanjeev, Pattillo, Catherine A., and Wagh, Smita. 2009. "Effect of Remittances on Poverty and Financial Development in Sub-Saharan Africa," *World Development* 37: 104–115.

Gwartney, James, Lawson, Robert, and Hall, Joshua. 2015. *Economic Freedom of the World, 2014 Report*. Vancouver: Fraser Institute.

Gwartney, James, Lawson, Robert, and Hall, Joshua. 2017. *Economic Freedom of the World, 2016 Report*. Vancouver: Fraser Institute.

Hall, Joshua, and Lawson, Robert A. 2014. "Economic Freedom of the World: An Accounting of the Literature," *Contemporary Economic Policy* 32: 1–19.

Hall, Robert, and Jones, Charles. 1999. "Why Do Some Countries Produce So Much More Output per Worker than Others?," *Quarterly Journal of Economics* 114: 83–116.

Hansen, Henrik, and Tarp, Finn. 2001. "Aid and Growth Regressions," *Journal of Development Economics* 64: 547–570.

Hassoun, Nicole. 2012. *Globalization and Global Justice*. New York: Cambridge University Press.

Heath, Joseph. 2016. "Caring about Climate Change Implies Caring about Economic Growth," Working paper. University of Toronto.

Hubbard, R. Glenn, and Duggan, William. 2009. *The Aid Trap: Hard Truths about Ending Poverty*. New York: Columbia Business School Publishing.

Huemer, Michael, 2010. "Is There a Right to Immigrate?" *Social Theory and Practice* 36: 429–461.

Huemer, Michael. 2013. *The Problem of Political Authority*. New York: Palgrave-MacMillan.

Huemer, Michael. 2016. "Confessions of a Utopophobe," *Social Philosophy and Policy* 33: 214–234.

Hufbauer, Gary, and Elliott, Kimberly. 1999. "Same Song, Same Refrain? Economic Sanctions in the 1990s," *American Economic Review* 89: 403–408.

Irwin, Douglas. 2007. *Against the Tide; An Intellectual History of Free Trade*. Princeton, NJ: Princeton University Press.

James, Aaron. 2012. *Fairness in Practice: A Social Contract for a Global Economy*. New York: Oxford University Press.

Janis, M., Kay, R., and Bradley, A. 2008. *European Human Rights Law: Text and Materials*, 3rd ed. New York: Oxford University Press.

Kapur, Devesh. 2013. *Diaspora, Development, and Democracy: The Domestic Impact of International Migration from India*. Princeton, NJ: Princeton University Press.

Karlan, Dean, and Appel, Jacob. 2011. *More than Good Intentions: Improving the Ways the Poor Borrow, Save, Learn, and Stay Healthy*. New York: Plume.

Kerr, Sari Pekkela, and Kerr, William R. 2011. *Economic Impacts of Immigration: A Survey*. No. w16736. Cambridge, MA: National Bureau of Economic Research.

Kershnar, Stephen. 2000. "There Is No Moral Right to Immigrate To the United States," *Public Affairs Quarterly* 14: 141–158.

Keynes, John Maynard. 1972. *The Collected Writings of John Maynard Keynes, vol. 9: Essays in Persuasion*. London: MacMillan.

Kimura, Mitsuhiko. 1995. "Economics of Japanese Imperialism in Korea, 1910–1939," *Economic History Review* 48: 555–574.

Koechlin, Valerie, and Leon, Gianmarco. 2007. "International Remittances and Income Inequality: An Empirical Investigation," *Journal of Economic Policy Reform* 10: 123–141.

Krugman, Paul. 1993. "What Do Undergrads Need to Know About Trade?," *American Economic Review, Papers and Proceedings of the AEA* 83: 23–26.

Kukathas, Chandran. 2003. "Responsibility for Past Injustice: How to Shift the Burden," *Politics, Philosophy and Economics* 2: 165–190.

LaFave, Wayne. 2003. *Criminal Law*, 4th ed. Washington, DC: Thomson-West.

Lal, Deepak. 2005. *In Praise of Empires: Globalization and Order*. New York: Palgrave-MacMillan.

Landes, David. 1999. *The Wealth and Poverty of Nations: Why Some Are So Rich and Some are So Poor*. New York: Norton.

Leeson, Peter. 2010. "Two Cheers for Capitalism," *Society* 47: 227–233.

Lensink, R., and White, H. 2001. "Are There Negative Returns to Aid?," *Journal of Development Studies* 37: 42–65.

Lomasky, Loren, and Tesón, Fernando. 2015. *Justice at a Distance*. Cambridge: Cambridge University Press.

Longhi, Simonetta, Nijkamp, Peter, and Poot, James. 2005. "A Meta-Analytic Assessment of the Effect of Immigration on Wages," *Journal of Economic Surveys* 19: 451–477.

Longhi, Simonetta, Nijkamp, Peter, and Poot, James. 2006. "The Impact of Immigration on the Employment of Natives in Regional Labour Markets: A Meta-Analysis," IZA Discussion Papers 2044, Institute for the Study of Labor (IZA). https://ideas.repec.org/p/iza/izadps/dp2044.html.

Longhi, Simonetta, Nijkamp, Peter, and Poot, James. 2010. "Joint Impacts of Immigration on Wages and Employment: Review and Meta-Analysis," *Journal of Geographical Systems* 12: 355–387.

López-Córdova, Ernesto, Tokman, Andrea, and Verhoogen, Eric. 2005. "Globalization, Migration, and Development: The Role of Mexican Migrant Remittances," *Economía* 6: 217–256.

Macedo, Stephan. 2007. "The Moral Dilemma of US Immigration Policy: Open Borders versus Social Justice," in *Debating Immigration*, ed. Carol M. Swain, 63–84. New York: Cambridge University Press.

Maddison, Angus. 2007. *Contours of the World Economy, 1–2030 AD: Essays in Macro-Economic History*. New York: Oxford University Press.

Malfliet, Katlijn. 2002. "Property Rights as Human Rights: A Post-Communist Paradigm?," in *Human Rights in Russia and Eastern Europe*, ed. F. Feldbrugge and W. N. Simon, 97–119. The Hague: Kluwer.

McDonald, Paul. 2009. "Those Who Forget Historiography are Doomed to Republish It: Empire, Imperialism, and Contemporary Debates about American Power," *Review of International Studies* 35: 45–67.

McKenzie, David, and Rapoport, Hillel. 2007. "Network Effects and The Dynamics Of Migration and Inequality: Theory and Evidence From Mexico," *Journal of Development Economics* 84: 1–24.

Miller, David. 2005. "Immigration: The Case for Limits," in *Contemporary Debates in Applied Ethics*, ed. Andrew I. Cohen and Christopher H. Wellman, 363–375. Oxford: Blackwell.

Miller, Richard. 2002. "Too Much Inequality," *Social Philosophy and Policy* 19: 275–313.

Moellendorf, Darrel. 2014. *The Moral Challenges of Climate Change*. New York: Cambridge University Press.

Morgan, T. Clifton, and Campbell, Sally Howard. 1991. "Domestic Structure, Decisional Constraints, and War--So Why Kant Democracies Fight?," *Journal of Conflict Resolution* 35: 187–211.

Morsink, Johannes. 1999. *The Universal Declaration of Human Rights: Origins, Drafting, and Intent*. Philadelphia: University of Pennsylvania Press.

Moyo, Dambiso. 2009. *Dead Aid: Why Aid Is Not Working and How There Is a Better Way for Africa.* New York: FSG.

Mueller, Dennis. 2003. *Public Choice III.* New York: Cambridge University Press.

Nickel, James. 2005. "Poverty and Rights," *Philosophical Quarterly* 55: 385–402.

Nickel, James. 2007. *Making Sense of Human Rights.* Malden: Blackwell, 2007.

Nordhaus, William. 2010. "Economic Aspects of Global Warming in a Post-Copenhagen Environment," *Proceedings of the National Academy of Sciences* 107: 11721–11726.

Nordhaus, William. 2013. *The Climate Casino.* New Haven, CT: Yale University Press.

North, Douglass. 1990. *Institutions, Institutional Change, and Economic Performance.* Cambridge: Cambridge University Press.

North, Douglass. 2012. *In the Shadow of Violence: Politics, Economics, and the Problems of Development.* New York: Cambridge University Press.

North, Douglas, Wallis, John Joseph, and Weingast, Barry. 2012. *Violence and Social Orders.* Cambridge: Cambridge University Press.

Nowrasteh, Alex, and Cole, Sophie. 2013. "Building a Wall around the Welfare State, Instead of the Country," Cato Institute Policy Analysis #732. http://www.cato.org/publications/policy-analysis/building-wall-around-welfare- state-instead-country.

Nozick, Robert. 1974. *Anarchy, State, and Utopia.* New York: Basic Books.

Oberman, Kieran. 2013. "Can Brain Drain Justify Immigration Restrictions?," *Ethics* 123: 427–455.

O'Brien, Patrick. 1988. "The Costs and Benefits of British Imperialism, 1846–1914," *Past and Present* 120: 163–200.

OECD. 2013 "The Fiscal Impact of Immigration in OECD Countries," in *Organisation for Economic Co-operation and Development, International Migration Outlook 2013.* Paris: OECD Publishing. http://dx.doi.org/10.1787/migr_outlook-2013-6-en.

Offer, Avner. 1993. "The British Empire, 1870–1914: A Waste of Money?," *Economic History Review* 46: 215–238.

Okkerse, Liesbet. 2008. "How to Measure Labour Market Effect of Immigration: A Review," *Journal of Economic Surveys* 22: 1–30.

Ottaviano, Gianmarco, and Peri, Giovanni. 2008. *Immigration and National Wages: Clarifying the Theory and the Empirics.* No. w14188. Cambridge, MA: National Bureau of Economic Research.

Peri, Giovanni, and Sparber, Chard. 2009. "Task Specialization, Immigration, and Wages," *American Economic Journal: Applied Economics* 1: 135–169.

Pevnick, Ryan. 2009. "Social Trust and the Ethics of Immigration Policy," *Journal of Political Philosophy* 17: 146–167.

Pfutze, Tobias. 2012. "Does Migration Promote Democratization? Evidence from the Mexican Transition," *Journal of Comparative Economics* 40: 159–175.

Pogge, Thomas. 1997. "Migration and Poverty," in *Citizenship and Exclusion*, ed. V. Bader, 12–27. Basingstoke: Macmillan.

Pogge, Thomas. 2001. "Eradicating Systemic Poverty: Brief for a Global Resources Dividend," *Journal of Human Development* 2: 59–77.

Pogge, Thomas. 2002. *World Poverty and Human Rights*. New York: Polity Press.

Pogge, Thomas. 2005. "Real World Justice," *Journal of Ethics* 9: 29–53.

Pogge, Thomas. 2011. "Are We Violating the Human Rights of the World's Poor?," *Yale Human Rights and Development Journal* 14: 1–33.

Powell, Benjamin, and Skarbek, David. 2006. "Sweatshops and Third World Living Standards: Are the Jobs Worth the Sweat?," *Journal of Labor Research* 27: 263–274.

Pritchett, Lant. 2006. *Let Their People Come: Breaking the Gridlock on International Labor Mobility*. Washington, DC: Center for Global Development.

Putterman, Louis, and Weil, David N. 2010. "Post-1500 Population Flows and the Long-Run Determinants of Economic Growth and Inequality," *Quarterly Journal of Economics* 125: 1627–1682.

Queralt, Jahel. 2017. "Are Economic Liberties Basic Rights?," in *The Routledge Handbook of Libertarianism*, ed. Jason Brennan, Bas van der Vossen, and David Schmidtz, 283–300. New York: Routledge.

Radzik, Linda. 2001. "Collective Responsibility and Duties to Respond," *Social Theory and Practice* 27: 455–471.

Radzik, Linda. 2009. *Making Amends*. New York: Oxford University Press.

Rajan, Raghuram G., and Subramanian, Arvind. 2008. "Aid and Growth: What Does the Cross-Country Evidence Really Show?," *Review of Economics and Statistics* 90: 643–665.

Rawls, John. 1955. "Two Concepts of Rules," *Philosophical Review* 64: 3–32.

Rawls, John. 1971. *A Theory of Justice*. Cambridge, MA: Harvard University Press.

Rawls, John. 1996. *Political Liberalism*. New York: Columbia University Press.

Rawls, John. 1999. *The Law of Peoples*. Cambridge, MA: Harvard University Press.

Rawls, John. 2001. *Justice as Fairness: A Restatement*. Cambridge, MA: Harvard University Press.

Raz, Joseph. 1986. *The Morality of Freedom*. New York: Oxford University Press.

Reddaway, T. F. 1940. *The Rebuilding of London after the Great Fire*. London: Jonathan Cape.

Risse, Mathias. 2005a. "Does the Global Order Harm the Poor?," *Philosophy and Public Affairs* 33: 349–376.

Risse, Matthias. 2005b. "Do We Owe the Global Poor Assistance or Rectification?," *Ethics and International Affairs* 19: 9–18.

Risse, Mathias. 2012. *On Global Justice*. Princeton, NJ: Princeton University Press.

Rodrik, Dani (ed.) 2003. *In Search of Prosperity*. Princeton, NJ: Princeton University Press.

Rodrik, Dani, Subramanian, Arvind, and Trebbi, Francisco. 2004. "Institutions Rule: The Primacy of Institutions over Geography and Integration in Economic Development," *Journal of Economic Growth* 9: 131–165.

Roland, Gérard. 2014. *Development Economics*. New York: Pearson.

Rosenberg, Nathan, and Birdzell, L. E. 1986. *How the West Grew Rich*. New York: Basic Books.

Roser, Max, and Ortiz-Ospina, Esteban. 2017. "Global Extreme Poverty," in *Our World in Data*. https://ourworldindata.org/extreme-poverty/.

Sachs, Jeffrey. 2005. *The End of Poverty*. New York: Penguin.

Sachs, Jeffrey, and Warner, Andrew. 1994. "Economic Reform and the Process of Global Integration," *Brookings Papers on Economic Activity* 26: 1–118.

Schmidtz, David. 1994. "The Institution of Property," *Social Philosophy and Policy* 11: 42–62.

Schmidtz, David. 2006. *Elements of Justice*. New York: Cambridge University Press.

Schmidtz, David. 2008. *Person, Polis, Planet: Essays in Applied Philosophy*. New York: Oxford University Press.

Simmons, A. John. 1979. *Moral Principles and Political Obligations*. Princeton, NJ: Princeton University Press.

Singer, Peter. 1972. "Famine, Affluence, and Morality," *Philosophy and Public Affairs* 1: 229–243.

Singer, Peter. 2005. "Ethics and Intuitions," *Journal of Ethics* 9: 331–352.

Singer, Peter. 2010. *The Life You Can Save*. New York: Random House.

Smith, Adam. 1904 [1776]. *An Inquiry Into the Nature and Causes of the Wealth of Nations*. London: Methuen and Co. http://www.econlib.org/library/Smith/smWN.html#.

Spolaore, Enrico, and Wacziarg, Romain. 2013. "How Deep Are the Roots of Economic Development?" *Journal of Economic Literature* 51: 325–361.

Stark, Oded, Taylor, Edward, and Yitzhaki, Shlomo. 1986. "Remittances and Inequality," *Economic Journal* 96: 722–740.

Stern, David I. 2005. "The Rise and Fall of the Environmental Kuznets Curve," *World Development* 32: 1419–1439.

Stern, Nicholas. 2007. *The Economics of Climate Change: The Stern Review*. New York: Cambridge University Press.

Stringham, Edward. 2015. *Private Governance*. New York: Oxford University Press.

Taylor, Edward J. 1999. "The New Economics of Labour Migration and the Role of Remittances in the Migration Process," *International Migration* 37: 63–88.

Tesón, Fernando. 2014. "When Philosophers Misdiagnose," *Analysis* 74: 107–118.

Tesón, Fernando, and van der Vossen, Bas. 2017. *Debating Humanitarian Intervention*. New York: Oxford University Press.

Tomasi, John. 2012. *Free Market Fairness*. Princeton, NJ: Princeton University Press.

Wagner, Gernot, and Weitzman, Martin. 2015. *Climate Shock: The Economic Consequences of a Hotter Planet*. Princeton, NJ: Princeton University Press.

Waldron, Jeremy. 1988. *The Right to Private Property*. Oxford: Clarendon Press.

Waldron, Jeremy. 2010. "Two Conceptions of Self-Determination," in *The Philosophy of International Law*, ed. S. Besson and J. Tasioulas, 397–416. New York: Oxford University Press.

Wall, Howard J. 1999. "Using the Gravity Model to Estimate the Costs of Protection," *Federal Reserve Bank of St. Louis Review* 81: 33–40.

Weil, David. 2013. *Economic Growth*, 3rd ed. New York: Pearson.

Wellman, Christopher H. 2005. *A Theory of Secession*. New York: Cambridge University Press.

Wellman, Christopher H. 2008. "Immigration and Freedom of Association," *Ethics* 119: 109–141.

Wellman, Christopher H., and Cole, Philip. 2011. *Debating the Ethics of Immigration: Is There a Right to Exclude?* New York: Oxford University Press.

Wenar, Leif. 2015. *Blood Oil*. New York: Oxford University Press.

Unger, Peter. 1996. *Living High and Letting Die*. New York: Oxford University Press, 1996.

United Nations, Department of Economic and Social Affairs, Population Division. 2015. *World Population Prospects: The 2015 Revision, Key Findings and Advance Tables*. Working Paper No. ESA/P/WP.241.

van de Walle, Nicolas, and Johnston, Timothy. 1996. *Improving Aid to Africa*. Baltimore: Johns Hopkins University Press.

van der Vossen, Bas. 2015. "Immigration and Self-Determination," *Politics, Philosophy and Economics* 14: 270–290.

van der Vossen, Bas. 2016. "Self-Determination and Moral Variation," in *The Theory of Self-Determination*, ed. Fernando Tesón. New York: Cambridge University Press.

Zwolinski, Matt. 2007. "Sweatshops, Choice, and Exploitation," *Business Ethics Quarterly* 17: 689–727.

Index

References to tables and figures are indicated by an italic *t* and *f* after the page number. References to notes are indicated by an italic *n* between the page number and the note number.

Index